Heaven Knows I'm Miserable Now

For Julie

Heaven Knows I'm Miserable Now

My Difficult 80s

Andrew Collins

EBURY
PRESS

1 3 5 7 9 10 8 6 4 2

Copyright © 2004 Andrew Collins

Andrew Collins has asserted his moral right to be identified as the author of
this work in accordance with the Copyright, Designs and Patents Act 1988.

First published 2004 by Ebury Press.

This edition first published 2005 by Ebury Press,
An imprint of Random House,
20 Vauxhall Bridge Road, London SW1V 2SA
www.randomhouse.co.uk

Random House Australia (Pty) Limited
20 Alfred Street, Milsons Point, Sydney,
New South Wales 2061, Australia

Random House New Zealand Limited
18 Poland Road, Glenfield, Auckland 10, New Zealand

Random House South Africa (Pty) Limited
Endulini, 5a Jubilee Road, Parktown 2193, South Africa

The Random House Group Limited Reg. No. 954009

www.randomhouse.co.uk

Printed and bound in Great Britain by Cox & Wyman Ltd, Reading, Berks

A CIP catalogue record for this book is available from the British Library.

Cover designed by
Interior by seagulls

ISBN 0091897483

contents

acknowledgements

First, I'd like to apologise to Northampton. If my previous book was a love letter to my home town, this one is more of a difficult but lengthy phone call confessing an affair.

Heaven Knows I'm Miserable Now is about a boy leaving behind the provinces to be seduced by London. In the course of this journey, I say one or two disparaging and dismissive things about Northampton, the town that raised and shod me and, to this day, houses my entire family. What an ungrateful bastard. Especially as I wouldn't even have written this current book had it not been for my childhood hymn to Northampton: *Where Did It All Go Right?*

Of all the kindness and interest extended to me since it first hit the shelves, the most heartening has come from my home town. So let me thank all of you: Mel Harris and the staff of Waterstone's in Abington Street; Anna Murby and all at BBC Radio Northampton; Sarah Freeman (now departed), Perrie Balthazar, Paul Jeeves and the staff of the *Chronicle & Echo*; Neil Rowland at Northamptonshire Libraries, everyone connected with the WordWorks festival and all at Kingsthorpe Library; the Ebury reps who made the book so available and visible; and Robert Webb, the Kingsthorpe Book Shop Supper Club and the Lime Trees Hotel. A warm vote of thanks to the old friends, teachers, parents and local people who turned out or contacted me – especially Dave Walman for inviting me to speak at the wake for Abington Vale Middle School. To all of you, I'm sorry about some of the disloyal things I thought about Northampton during the Eighties. It was a difficult time.

I started writing the book in London and, following a house move, finished it in Surrey. This seems poignant. It would be too hasty to say that I have finished with London now, because I still work there for much of the time, but having lived my first nineteen years in Northampton, I can now say with some finality that I lived the next nineteen in London, before opting out to the suburbs.

If I'd never reached this book without the other one, I wouldn't have written *either* without Andrew Goodfellow, whose name is so apposite he could apply to be a character in a Martin Amis novel. Having teased out my childhood, a process miraculously free of pain and revision, he was surprised to have to wrestle the student years out of me. I always used to imagine that authors who thanked their editors were merely fulfilling a polite contractual etiquette. Now I know otherwise. A high state of appreciation is observed for the rest of the Ebury gang: Sarah B, Caroline, Di, Hannah, Dawn, Alex, Jake and Martin Noble.

We seem to be in the approximate area of deal-making, so thanks once again to my agent and great friend Kate Haldane, and cigars all round at Amanda Howard Associates.

Closer to home now. To Julie, for the best eleven years of my life so far – thanks for letting me wallow once again in the past, when the present and the future is where our partnership lies. To the extended Collins family, Mum, Dad, Simon, Melissa, Lesley, Graham, Charmaine, Natasha, Ben,

Jack and William. To the family I married into, Eileen, Mary, Paul, Steve, Kim, George, Katie, Danielle, Steven and Oliver. And to that great big family that is the BBC.

In revisiting another chunk of my past, I found the shared reminiscences of the following old pals invaluable: Rob Mills, Paul Garner, Kevin Pearce and David Keech. My *alma mater* Chelsea School of Art and its fine Alumni Association were instrumental in hosting a memorable reunion in 2003 at which I was able to relive the past with Rob, Jane Chipchase and David Strickland, and another in 2004 when our old building was decommissioned, and Stephen Clasper and Stuart Mackenzie blasted in from the past. What used to be Nene College when I was there in 1983-84 is now University College Northampton (fancy!), and I wish them well in all their endeavours.

Further props to Kevin for the website, and all who sail in her.

Andrew Collins, Reigate, 2004
www.wherediditallgoright.com

In stark contrast to my first volume *Where Did It All Go Right?*, I have protected the identity of certain players in *Heaven Knows I'm Miserable Now* by changing their names. *I'm* comfortable with the shallow, impetuous, self-serving melodrama of my college years; they may not be. I aim to embarrass nobody but myself. The events in this book occurred as I remember them, or as they were relayed in my diaries and letters home. My aim has been to re-inhabit my 80s self and tell the tale from there. Though I regret dismissing Northampton, I make no further apologies for thinking the things that I thought. It was, after all, 2,000 light years ago.

prologue

The End
of History

It's the last day of school. Friday. Day 1 of the rest of my life and it's all a bit disappointing – an afternoon 'informal sixth-form buffet' in our own common room: all mufti and enforced jollity.

'I *am* coming back here in September,' says Mick.

'I *will* be needing my blazer again,' rejoins Dave.

It's one of those.

'I *am* going to miss this place,' I throw in, never to be outdone. I'm not going to miss this place (or at least that's what I'm saying) – that's the point. Sarcasm is the highest form of wit in sixth form, or has been, as sixth form is one informal buffet away from being past tense.

I'm eighteen: henna-ed hair, Bunnymen shirt, kung fu pumps: all conspicuous angst and attitude. We're all eighteen and have been for some time as far as the landlord of the Bold Dragoon's concerned, even Neil Lawrence, who still isn't.

This is the way school ends, not with a bang but a whimper. T.S. Eliot quotes are one of the few really practical things I shall be taking away from these two extra years at Weston Favell Upper School. I plan to drop them casually into conversation when I get to wherever I'm going. I fancy that couplets from *The Hollow Men* will serve me well in the outside world.

The final chapter of school has been made vague and messy by exams which ought to bring their own melodrama but in fact create an in-built anticlimax. Two years of study eaten up by two disjointed, anxious weeks sat in the gym or else at home in the back garden sunning yourself with Gerard Manley Hopkins and plant tissue, listening to the Fun Boy Three. All that coursework, homework and fieldwork, all that hothouse revision, gone, like sinkwater gurgling down a plughole. Except the quotes. I'm taking those.

We line up for a group snap. A rictus smile or wacky grin. Rabbit ears. V-signs. Peace signs. Then we return to milling awkwardly in our stretch jeans around the common room that has been our bolthole for so long; balanced at the end of the ordered, timetabled, maroon-blazered world as we know it, wishing there was alcohol when of course there's only tea or coffee; wondering if it's fear or melancholy we feel in the pits of our stomachs. It may well be too many Belgian buns and doughnuts, bought in with petty cash by the staff as an attempt at a devil-may-care send-off.

The more sociable among our teachers hover and nibble buns and nod approvingly as they witness the final send-off of another consignment of pupils into the real world. They've seen it all before. And somewhere back in the mists of time it no doubt happened to them too. They'll have another intake of maroon blazers to worry about in one summer's time – just like us. But not us.

'Tuck in, everyone!' trills bald head-of-sixth Mr Cole. 'Help yourselves to another bun! They're all to be eaten!' He was such a sport allowing Mick to get away with micking him so relentlessly in the sixth-form revue at Christmas, the last hurrah of indulgence before the mockery turned to mocks.

My form teacher, the virile Mr Bradshaw, arms tightly folded across his chest, is here too in his trademark pale blue tweed jacket. He's rumoured to be shagging one of the PE mistresses, Miss Hill, which ratchets up his one-of-us cool no end. I used to clumsily fantasise about Miss Hill seducing me when she was my form teacher, mainly because she wore a short skirt and was sometimes still slick with perspiration when she took afternoon register. I know, PE teacher, hardly original, but I was a thirteen-year-old virgin at the time. Is he married? (*She* can't be, not with a name like Miss.) We don't even know Bradshaw's first name. He signs himself KB on our reports. Keith? Ken? No way is he a Ken. Mr Bradshaw isn't really one of us at all. Just compared to Mr Cole.

It has to be Keith. I wonder how old he is? Younger than my dad, younger than all our dads. It's difficult to age the teachers. For all we know Keith might be no more than a couple of years out of teacher training college.

College. We're all going to college. When *we're* a couple of years out of college – which is only a couple more years away – we'll be Mr Bradshaw and Miss Hill. That *is* a comforting thought. I won't be wearing pale blue tweed, I know that much.

The buffet grinds informally on. Something out of the ordinary needs to happen. Something to mark the end of history, the end of biology, the end of English. We laugh and in-joke and reminisce about a part of our lives which is barely over and say the opposite of what we mean.

Eventually, because you have to make your own moments in Northampton, Mick and I break ranks and give them what they want. A slapstick bun fight. It's a half-hearted comic tussle and hardly John Belushi in *Animal House*. Belgian buns don't even make much mess.

'You lads,' tuts Bradshaw approvingly.

Mick and I grin for more snaps and cream-covered peace signs and it's soon time for us all to disperse into the bright afternoon, there to begin the waiting, our university places and our futures up in the air until the results come back in August.

One last look around before I leave behind the cotton wool and invisible force-field of the common room with its low comfy chairs and low coffee tables, its tuck shop (Outer Spacers and Opal Fruits), its grown-up kettle and its out-of-date Incredible Hulk mural. I missed a lot of lessons here.

'Seeya.'

'Bye.'

'Ta-da, mate.'

Short goodbyes, said without feeling or sarcasm, trying to make a moment out of a minute. It's not easy. After all, the whole lot of us will reconvene at the big party on Sunday night at the Masonic Hall in town.

I'll be there with Sally.

one

The Long Way

ROCKERS ARE GETTING COOL FEET
*If you want to look like a rock star this summer,
fellas, throw your socks away. Most of Duran Duran
seem to favour the sockless look. Even Echo and the
Bunnymen's moody Ian McCulloch has chucked
away his socks. I was so impressed that I tried it over
the weekend and all I can say is that it has to be the
most uncomfortable fashion yet invented!*

John Blake's Bizarre column, The Sun, *28 July 1983*

'Dave Griffiths doesn't go out looking like that!' Mum snipes, slamming the cutlery drawer to underline her point.

We're having one of our free and frank exchanges of views, becoming ever more frequent as my need for fumbled self-expression increases. I'm on my way out to collect Sally for tonight's big party. Why does she *always* wait until I'm on my way out to challenge me? Why do all mums do that? In the old house at Winsford Way you could get from the stairs to the front door without passing the kitchen ('I'm off out, won't be late, bye!' *slam*). Not at Kestrel Close. The kitchen's between the stairs and the door, like a sentry box.

'I don't want to look like Dave Griffiths,' I protest. Dave Griffiths is my ultra-straight friend who is leaving sixth form not for university but the RAF. Where's Dad when you need him to arbitrate? He usually dries as she washes.

'I sometimes wish you *were* Dave Griffiths,' she shouts. Ah good, she's strayed into fantasy. I give her an eye-rolling look of derision and reach for the door handle. The argument is over. I have won the battle, and so, in her mind, has Mum.

'Won't be late, bye!' *slam.*

I was, to be fair to Mum, beginning to put my head above the parapet in fashion terms that year. I wore my hair increasingly blow-dried and lacquered, in deference to Ian McCulloch and Robert Smith and other pop peacocks whose aromatic, dark music I'd fallen in love with on *Switch* or *The Tube*. Boots on the Market Square did brisk business with their gender-unspecific green hair gel that year. Black pumps were *de rigueur*, even when it got too chilly to wear them sensibly *sans chausette*. October was the reluctant start of the sock season, by which time I'd be off.

There is something about me in plentiful Truprint photos from the time that suggests I am not content merely to be part of a group that stands out from the crowd. Either my jeans are rolled higher than everybody else's, or I am wearing my hair spikier, or the sleeves have been more roughly hacked from my T-shirt for that Bono soldier-of-fortune effect. And no one else seems to be wearing fingerless gloves.

You couldn't play the drums in fingerless gloves, more's the pity. The local band I drummed for and gigged with had risen from the ashes of a previous band, Absolute Heroes. We were called, with no hint of embarrassment, Sketch For Dawn, after a Durutti Column track that bassist Craig and I particularly loved. All four of us in the band backcombed our hair to varying degrees, as did the knot of kids who came to see us play at the Black Lion in town. In fact, only Dave Griffiths stayed completely square, as if he were perhaps in the pay of my mum.

It was a Northampton thing. Provincial, Middle English, suburban, it was fertile soil for the sombre flowering of a generation too young to have experienced punk first-hand and too far away from the nearest city to affect New Romanticism. A tartan cape and jodhpur ensemble would have got you kicked in down town, and perhaps rightly so. It was all right for the actual New Romantics – they lived in London and got taxis. Their look and lifestyle was never going to translate to Northampton. But second-hand overcoats, check shirts and cheap hair gel? Bring them on.

You needed nothing much to do and nowhere much to go in order to get a fix on this moody new music's A-level-friendly ennui. Minor chords and wailing vocals, it was a custom-made soundtrack for our wannabe disaffected, misunderstood years. The movement's Beatles and Stones, The Cure and Echo & the Bunnymen, were in the process of going awkwardly overground in 1983 – fixtures suddenly of *Top of the Pops* and *Smash Hits* – but their sartorial influence was, it seems, much more heavily felt outside London. Macs, multiple T-shirts and heavy fringes were anything but the uniform of an ostracised cult in Northampton. They were everywhere, or seemed to be. Though big hair and outdoor slippers were not welcome at the town's only notable night-club, Cinderellas, we successfully colonised select pubs and newly minted wine bars and kept our overcoats on, however hot it got.

Cinderellas – or Cinderella Rockefellers, to use its full, disagreeably aspirational title – remained off-limits. Until, that is, it opened its doors to the great unsocked by advertising its first ever Alternative Night. This meant no door policy, and Northampton's raincoat brigade jumped at the chance actually to see inside the place. They were playing 'Mad World' by Tears For Fears – an approved record – as we pushed through about the third set of silver-laminated double-doors, but the mythical Cinderellas was no better than a hotel disco really. And no bigger either – once you'd taken into account the ubiquitous mirrored surfaces. It was not a wild success. The dance floor was too keen and obvious and needy, with its puls-ing floor and flashing lights and remained forbiddingly empty for much of the night. On reflection, we preferred the dour ambience of the Masonic Hall.

Northampton's more conservative soul boys, who were legion, might have considered us avant garde – actually, poofy's more accurate – but despite an isolated attack on Richie Ford at a house party after a Dentist Chair gig, violence rarely broke out. If you wore a tie you were, in our parlance, a 'rugby player': you went to Cinderellas and lived out the unfolding Eighties dream of chrome and money; if you wore the ripped-off hem of a T-shirt wrapped round your wrist as a kind of bangle-cum-bandage, you went to a house party in one of the terraced streets near the Racecourse and feigned existential doom. Nobody got hurt.

One member of our big-haired circle, John Lewis, had made a premature break for it at Weston Favell. Mistaking the relative *laissez faire* of sixth form for real freedom, he turned up to school one morning with his hair intricately beaded into plaits, like some Vivienne Westwood clone out of *The Face*. He looked a bit silly – he looked bloody stupid – but the rest of us would have defended to the death his right to do so. He was promptly sent home by Mr Cole to reconsider his position.

I now realise that what we were doing that summer was pretending to be students. Which, apart from Squadron Leader Griffiths, is what most of us were about to be. If by throwing away our socks we were trying to look like rock stars, then it was the type of rock star who looked like a student! Why? Because student life, with all its imagined freedoms and possibilities and subsidy, is as aspirational to fifth- and sixth-formers as Cinderellas is to rugby players. It meant leaving home, wearing second-hand clothes and attempting to become an interesting but sensitive individual – another Eighties dream for some of us.

The Metro is neatly parked outside and Sally and I quietly decorate the dark shallows of the Masonic Hall. I don't know if it's the weight of expectation, but tonight it's just not working. Too many interchangeable sixth-form parties have been held here, each with the same, almost Masonic codes and practices, the same cliques and sarcastic catchphrases, the same dash for the dance floor when 'our' music comes on. The evening seems destined to be fogged with the same mood of anticlimax as the informal buffet. Celebration brought down with the anxiety of major change.

A tyre exploded in Bert Tilsley's face on *Coronation Street* tonight. He might die. But nobody's talking about it – we're too cool for that. The talk is of Ian McCulloch on *Top of the Pops* and Richie Ford getting beaten up for trying to look a bit like Ian McCulloch. I might have been at that ill-fated house party if me and Sally hadn't been babysitting my sister. I might have had *my* head kicked in. I lean towards Sally as 'Billie Jean' starts to fade out.

'You OK? Let me know when you want to make a move,' I ask in the quiet voice reserved for talking to your girlfriend amid a larger group.

Of late, it's increasingly me who wants to make a move, and Sally who wants to stay.

The sixth form marked the start of what we view as 'serious relationships' – Craig went out with Jo, I went out with Jo, Neil went out with Liz, Mick went out with Lynsey, Craig went out with Lynsey, Craig went out with Jo's sister, I went out with Jo's sister, Pete always looked like he'd go out with Het but never actually did. We've grown used to couples becoming the prime unit within our gang. That's cool, as long as *they* don't interfere with our catchphrases. We drink cider or Fosters or Britvic for the drivers and dance to whatever approved records the DJ has.

Tonight's bash is called the Hello Goodbye Party, in that it sees off one year of maroon blazers and welcomes another. I'm ready to say goodbye. Sally wants to say hello for a bit longer.

Our conversation is curtailed when we hear the frenetic opening guitar on 'The Back of Love'. Our siren call, we all rise reflexively and head to the floor for the allotted three minutes of elbows-out raincoat dancing. It ends with that sustained chord. We repair to the edges of the hall. It's back to Shalamar.

I return to pretending I'm having a good time and manage to sustain it for another half-hour before subtly renewing my theme.

'Ready to go?'

My Great Escape mood is hardly alleviated by the fact that it seems I'm the only one who's spotted a couple of blokes from the gang who reportedly jumped Richie. They're not in the sixth form, nor are they about to be (it is, after all, for poofs), but they got in to the party somehow, skulking in their white shirts and Sta-Prest trousers. My desire to go is heightened.

'Why do you want to go so early?' Sally looks at me slightly pityingly. 'It's your party.'

I return to my previous tactic, made a little more nervous by the scent of imminent violence.

Eventually Sally will give in and I'll drive us both home 'the long way' in Mum's Metro – putting the clock back to nought to conceal the extra miles. A detour for snatched, self-educating sex, seats reclined on an unlit lane near Billing Aquadrome in sniffing distance of the sewage farm. Meanwhile, until then, the party grinds informally on, unapproved records booming out in the main hall as we suck our drinks to make them last.

'Shall we go?'

'OK.'

While today is supposed to be the first day of the rest of my life, tomorrow is the first day of the rest of Sally's. She turns sixteen. Which means that after seven months of going out – four of those taking 'the long way' – she'll be legal. She's been a tender but mature fifteen, so mature in fact that we never really considered what we were doing on a fairly regular basis as illegal. I was simply her biggest thrill, and she was mine.

We first got off with each other at the fag end of a house party at the end of 1982. I had no reason to believe that the girl underneath me on the floor of Alan's flat would turn out to be my first proper girlfriend. Sally seemed, on the face of it, to be like the others: a doll-eyed, big-skirted schoolgirl with whom I could wetly snog and fitfully grope until we tired of writing each other's initials on our exercise books. And our relationship was textbook term-time training-bra love, the kind I'd grown to know. Barely thought through, it was in truth more that we had the right look and listened to the same music than any real kismet. But the weeks went by. And the months. Sally and I started marking anniversaries. It was a sweet-natured, well-meant, mutually rewarding, highly decorative relationship, the first for both of us with any staying power, and certainly our first with anything even approaching sex.

Trading *Young Ones* catchphrases and Bauhaus lyrics like a couple of boys and sharing a penchant for big hair and espadrilles and latterly, each other's bones, Sally and I were working out fine; 1983 had our name on it. We were a foundation course in young love.

Then comfort set in. Comfort and conformity. I hadn't expected staying in to become so attractive so soon in my life, having spent most of puberty trying to get out, but romantic security – and a warm body on tap – tend to keep you indoors. This is the great irony of teenage love: when you're single you go out in order to find somebody to go out with and then, when you have, you stay in with them.

So take away the homework, the curfew and the fact that sex could only last as long as we dared and it was like a marriage.

SCENES FROM A PRETEND MARRIAGE (1)

The Beginning

We're in the living room, Winsford Way. January. My parents are having a noisy, grown-up house party to celebrate Mum's fortieth and the fact that they've put the house up for sale. Sally and I are invited: the token young people. I'm not sure it's such a great idea but we have to 'come out' as a couple at some stage. The living room is full of friends, neighbours, uncles, aunties and people from Dad's work getting merry on snowballs, eating cocktail sausages and jiving to old rock 'n'roll records. Me and Sally sit in the corner of the extension, draped over each other just enough to provide comfort without raising eyebrows. Sally is shy by nature and barely even knows me, let alone my parents or their hot-faced friends and, as such, her opportunity to shine in public as My Girlfriend is limited to looking pretty. She does look pretty though in voluminous skirt and vest top and her doll's face suits demure. Chris from up the road staggers past and, nodding to me, indicates the buffet.

'That's your fucking breakfast!' he slurs.

We laugh. I've never heard any of Mum and Dad's friends say the f-word before.

Gesturing to her half-empty glass of Bacardi and Coke, I ask Sally if she wants a top-up.

'Yes please. Don't be too long though.'

I undrape myself and take our empty glasses into the kitchen, avoiding Dad and Chris's wife Carol giving it the full rock around the clock.

The kitchen is rammed with party guests. I squeeze through to get to the table, laden with drinks. As I pour out two more Bacardis, I am accosted by a group of women.

Auntie Pat says, 'Your girlfriend's very pretty.'

'So pretty,' concurs Auntie Sue.

Neither of these women is actually my auntie, just old friends of Mum.

'Thanks,' I say, not sure how else to react.

'Where does she go?' asks Denise from next door.

'The girls' school.'

'Well, she's really pretty,' says Auntie Pat, adding, with a twinkle in her eye, 'well done.'

They laugh, not unkindly.

I feel oddly buoyed, simply by the fact that drunk adults, who know next to nothing about me, think it's a good idea. It's official then.

SCENES FROM A PRETEND MARRIAGE (2)

The Middle

March. Sally and I are listening to a tape of Echo & the Bunnymen that I've recorded off the telly – a live gig at Sefton Park in Liverpool. We're in my room. She's wearing my lumberjack shirt. We long-haul snog and gently paw at each other with the anglepoise lamp aimed at the wall for mood lighting. It is all very innocent. Mum and Dad are downstairs watching *Auf Wiedersehen, Pet.* I discover through the miracle of touch that Sally, though fully dressed, is not wearing a bra. She always wears a bra. I stop and pull back to look at her. The other person is often strangely absent during full-on teen snogging.

'I thought you'd like it,' she says.

She has been waiting all evening for me to find out and enjoys her moment of triumph.

'I do.'

'It's a late birthday present.'

We stare at each other.

'I love you.'

'I love you too.'

This is the first time we have said it. It makes us feel all warm and special. It suddenly feels like we've made a pact. No going back. Andy and Sally against the world. AC4SP 4EVER. It makes us feel like we always thought it would feel when the moment came. Perhaps we were encouraged by Russell Grant's horoscope page in the *Chronicle & Echo*. Love, he told us, was in store for both Pisces (Andy) and Leo (Sally). Hers read, 'A lion in love is a happy one.' It's ten weeks and three days.

SCENES FROM A PRETEND MARRIAGE (3)

The End

We're in Sally's living room. It's August. The beginning of the end of summer with the start of college breathing down our necks. Sally's back from her holiday in the Isle of Wight with her friend Charlotte today. I've been away too, with my family to Jersey, where I picked up a deep tan and some cockney catchphrases from a taxi driver called Dave who we met at the hotel. Sally's freckles have spread in the south coast sun – she looks more bohemian. We're exchanging presents. Love tokens.

Removing a bottle wrapped in crepe paper from the plastic bag, she says, 'I know what this is …'

It's a bottle of Malibu. Safe bet. She gives me a kiss.

'Thanks. This is for you.'

I unwrap something worryingly small and saucer-shaped. It's a small craft-shop ceramic saucer with a fish design.

'Wow,' I say, just able to mask my underwhelmed indifference.

'It's Pisces.'

'Thanks, it's really sweet.'

I'm not sure what to do with it.

'You could put your change in it.'

'Brilliant.'

We cuddle up on the sofa, aware that Sally's mum is hovering in the background, folding clothes. We haven't seen each other for a grand total of seventeen days, the longest we've been apart in eight months of going out.

She says, 'You smell different.'

'Do I? Well you sound different.'

I sound like Dave. Sally sounds a bit like Charlotte. She smells like the world outside.

By October it was over. At a new seat of learning, enjoying new friends and new ways, Sally suddenly felt more of a schoolgirl. But we'd truly lost our shine while she was in

Ryde and I was in St Helier. The magic faded as fast as a British summer. When hanging out at the right places, looking a certain way and dancing to appropriate records is the beating heart of your very existence, distraction is likely. When life is essentially shallow and cosmetic and responsibility-free, changing partners is like changing hair colour. That Sally and I lasted so long is the amazing thing. Perhaps because we had exchanged the prized property of our mutual virginity we felt a nagging guilt about going our separate ways.

While we both knew it was over, it takes one person to act – to unilaterally push the detonator – and if I'm honest with myself, Sally wanted out more than me. At the beginning of our relationship I had been quite the catch – an older, wiser, spiky-haired drummer with a Mini Metro. What more could a Northampton girl want? While I was initially more wary, expecting the usual, I soon took the relationship to heart. Now *I* wanted to stay at home and play at couples in a safe domestic vacuum, unthreatened by the maelstrom of hormones 'out there' – particularly if 'in here' involved sex education. But as I've since learnt, what women want is not as simple as that. Sally, having achieved her initial goal, increasingly wanted to go out. First to show us off, and then, once we'd shown ourselves off, to tear off with her friend Rachel dressed like twins in search of … in search of, I'm not sure what: the joy and freedom of being sixteen, I suppose. She wanted to have her cake and eat it and I became, even if only in my own eyes, that loathed object: the proprietorial husband.

* * *

'Sometimes I think you should be out at hipfreakntrendy parties with Rachel, not sitting in watching telly with me,' I explain, tugging at the tail of her checked shirt – my checked shirt actually – hoping for a denial. She says nothing.

Our latest Little Talk is not going well. Hipfreakntrendy is our catch-all term for the life Sally isn't leading, by the way. The life 'out there'. A life less ordinary. For all our crazy hair and exposed rock-star ankles, we spend an awful lot of time sitting in and watching telly. And when we do go out, we're driving to parties in Mum's Metro, not drinking and leaving early while other people roll in the coat room. I'm ashamed to admit it suits me, but not her.

'I know you feel you're missing out on a lot of … stuff.'

'I didn't say that,' she says, after an age.

'It's true though,' I counter, because it is.

More silence. Her perfect face as still as a doll's.

'If you want to finish it just tell me.' Urgency in my voice now – a rare visitor.

'I don't.'

She does, but then there would be no more lifts and even girls in the prime of their life can get used to stuff after ten months.

The Little Talks, which are talks for me and don't-talks for Sally, are becoming more frequent. In the early stages of our relationship, Rachel coveted Sally's prize – not me specifically, but a boyfriend in a band. Now she covets Rachel's freedom. The freedom to eye people up from under your fringe. The freedom to get falling-over drunk and not even know whose house it is. The freedom to get off with other people – taller boys, boys with jobs.

I honourably put us out of our misery.

'I think it would be better for *you* if we finished it.'
Silence. Doll face.

After a brief honeymoon period of singledom, Sally went out with a tall bloke who had a job. Whether he was her biggest sixteen-year-old thrill I neither knew nor cared by Christmas.

Sally and I went out for 287 days. The long way.

two

Painted Green with a Teapot on Your Head

Free at last from the shackles of school and now Sally too, I was off to college. Like the rest of my friends – who were heading for the great cities: Manchester, Bristol, Stoke – off to taste the real world. One snag: I was heading for Nene, the local technical college ten minutes down the road in Mum's Metro.

With my sights set on 'going to art school' – a vague notion at this time based on a penchant for drawing pictures – I had secured a place on Nene's one-year foundation course. I would be a student, just like the Young Ones, except I would continue to live at home and have cutlery-slamming rows with Mum.

'Can I borrow some towels and a deckchair?'

'What d'you want those for? It's freezing outside!'

'We're turning the hall at college into a beach.'

I delight in disarming Mum and Dad with these everyday bulletins from the frontline of art school, hoping to shock them to their very Middle English marrow but only really eliciting rolled eyes and patient tuts.

Bearded men with first names looked at my work and interviewed me way back in February. 'Quite a strong little folder you've got,' was one comment about my work – unless he actually meant my folder.

It might only be ten minutes from home but Nene is another planet. The goal of the one-year foundation art course – similar to that of the basic army training my brother Simon's doing as we speak – is to reduce you in the first weeks to jelly and rebuild you from the ground up; deconstruct, then reconstruct. It strips away everything you think you know until you are left with nothing, then hands you a pencil and says, 'Draw with the other end.' It's all about confronting your preconceptions of *drawingness*.

Mum and Dad barely look up from their toast.

'Airing cupboard; back of the garage.'

Pete Hepworth is dressed as a giant penis. He's in a ribbed fabric tube fashioned from an old candlewick bedspread that runs from his ankles up to his ears and a pink papier mâché skullcap with a hole in the top. At his feet rest his testicles – two pink pillowcases, stuffed with newspaper and attached to the bedspread shaft. To complete the look, he's wearing a mud-brown flasher mac and a red tabard emblazoned with a black and white swastika. His face, squashed under a black stocking, pokes out of a slit so he can see where he's going.

'What have you come as?' asks bearded, first-named John Harper as he walks around like Professor Yaffle taking it all in.

Pete replies with conviction. 'A tool of the fascist dictatorship.'

Pete is fulfilling a brief set at art school. The performance begins, captured on the college video camera which is the size of a Korean airliner. As Pete shuffles along (to the muffled strains of Wagner's *Ride of the Valkyries* coming from the tape machine in my army surplus backpack), one of his arms slides from the sleeve of his mackintosh and drops to the floor. It appears he has been maimed, presumably by the aeroplane – Alison and Jenny are in a handmade aeroplane costume – buzzing around us. Gaynor and Catherine, walking behind Pete, gather up his limb and dispassionately place it in a basket. This seems to be their job. I bring up the rear, supplying the evocative soundtrack, dressed in fatigues and covered from head to toe in camouflage strips.

It's only week two.

'Weird, isn't it?' Alison giggles afterwards, motioning with her eyes as if to say, 'All this.'

I gaze around the quad, flicking camouflage strips out of my face like an unruly fringe. It is weird to be among so many people dressed as living sculptures on a Friday afternoon in a quad in Northampton, but I don't want Alison to know that I think that. I want her to think that I think it's perfectly normal, even though I'm haunted by Alexei Sayle's parody of an art student, 'walking round a shopping precinct painted green with a teapot on me 'ead!'. Such bollocks seems but a short step away.

Nene's new intake comprises 64 of us, similar age, similar temperament, fresh out of A levels. Ripe for plucking.

Unlike school where it was strictly fifty-fifty, there are a lot more girls, who tend to have either very long, unruly hair or tight, shaved-neck bobs, and favour baggy jumpers, big earrings and dungarees. Dungarees are quite sexy in their own way. Something in the knowledge that if you unhooked the straps the trousers would fall to the floor in a heap. The boys – a conspicuous minority, all no doubt thinking about that heap – dress more conservatively in jeans and granddad shirts. I'm in Hush Puppies today. (I don't know where I got *that* from.)

Jenny, one half of the aeroplane, was the first girl I spoke to on day one – dumpy, feather-cut, in no way unattractive – and she keeps hinting at how unhappy she is in her relationship with the boyfriend 'from home'. Is she flirting with me? Am I flirting with her?

The transformation Nene would effect upon my still-spotty soul had already begun. Before the living sculptures was the beach and before that the tents. We were instructed to build our own tents – turning the college hall into a refugee camp for the trainee pretentious – and to spend two days sitting inside them, 'describing the space'. These days, you'd be looking around for the hidden cameras, but we had no choice other than to take these ostensible practical jokes at face value. We weren't in sixth form any more.

It felt a bit like a holiday for the first few weeks. Perhaps it was the camping and the deckchairs. It was a holiday for Mum and Dad too, but not for long. Art education, the route down which they had guided and encouraged me, was very soon playing fast and loose not just with my preconceptions of *drawingness*, but with my already unacceptable appearance. Having borrowed a pair of Simon's out-of-service army trousers when I dressed as the Vietnam War in week two, I decided I liked the cut of them and adopted them as daywear. This was the start of the slippery slope to full-blown artisthood and with it pariah status at 6 Kestrel Close.

It might have been 'pretty potty' in the Young Ones' student house, but not in mine. Mum and Dad, for all their admirable open-mindedness about their eldest pursuing art as a career, were – and still are – benign Tories at heart. Free-thinking in many ways, and, since Dad's retirement, rather well travelled and urbane, but back in 1983 they were basking in the rays of Thatcher's second landslide, a 144-seat majority, and didn't relish having the view spoiled by their eldest son walking out of the front door each morning looking a sight.

We had moved house that summer, trading up (as it wasn't yet known) from the functional, semi-detached estates of Abington Vale to the more spacious cul-de-sacs of Weston Favell village. Kestrel Close was – and still is – a picturesque little no-through-road in attractive brick, a Shangri-La for those who have saved and invested well: middle-aged or retired couples whose kids have flown the nest, leaving more time to garden and golf and write stiff letters to the *Telegraph*.

Unfortunately, its depilated gravel drives and wooden garage doors lulled my mum into a false sense of superiority. It wasn't so much that *she* changed once across the threshold, but that she imagined the class of next-door neighbour had and she adjusted accordingly. Mum felt watched and scrutinised in the new house, as if those who had moved in before us formed some sort of critical cabal. Observing our every move, they had the power to ostracise and even exile new residents if they didn't meet stringent Kestrel Close standards. Social climbers would be repelled. Families with scruffy artist sons would have a red cross painted on their garage door. Mum took my worsening appearance personally, as if perhaps I was single-handedly plotting to destroy her reputation before Dad had even got round to putting up a toilet-roll holder in the second loo. I wasn't. I was just doing the same as everyone else. And it wasn't like I looked as bad as Paul Garner.

Paul and I had been bosom buddies at school since 1980, thrown together initially by Saturday morning art classes. I first became aware of Paul when his drawing of sleeve artwork for 'Rat Trap' by the Boomtown Rats was displayed in the corridor leading to the art block. I was equal parts impressed and jealous: it was a leering rat's face, echoing the illustration from the cover of the James Herbert novel we were all reading, but it was so detailed and better than anything else up there.

A somewhat gangly, less than aerodynamic young man, Paul was cursed with trickier skin, more problematic hair and riper bodily oils than most, which put him out of the race for the ladies and allowed him instead to concentrate all his adolescent energies into the wrist. (Stop it!) In the Venn diagram of my daily existence, I never tried to assimilate Paul into my music and girl-obsessed circle of friends. I did invite him to my sixteenth birthday party and he sat unselfconsciously in the corner and ate the food. I felt certain that my other mates would have misunderstood his artistic tunnel vision and that he in turn would find them shallow and frivolous. Somehow, thanks to a modicum of plate-spinning, I managed to occupy both worlds, content that I would never be quite as good as Paul at drawing caricatures, but at least I might get a snog occasionally.

When sixth form came around in 1981, Paul opted out and signed up for Nene's three-year graphics diploma. While I spent the next two years trudging to and from the biology lab in a tie, he was a real student. And when I finally caught up with him at Nene in September 1983, I had a lot of catching up to do.

Paul had turned into a werewolf. He had transformed himself – or had *been* transformed – from super creep into scary monster, as visibly and spectacularly as David the backpacker in *An American Werewolf in London*. He entered Nene a mild-mannered sixteen-year-old with hair that curled outwards if he didn't palm it down flat, a wearer of nondescript cords and black jumpers,. A creative whirlwind, yes, but disguised as the boy next door. Two years down the higher-educational line, he had turned himself into a creature of the night. He sometimes quite literally barked as he walked down the corridor, a cascade of unkempt black hair, some of it pinched into random pigtails, unshaven face, staring eyes, exposed teeth, baseball boots, camouflage trousers, and he was so ... big. The boy had shot up since school, as if perhaps Weston Favell had been physically repressing him, squashing him down into a more manageable shape, keeping a foot on his head. He drew pentangles on everything and entertained unsavoury fantasies about Linda Blair in *The Exorcist*.

We were all going through a painful transformation, but Paul's was a caricature, like one of his drawings. He hunched I suspect to disguise his new height. Even though they can't have been, Paul's friends from the graphics diploma course all seemed taller than those of us on foundation – and of course *pottier*. They had a habit of cuddling each other – just doing it, right there in the Union Bar, for the hell of it. I dare say they stayed up until one o'clock some nights too. One of them, called Jimbox, could fit an entire protractor in his mouth, creating a smile or a frown depending on which way he put it in.

They'd been through two years together and now they thought and moved as one. Paul sometimes seemed like the ringleader. He had once been my bedroom buddy; now I was in awe of him. He was also Mum's worst nightmare. What's worse, Paul lived round the corner and called for me every college morning. I would sometimes sit at the front window and watch him stomping up Kestrel Close, just for the fun of imagining what the new neighbours would think.

Here he comes. Walking up the close. In broad daylight. Head down, carrying that plastic toolbox. It's filled with magic markers and Winsor & Newton inks, but the neighbours probably suspect body parts. He has *things* drawn on his clothes, and rubber bands wound round clumps of his hair, streaked with genuine white since that nasty business with his appendix. Mum's upstairs making the beds. She's already done me some egg sandwiches and put them in a Tupperware tub.

Ding-dong!

'I'll get it – it's Paul!' I shout up the stairs. You can see his face distorted through the textured-glass window in the new door. It's probably how he sees himself.

'Wotcha,' I chirrup.

Paul just pulls a horrible face by way of a returned greet-ing, narrowed eyes, huge teeth. I wonder if he'd do the same if Mum got to the door first? I don't invite him in: more fun to leave him out on display.

'I'm off, seeya!'

'Bye!' she calls, from a safe distance. 'Have you got your towels?'

I have, stuffed in a large Beatties bag. And a deckchair which I am going to love carrying incongruously down Kestrel Close in September, taking my time on the gravel drive, while Mum hides in the en suite shower room and prays to Margaret Thatcher that Mrs Smith at No. 7 isn't looking out of her front window.

Paul and I stand at the bus stop and wait not for the bus to college, but for one of the girls with cars – sometimes Gaynor, sometimes Steph – who all seem to drive 2CVs. They go with the big earrings.

'Morning!' Gaynor chimes as Paul and I climb in, filling the back seat with our paraphernalia. 'Morning!' I chime back on behalf of both of us. Paul makes his Alien face, and even she – a girl with a lisp and brightly coloured print trousers and a slash-neck Breton shirt – understands that he's being friendly. So why can't Mum?

At least, having come between us, Nene took my mind momentarily off Sally. There was, after all, a new woman in my life now. A naked woman.

Daryl was the foundation course life model.

'Come on, Madame Arcarti,' bronchial head-of-course Frank Cryer would say to her, playfully, as he put her to work, a baffling reference to the fake spiritualist in Coward's *Blithe Spirit*. Margaret Rutherford played her in the film. Daryl looked nothing like Margaret Rutherford. Not that I'd ever seen Margaret Rutherford in the nude.

Daryl was my first ever real-life nude woman, not counting my own mother. (I'd barely seen Sally in the nude – it's not *that* kind of sex when you live under the parental roof.) Daryl's job was to sit perfectly still, perfectly blithe, perfectly naked except for an Alice band, usually on a wooden box draped in a dust sheet, sometimes herself draped across a covered mattress, there to be gawped at and studied in a fundamental way by eighteen-year-olds wielding charcoal. Antique five-bar electric heaters were always thoughtfully and strategically arranged around her (those big rooms never heat up) and a screen placed decorously by the door. So it went. We never saw Daryl undress – that would have seemed intrusive somehow – instead she just appeared out of a cupboard in a pale robe and slippers, as if she was perhaps turning in for the night: Madame Arcarti. Nothing fake about her. What you saw was what you got, and you saw everything.

We would come to know Daryl in a way that we would never know our own mothers. Every Tuesday we would inspect and reproduce her every nook and cranny for solemn hours at a time. It would be wrong to say that we ever really *knew* Daryl – in that we hardly spoke to this mysterious, mousy, long-limbed woman, other than to say a respectful hello, and to listen to her occasional gripes about the temperature of the room – and yet we knew when she was on her period, whether we wished to or not. A strange pact, to be sure, but one to which art students become inured, while the rest of the world sniggers behind its hand.

Sally and I had never talked about it, so I have no idea whether it disturbed her or not that I came home with detailed drawings I had made of another woman, naked. It may just be coincidence that we terminated the relationship after three Tuesdays of life class.

We drew a bloke occasionally, who once experienced what I can only imagine was an unwanted semi, but it was usually Daryl. Lanky, tired-looking, not-my-type Daryl with a voice like Candice Marie's off *Nuts in May*. She did something for me that no other woman could: she objectified the female form. Not womankind, just the interconnected shapes of the body, where they joined, how they fell, the weight of an unsupported breast, the shadow created by an untoned thigh come to rest on another, the light behind pubic hair in profile.

If Madame Arcarti had foreseen the end of my cosy, photogenic relationship with Sally, she kept it to herself.

With almost mundane inevitability I got off with Jenny on the grubby lino floor of Pete's kitchen after a college party at Christmas. It was rather sordid and desperate but hey, I was a single man. It wasn't me who'd angled for the 'freedom' to do this – but since I *was* doing it, I had to assume Sally was also doing it, on another floor in a different kitchen, which wasn't a happy thought for me. Jenny was still going out with her boyfriend 'from home', by the way. He was elsewhere that night, at the very back of Jenny's mind. She and I remained friends for the rest of the course (this night was never spoken of again), and she probably finished with her boyfriend when she got to big college anyway. Proper college. *College* college.

* * *

31

All this change, all this friction, all this art. It seems ungrateful to admit that by somewhere around week four of the course, I was bored. I was eighteen years old; eighteen-year-olds get bored for a living. But it wasn't just nature. To keep the culture-shocked interested, you must continually raise the bar. By week four, having pitched a tent, created a hall-beach and dressed as a South-East Asian conflict, the extraordinary had become ordinary.

On the last day of the last week of that first term, out of 64 of us on the course, only fifteen rolled into college. Fifteen! Perhaps the rest of them had trouble choosing their outfit that morning. Or perhaps we were proper students after all. *Student* students.

Pass the protractor.

three

Six
Blackcurrant
and Lemonades

Kevin is squirting anti-static solution all over *Blue Sunshine*, first album by The Glove. But we're not talking about The Glove. We're talking about another band.

'They're depressing,' he says, throwaway.

'Whaaaa-aat?'

'Whaaaa-aa-aaat?' Kevin mimics, playfully, not looking up from the task. ('Whaaaaat' is one of our words.) 'I don't like them. They're depressing.'

'And what are Death Cult and Sex Gang Children and X-Mal Deutschland?'

'I dunno. They're punk. They're not poofy.'

It's come to this. I knew it would.

You're supposed to apply the liquid, which can be purchased from any branch of Boots, to the anti-static brush, not directly onto the disc – but we have become obsessed with eliminating crackle from our records. Now delusional, neither of us is convinced of the positive effects of this solution beyond one or two plays – despite the record being visibly slick with the stuff. We're serious addicts and we can't go back to casual use of an anti-static cloth *now*.

'Sex Gang Children are poofy. And they're intrinsically depressing!'

We've just discovered the word 'intrinsic' and are trying to crowbar it into regular conversation.

'You egg.'

Teenage musical appreciation is all about the ratification of your peers. Kevin *is* my peers. He is Kevin Pearce. And what joins us at the hip is music: post-punk, dark, Gothic-sounding music with – ideally – thumping tribal drums, the odd pompous choir and an extended mix on the 12-inch. The choosing and buying of it, the taping of it, the careful designing of the cassette inlay cards and our fixed opinions of it.

Through the ever-present evening mist of Sunsilk hair-spray, a new band has entered our orbit that Kevin doesn't like and I do. He says they're depressing and poofy – even though they're not – and calls me an egg.

We agree to disagree and return to common ground: The Glove. We both like The Glove. He places the glistening album on the turntable. The stylus goes down onto track one: 'Like an Animal'. It's crackle-free. For now.

I fell in love with The Smiths on 4 November 1983. The day they interrupted my tea of fish-finger sandwiches. The day they appeared on *The Tube*.

The Tube ran a specially shot video for the group's new single 'This Charming Man'. Flowers. Beads. Oxfam couture. Morrissey quite unlike any pop singer I had ever seen. They had arrived at exactly the right time in my life. I was just starting to feel the first tug of self-imposed woe after the split with Sally.

The Smiths filled the gaping hole left by Sally. The bit not filled by Kevin.

My earliest recollection of Kevin Pearce is that of a mild irritant, which just goes to show that first impressions are unreliable, that circumstance is everything, and that you *can* steal your younger brother's best mate.

Without it being poofy.

Kevin and Simon had become inseparable in the fifth year: catchphrases, double-dates, masterplans, the textbook male teenage friendship. Like all good duos, they were symbiosis in motion, evolving into mirror images of one another, adopting identical Top Man style, going out with similar-looking girls.

Simon and I had of course once been mates ourselves, but puberty put paid to that, and the faultline of two years' age difference opened up into a chasm. So when Mum and Dad bounced the idea of building an extension and granting Simon and I separate rooms, I jumped at the chance. It was getting increasingly difficult to explore my own burgeoning sexuality with Simon in the bunk above me.

'What are you doing?' he asked one night after lights-out, when the bed seemed to be rocking about.

'I'm dancing,' I replied, quick as a flash.

'Well pack it in.'

We didn't do locks on bedroom doors in the Collins

household – it's not a prison you know! – but sovereignty was recognised, and after the extension Simon didn't go into my new bedroom or touch my stuff when I wasn't there. He certainly wouldn't play *my* records on *my* stereo at lunchtimes while I was at school. The Hitachi SDT-1000 had been my seventeenth birthday present, monolithic in both structure and significance, the metallic, faux-stack altar at which I worshipped. Turntable, tuner, cassette deck with 'full auto stop mechanism', Dolby logic … if I could have padlocked its lid down I would have. Sally and I lost our virginity to that stereo. I like to think 'The Drowning Man' by The Cure was playing, but it might equally have been 'We Are Detective'.

I got home from school one day to find the telltale green power light on, speakers still buzzing. Simon and Kevin had been in there. They had, I discovered, regularly been violating my airspace. But a teenager's bedroom is his castle and I had them bang to rights, taking their misdemeanour to the highest authority. Mum and Dad gave Simon a 'good telling off'.

'You're not to go into Andrew's room and play with his stereo.'

'We didn't scratch anything.'

'I don't care, Simon. You've got your own records.'

Yeah, 'Poison Ivy' by the Lambrettas. Enjoy.

I secretly blamed Kevin, who I imagined to be the ringleader.

Simon went into the army the week I started Nene College. It was a big week, full of contrasts. Militarily obsessed since Action Man, he'd been in the cadets for years, and had

pretty much screwed up his O levels so it was a na
progression to join up. But this didn't make it any easier for
poor Mum. The one son who was well turned out and
responsible and the neighbours would never get to see him!
My little brother was off to Shorncliffe Barracks to be what
army lingo called, with typical erudition, a 'crap-hat'.

Before he went though, Kevin threw Simon a bon-voyage
party in his parents' double garage. It was a noble gesture, if
a rather ill-attended do, but I dragged Sally along in Simon's
honour, there to drink cider and watch him snog a girl with
the exotic name of Gordana, a kind of going-away present.
To my surprise I found I liked what I saw of Kevin that night.
Full marks for decorating the garage and fixing up the
speakers, and what's more, he seemed like a good friend. He
was also playing his own records on his own record player.
That said, I didn't want him as my mate. I had plenty of
mates in September 1983 – not to mention a girlfriend – *I*
didn't need another.

Kevin did. He was just about to lose Simon. Which is how
we ended up sharing a school-leavers' pint down the Bold
Dragoon one Tuesday night and realising we had chemistry.
Happy coincidence meant that he'd just started a two-year
Building Studies diploma at Nene, so, despite being two
years apart, we were both new intake. Any residual older-
brother awe arising from the age difference quickly evaporated. We simply got on, from the word go: the catchphrases, double-dates and masterplans were not far behind.

I considered Kevin my replacement brother, if that
doesn't sound too harsh on Simon, who was by that time
being made to eat a spoonful of instant coffee by some sadist
of a sergeant and jump as high as he could in a doorway

without banging his head on the jamb. Or at least standing by while some other poor crap-hat did. Kev and I were down the wine bar on Bridge Street, preening. Although I would have been loath to admit it, he really became my replacement girlfriend, my replacement Sally.

Around this time I also changed my name. No longer was I Andrew Collins, son of John and Christine Collins, brother of Simon and Melissa Collins – but Andy Kollins. A subtle and rather ludicrous adjustment, granted – but one full of significance. With a gothic 'K' I was unconsciously detaching myself from the family, striking out for independence. Kollins also looked miles better next to Kevin – my new brother.

As alternative and outcast as Kevin and I might have fancied ourselves, Saturdays for us followed a routine as conservative and unbending as any rugby player's: drive down town in the afternoon, park Mum's car on the same floor of the multi-storey car park, mooch around the same shops, say hello to Goz in Habitat, buy some hairspray and Dextrasol tablets in Boots (we eat Dextrasol as a kind of frothy affectation), given sufficient funds buy a record after ages spent flicking through the racks, have a strip of photos taken in the Photo-Me booth at the bus station, walk to and fro past the bakery and try and catch the eye of the girl who works in there – if we ever did or actually talked to her it would ruin it! – take the record back to mine and play it again and again, drive Kevin home for his tea, reconvene later at his house, spend at least an hour crimping and spraying each other's hair into solid haystacks, undisturbed by his parents, drive into town, park in the same spot on George Row, get to the wine bar

earlier than anyone else, order six blackcurrant and lemon-
ades so that once we're installed at our table and the place
fills up with Northampton's spiky people, we won't have to
get up again and fight our way to the bar. (I drink blackcurrant and lemonade because I'm driving; Kevin does so out of
loyalty and symmetry. And purple drinks look cool.) We
might meet a girl in there or at a house party afterwards. If
we meet two, we might talk them into coming with us to
Abington Park, there to sit at the top of the slide in the pitch
black or the bandstand and scare ourselves with talk of
werewolves. Once, in a big four-way huddle, Kevin and I
ended up holding each other's hands by mistake. Well, we
did have gloves on. Maybe it wasn't a mistake. We'll split into
pairs if the girls are up for it and snog them with sweet,
blackcurrant breath. Often I'll take the parked car with my
girl and Kevin will disappear into the dark with his. Nothing
carnal will happen: too cold, too many layers. We'll deliver
the girls home – and rarely will a phone number be
exchanged – then I'll deliver Kevin home and by the time I
get in Mum and Dad will be fast asleep and won't see how
big my hair has been. By the morning it will be flattened
somewhat and that which they don't know can't hurt them.

'Did you have a good night?'

'Yeah.'

'Where did you go?'

'Wine bar.'

'What time did you get in?'

'Not too late.'

'Meet any nice girls?'

'Not really.'

'Don't you think it's time you had that cut?'

'It's just getting good!'

Why won't they leave me alone? It's not as if we crash the car or get off our heads on drink and drugs – *whaa-aaa-aaat* drugs? – and we never stay out all night, even if we cruise for a bit in the Metro, listening to Kevin's weird German punk tape with no band names on it. *Die neue Deutsche welle.*

One Saturday, Kevin slept over. We stayed up till the small hours talking bollocks and drinking duty-free Pernod and eventually passed out on my bed. Mum discovered us there in the morning, curled like embryos, and, even though we were fully clothed, *on* the bed, she flew into a high huff. While Kevin put his boots on and cleaned his teeth, I found myself at the breakfast bar effectively defending myself against the trumped-up charge of homoerotic shenanigans. With Kevin! Who dismisses bands for being poofy! Who's studying to be a bricklayer! It was so ridiculous it wasn't worth the oxygen of a proper row.

'Well, what were you both doing on the bed?' she sniped.

'Sleeping,' I replied, quick as a flash. 'What do you *think* we were doing?' (Come on, say the words …)

'I don't *know*!'

'It's Kevin, Mum! Ke-vin!'

Honestly, it was like Alan's flat all over again. I'd been out with Sally for months. What did I have to do to convince them that I was interested exclusively in having sex with girls?

four

A Devil of an Ulcer

I'd rather not but I don't know what else to do. I push open their bedroom door. She's making the bed.

'Mum?'

She'll think from my tone that I want money or to borrow something. I want neither.

'It hurts when I do a wee.'

Jesus, I sound about ten years old.

Her reaction is immediate and calm.

'You'd better talk to your dad … John!'

Dad emerges from the en suite shower room, where he has been cleaning his teeth.

Mum repeats the news: 'It hurts when he wees.'

Dad doesn't even look shocked. I know he's sanguine and pragmatic by nature but I thought this might do it. And yet it's almost as if he's been waiting to hear these words. Of course it does. It was only a matter of time.

'Does it feel like you're peeing razor blades?' he enquires, matter-of-factly, like a doctor.

'Yes,' I confirm. That's precisely how it feels.

'We'd better ring Dr Randall.'

I sigh deeply, shrinking with the exhalation. It seems we all understand what's just taken place in this room, without resorting to sordid terminology – that will come later, with Dr Randall.

Dad springs into action; he phones the surgery, books me an appointment and takes an hour off work to drive me down there. We sit in the waiting room together, too dazed to look at the magazines, and I'm called in. Dr Randall, our family doctor, the man who once looked in my mouth and told me I had a devil of an ulcer, asks me what the problem is.

'It feels like razor blades when I urinate.'

I'm an old pro at this already.

We establish that there is also 'a discharge'. He asks me if I have had unprotected sex in the past few weeks. Nobody has ever asked me this before. I tell him yes. I've never had *protected* sex, but I don't tell him that. He knows what I've got. So do I and so do Dad and Mum.

I can only assume that *she* doesn't know. *She* is going to find out.

Here's the good news: Dr Randall works one day a week at the 'special clinic' at the hospital so when I pay it a visit, as I must, forthwith, I will at least get to see a familiar face. I still feel like a leper though. My disease has a name and it's like diarrhoea with the word 'goner' in.

On the drive home Dad gently interrogates me.

'How do you think you might have got it?' he asks. He doesn't mean how, he means who.

'Abigail.'

Dad guessed as much. When I brought her back to the house to catch VD off her late last Saturday he was still up and about and introductions were formally made over the kettle in the kitchen. You could tell he thought she was really something – he even said so at breakfast the next morning, risking a 'John!' from Mum.

In my diary I call Abigail my 'bilingual film star' as she is studying languages at college in nearby Kettering and looks stunning. Quite unlike Sally, Abigail is tall and mature and wears lots of make-up. (She also works in Boots.) Even though she's only nineteen, she *looks* like a woman. Which is why Dad was, I think, so taken aback last Saturday: Andy's brought a woman back to the house instead of a girl. He was proud of me then, although I suspect some of the glitter has come off *that* this morning.

Well, Abigail certainly turned out to be special. I'm going to the clinic to prove it.

The facts are repeated for Mum when we return. Suddenly we're all very grown up, talking matter-of-factly about who I've been having unprotected sex with. I felt ten years old again when I went to the surgery; I have returned nineteen. Old enough to know better.

As it happens, and for much less dramatic reasons, I was on the brink of breaking it off with Abigail, days before Dr Randall made me a man. Burning pee simply gave me a better excuse.

She never did feel much like a girlfriend. I met her on a Friday, slept with her on a Saturday – in my bedroom, under the parental roof – and again a week later. The razor blades came a week after that: textbook gonorrhoea. All they showed you at school in the health education film about sexually transmitted diseases was a group of animated silhouettes moving past each other as if on a busy street and some kind of infection indicated by a pulsating red blob being passed randomly from one to another. No mention of discharge. If they'd showed the boys in our class what it's like to have a swab inserted into the end of your penis we would all have happily stayed virgins.

Kevin and I glimpsed the stunning Abigail across a crowded wine bar and we knew she was special. She had spiky hair and wore layers – our kind of girl – and she had a friend, Ange, less attractive than Abigail but frankly, who wasn't? We wowed them both with our rehearsed Andy and Kevin repartee, played the brothers act, made *two* drinks last all evening and half-arranged to be in the same place the following night: a goth double-header at the Black Lion (Seven League Red from nearby Market Harborough supporting Sister Crow, all the way from Leicester). This was how these things often worked out, except for one key detail.

After the gig I took Abigail home, rather than to the park.

Mum and Dad exercised a thoroughly modern attitude to my bringing girls home – thanks in part to the 'gay' scare I'd given them when I was seventeen. Hanging out with bigger boys at Alan's flat – the manager of our band Absolute Heroes and my first friend old enough to live in a flat – I refused to deny to my parents that I was gay when accused of this most heinous crime one night. It was around that time that Mum's Metro became almost constantly available to me, in the hope it would improve my prospects with girls.

There were no locks on doors in our house as we have established, but once I turned eighteen Mum and Dad never entered my bedroom without knocking, and if they knew I had company, they even had the dignity to conduct conversations through the door.

'We're going to bed now – don't be too late.'

'OK.'

I was aware even then how fortunate I was to enjoy this level of rumpoactive autonomy. Only my sister Melissa would sometimes break the knock-first rule – if, say, she wanted to borrow my scissors. But if anything private was afoot and she did open the door, the room would be lit only by a single red light bulb in my anglepoise lamp, so there was, in police parlance, nothing to see. It was still bloody annoying. She was twelve years old and inquisitive – perhaps it was subconscious mischief disguised as innocent borrowing. I'd rather not think about it, but suffice to say, 'I'll get them,' is something I had to say often. I should have bought her some scissors for her thirteenth birthday.

It became clear on VD Day that Mum and Dad imagined me to have been enjoying one long, continuous shagfest up in the red-lit room since we moved to Kestrel Close in the summer of '83. While going out with Sally it might have been the case – when we weren't having a Little Talk – but since then: nothing. Jenny on the lino was just a fumble.

Nothing, that is, until Abigail.

You could tell they were surprised. Disappointed? Maybe Dad was. Either way, we had reached a point of no return in our relationship, I had changed in their eyes, as had they in mine. They had admitted to me that they thought I was rutting away constantly under their roof, even though I wasn't. I had never given any thought to my own parents imagining me having sex. It's almost as squirm-inducing as imagining *them* having sex.

The reason I was going to give Abigail the cold shoulder was that she had pushed things too far. After just two Saturdays together, admittedly intimate ones, she wrote me a letter from Paris (something to do with her course) in which she sounded nothing less than infatuated. She couldn't bear to be without me, even though we'd only spent about six or seven hours alone together. I compensated for her over-enthusiasm by taking my romantic football home.

As I wrote in my diary, quoting Jack Nicholson from *Terms of Endearment*:

I'd rather stick needles in my eyes.

In fact, I got razor blades in my urine.

For the dreaded clap clinic, you'd hardly know it's here. It's just up some stone steps and through a nondescript blue door. A sign saying Special Clinic is reassuringly discreet but I still glance furtively up and down before entering. I am alone this time, no chaperone.

I was born here, Northampton General Hospital – a vast, gloomy old Victorian sprawl that sits between Billing Road and Bedford Road. I also had stitches here as an accident-prone child, in my head and my face, and now I have returned to have a plastic spatula inserted where no implement has been inserted before.

This is no place for Dad. This is my penance, and mine alone: to sit on an orange plastic chair in a waiting room papered with overly frank posters about heroin and condoms. I'm now wearing a wad of tissue in my pants. I am unclean. Abigail's in Paris.

I try not to catch the eye of the cagey middle-aged man seated opposite with a briefcase at his feet – what's *he* doing catching gonorrhoea?

I scan the room; if you didn't know it was special, you'd say it was just like any other waiting room. I consider a *Reader's Digest* but this is no time to improve my word power. I've learnt one new word this week already.

Then an amazing thing happens, something I instantly know I can never tell anyone about: *he* comes in. I think his name's Gavin but I only know him to look at; he's one of the cool blokes you see around at parties, older than us, maybe 22, heavy fringe, pushed up at the back and sides, denim jacket, suede boots, drives a van I think and DJs at nights. Looks like he wears eyeliner. Gavin, if that is in fact his name, is one of those blokes who all the girls our age fancy and all the boys want to be. And he's got VD.

Even though we don't know each other by name, or even to speak to, he nods at me by way of a greeting. I'm so proud. Gavin knows me.

''Cha.'

''Cha.'

This is the traditional manly Northampton greeting – it's short for wotcha. It says that all is well. Of course neither of us is well. Unfortunately I get called in first, so I never get to find out his actual name, but it doesn't matter – I have now entered into a sacred, unspoken pact with someone who DJs and wears eyeliner. Your secret's safe with me, Gav.

Then it's hello, pants down, spatula time, and I'm back feeling exposed, dirty and molested, despite Dr Randall's supreme nonchalance. What I've got is nothing special but I don't know anybody who even knows anybody else who's had it. How can I ever even snog a girl in the park again? She'll know! She's smell it on me! Kevin will have to find someone else to preen with at the Berni Inn.

'We'll soon have it cleared up with some antibiotics,' Randall reassures me. 'Pull your pants back up.'

The treatment isn't the real pain though. Apparently, even though I know precisely who I caught it off, I have to contact every girl I've had sex with in the past six weeks. That means the only other girl I've ever had sex with.

Sally and I had one for old times' sake in February.

Needles in my eyes.

Can life get much worse? I am riddled from head to toe with disease. My parents now know every detail of my sex life. And I have to call Sally – sweet, innocent sixteen-year-old schoolgirl Sally – arrange to meet tomorrow lunchtime without telling her why and then inform her, parked at a bus stop on the Lings estate that, through no fault of her own, she has to book her own appointment at the clap clinic and be humiliated just because I slept with a girl from Boots who slept with a dodgy bloke before me. It's Wednesday.

My interview at Chelsea School of Art is on Monday.

five

Eye Drops

I'm Pritt-sticking a picture of Morrissey into my diary. Carefully posed for the photographer from *No. 1* magazine, he's pretending to write on a pad with a biro – lyrics or a poem perhaps.

Customising the picture to suit my state of mind, I carefully add a single teardrop falling from his eye and write 'Dear Mum' on his pad, as if he's writing a letter home. Even though a rueful smile plays around his lips, he now looks sad and homesick. Morrissey is me. I am Morrissey.

Chelsea School of Art had accepted me. The interview went off fine. Dad accompanied me to London and back and we ate real fast-food cheeseburgers together at Euston Station. Mine had what I described in my diary as 'something green' in it, but I ate it anyway in the spirit of pioneering adventure.

I guess it was this spirit that drove me from the provinces: a thirst for the unknown, a yearning for the bigger picture. In truth, if Nene had done a degree course I expect I would have stayed there, but they didn't and, as much as anything else, it seemed time to go. It's what students did.

I'd been to London on day-trips, to the Natural History Museum, the Science Museum, Regents Park Zoo, the Tate Gallery, The Cure at Hammersmith Odeon. First being taken, and later taking myself, for my own reasons. The same pull that called Dick Whittington back was calling me down the M1. It would, I figured, be like a three-year day-trip. I could go to the Natural History Museum every day.

It was either go to London or get mixed up in what I had observed among my sixth-form peers as the Big Town Lottery. The decisions seemed largely random: Bath or Stoke? Hatfield or Newcastle? Chelsea had been my first-choice college. My second was Leeds Polytechnic, a place, quite frankly, I had no interest in going to. So, in fact, it was no choice at all. In the end, I'm not sure many of us really know how we finally make our big college decisions. For the record, my own particular random influence was the fact that, unlike all the other degree-course prospectuses, Chelsea's contained no pictures. I thought that was cool, and I already had a picture of London. It was a jigsaw of Piccadilly Circus I'd owned since childhood. That's where I wanted to be. This is something I had to keep telling myself as September loomed, London was *what I wanted*.

While on holiday with my family at the Merton Hotel in Jersey at the end of the summer of '84 – my final summer as a boy, my last ever family holiday, cleansed of VD but still wary of sex – Simon and I spent an unprecedented amount of social time with a gregarious, sprightly 84-year-old taxi driver called Bill from Redhill. Holidaying alone, he sort of adopted us for the week.

On learning that I was off to art school in London, Bill, a cockney by birth, told me I already had 'the Chelsea stroll' and promised to give me a free ride in his black cab if he ever spotted me on the streets of London. This cheered me at the time, but his offer gives me little comfort now, on my first night away from home.

So, here I am. My first night in London. I'm suddenly an individual, alone, isolated, picked up and put down and expected to start building the rest of my life. Sticking the seasonally adjusted Morrissey picture in my diary makes me feel, if not better, at least momentarily focused on my own misery and sense of displacement. Tomorrow morning, although it may as well be next year, I'm going to take the bus to Chelsea School of Art for the first time. I feel sick. Sick. Ill. Lost. Rudderless. Stranded. Scared. Hoodwinked. Homesick.

My new address – get used to writing it – is Room 317, Ralph West Hall of Residence, 45 Worfield Street, London SW11 8QZ. The third floor of a nine-storey Inner London Education Authority tower block in Battersea overlooking a council estate. It's the first address I've ever had which hasn't been Mum and Dad's.

The Ralph West Hall radiators aren't yet working. It's so cold I can almost see my Twiglet breath. I keep turning my radiator on, just in case it suddenly works. It doesn't. It's Sunday night and outside in the dark it is chucking buckets.

Last night was my final hurrah in Northampton with Kevin. Despite the familiar props – our usual parking space, our regular spot inside the doorway of the Berni Inn, the obligatory quest for a house party – there was an air of going through the motions, a strange anticlimax. I told all the regulars I'd be back.

This afternoon, after a steak send-off lunch at home – my last meal – I had one final row about clothes with Mum before leaving. She cried. Dad adjudicated. I understood. Mum and I kissed goodbye on the doorstep – recklessly for the Collinses, in full view of the neighbours – and Dad drove me down to London with my Hitachi stereo carefully propped between the old kettle, the portable telly and my bags in the boot. Leaving home, I discovered, is not like packing to go on holiday. You have to make informed, far-reaching decisions: which posters to transplant from one wall to another, whether or not to unscrew the anglepoise lamp (perhaps they supply one?), which LPs to leave behind for reasons of space. I left punk and New Romantic and packed only post-punk and The Smiths. Of my assorted Echo & the Bunnymen pics I carefully removed only the full-colour, glossy ones from *The Face* and *Smash Hits* and left the browning *NME* cuttings, fearful that the delicate parchment in its ageing, Blu-tack-stained state wouldn't weather being taken down and put back up again. I packed the red light bulb of course, my hairdryer and crimpers, and I bagged up the Pisces saucer Sally gave me – for old times' sake, and to keep my change in.

Mum packed me off with a few comestible luxuries to make my new life a little easier: Twiglets, cheesy biscuits, sugar cubes, Red Label teabags, a jar of Gold Blend (even though I never drink coffee; I suppose it was for entertaining – another alien concept) and an introductory bottle of Five Pints powdered milk. And as if that wasn't enough for a party, I also stashed a few miniatures from Jersey: Bacardi,

Pernod, Malibu. The old black and white TV was for continuity, so I could still watch *Brookside* and *The Tube* and, if I kept the door closed, pretend I was still at home and nothing's changed.

Everything's changed of course. My backdrop has been replaced, the rug pulled from under me, yet I'm expected to call this place home. I don't have a bedroom any more; I have a 'study bedroom'. It has unsightly orange curtains, a number on the door and a lock. (Did I really have to come all this way to merit a lock on my door?) I have my own sink, my own wardrobe with a sliding door and my own barrack-style bed. Simon would be proud. There's no duck-down continental quilt, it's sheets, hospital corners, a blanket and a brown bedspread, all contributing to the sense of, if not the armed services, then certainly boarding school.

Dad helped me settle in, which meant putting my sugar cubes away, artistically mounting my posters and wiring up my speakers. He also fixed a two-pin plug to an extension lead for me, so as to comply with halls voltage limits. You're not allowed to plug irons in, apparently, which will be a great loss.

We both knew it was an important moment when he finally left me there. I tried to match his stoicism as we stood and parted at the front door of the halls, wishing I was man enough to shake his hand when he dashed off to the car in the pouring rain – when all the dads dashed off to their cars in the pouring rain – but the whole wretched experience has taken years off me. I feel like I'm fourteen again. I've never needed my dad so much and he's halfway up the M1 with an empty boot.

Having christened the room – and tested the stereo – with a territorial too-loud spin of 'William It Was Really

Nothing', I lie on my bed and wait for my new life to begin. When it doesn't, I wander tentatively down the hard-tiled, dimly strip-lit corridor and past the lifts to inspect the toilets: unisex and communal, shaver sockets and tampon bins. I feel sick again. I may never go to the toilet here – a girl could be in the next cubicle, it just doesn't bear thinking about.

I return heavy-hearted to Room 317. As I am unlocking and opening my door the boy in the room opposite comes out. We cannot avoid making contact, as much as a part of me would like to hide away from everyone and have my meals pushed under the door.

'All right?' he says, a hairy-looking bloke in an uncool jumper.

'Yeah,' I reply, not yet fully conversant with reflex greeting etiquette: if someone enquires after your health your response is to enquire back.

'I'm Mike.'

He looks like a Mike.

'Andy.'

Conspicuous non-shake of hands.

'See you got the old telly?' he says, peering over my shoulder through my open door. I feel invaded by his prying eyes. How does he know it's an old telly?

'Yeah. It's only black and white though.' Don't want Mike to think I'm some rich kid.

'Still … Nice one.'

An unkind thought races through my head: if you think you're coming in to watch *my* telly you can fuck right off. Then in an instant it dawns on me that I need Mike; I need him not to fuck right off.

'You going down for food?' I enquire.

'Yeah,' he replies, evidently as relieved as I am to have found someone to go down with.

'Shall we go down together?'

'OK. I'll give you a knock in five minutes.'

'Nice one.'

I don't actually need five minutes; it just seems like the grown-up thing to do – to 'freshen up' perhaps? Now all of a sudden Ralph West feels like a hotel: going down for an evening meal. I have made my first friend and we're dining together. Fancy! Are things looking up? It's too early to say. I'm still a long way from Northampton in a strange, unheated block of flats. I play the b-side of 'William It Was Really Nothing', 'Please, Please, Please, Let Me Get What I Want', to get me in the mood for communal eating.

The dining room at the Merton Hotel it isn't. There are no Portuguese waiters making pidgin-English quips as they serve up *soupe de jardinière* and *Cassata Denise*. Though the copious wood-panelling gives the place the look of a Swiss chalet, the driving rain outside the high windows gives lie to that particular fantasy; it's a large canteen already abuzz with the chatter of students who all seem to know each other. How can that be? Did I start college a week later than everybody else? Of course not. We're all just in a hurry to get to know each other, frantic to impress, jockeying for position, finding out where we stand (and with whom) in this brave new world. But some of them look like they're having more fun than me. Better get a move on.

Mike and I continue our awkward small talk in the queue as we slide our wooden trays down the metal rail and shuffle past hot tin dishes of wet meat and mashed veg. I find myself asking a very adult question and it surprises me as the words escape my lips. 'Where are you from?'

'High Wycombe. Don't supposed you've ever heard of it.'

'I have actually,' I reply, making his day, 'I once went out with a girl from High Wycombe.'

He seems suitably impressed, 'What was her name?'

Mike thinks he might know her because they are both from the same Buckinghamshire town, population about 160,000. This is the kind of thing that happens when people from far apart are artificially thrown together for the first time. The only time I have ever met people not from Northampton is when I've met them on holiday. Like the girl from High Wycombe in fact.

'Paula.'

Mike mulls it over. 'What school did she go to?'

'I don't know. I met her on holiday a few years ago.' She came down for my sixteenth birthday party, the one where Paul Garner ate the food. She was the first girl to let me …

We reach the end of the metal rail, our trays now laden with warm food, and the filling of our plastic glasses with tap water distracts us from our conversational cul-de-sac. We search for two spare seats.

'Where are *you* from?' Mike asks. I tell him.

'Ah, the old Cobblers!' he chimes, in reference to Northampton Town FC, a team I have never followed. Another dead end.

If I were at home I'd probably have walked away by now, but here we have no alternative but to continue on our thankless path.

Turns out Mike's a textile designer, also at Chelsea, but in a different annex to the one I'm going to, in a different part

of London. I'm starting to think this might not be an al-
together bad thing and I'm hoping, for his sake, the jumper
he's wearing is not one of his own creations. He's also a
Queen fan. 'Yeah, love the old Queen,' he chirps. 'The old
Freddie. The old Brian. Simple Minds – love a bit of the old
Simple.'

Mike has a highly idiosyncratic Buckinghamshire way of
speaking and he likes some absolutely shite music, but
tonight, sat here in a canteen in Battersea while the rain
streaks down outside, I wouldn't have Mike any other way.
Tonight, he stands between me and loneliness. Me and
'Dear Mum'. Me and Morrissey. The old Moz.

Tomorrow will be better.

Higher education comes at exactly the right time: in the
twilight of your teens, you're just starting to coagulate as a
human being, to pull away from parental influence and find
your own feet. What better than three years in which to
explore the inner you, establish a feasible worldview, and
maybe get on *Blockbusters*.

I'll have a P please, Bob.

Well, you'd better get up early in the morning then
and make it quick, unless you want to find yourself listening
to a girl having a P in the next cubicle. We'll call this the
Gold Run.

Monday, 24 September 1984. My first day at college. I took
my maiden early-morning pee in the thankfully unpopu-
lated communal toilet and resisted the morbid temptation

to peer in the sanitary bin. I caught the 44 bus – my first red London double-decker – accompanied by three other new people from halls who turned out to be on the same course. There was Stephen, billeted in the room next door, 316. He'd arrived last night from the northeast, with his dad, too late to join Mike and me for dinner; Rob, an irritatingly self-possessed Kentish lad who dressed like an Oxbridge professor; and Chris who favoured aviator shades, said 'Keep well!' as a sign-off and had more of the air of an estate agent than an art student.

Ralph West housed students from five different London art schools, its dungareed residents trooping off in all directions each morning: some of them to the monolithic Central School of Art and Design in Holborn; some to the beauty contest that was St Martins in Covent Garden; others to the utilitarian London College of Printing in grubby Elephant & Castle; the rest to Camberwell School of Art, a building that looks like a giant radio. Chelsea was itself split into four separate sites for fine art and sculpture, graphics and illustration, textiles and foundation. It had no centre.

The far annex of Chelsea to which Stephen, Rob, Chris and I were off to was a former Victorian infants school in Fulham, just north of Wandsworth Bridge.

'Which stop do we get off at?' asks Stephen, wiping the condensation off the window with the sleeve of what looks like a really trendy cream jacket. Too good to be wiping windows with.

'Not this one, the next,' says Rob, authoritatively. If these people are my new family, I'm worried. Of the strangers with whom I have been thrown together so far, Stephen's the only one I can imagine myself being friends with. I'd fondly imagined Chelsea a paradise of like-minded artistic souls and instead I get a Queen fan, a mannered prig and an estate agent.

Rob presses the red button for the bell and we gather up our portfolios and alight at an inconspicuous bus stop in front of what looks like another council estate. The whole of London so far looks to me like one big council estate. Where are the landmarks? The museums? The Beefeaters? From where I'm looking it's just concrete and cars and people with their heads down going to work in the drizzle. It's no jigsaw.

As the four of us play chicken with the morning rush-hour congestion on Wandsworth Bridge, wishing that we had more than Chris's umbrella for protection, the heavens open and the rain turns from a light irritation into a downpour. We make a mad dash for it. Or at least the others do. In that laughably portentous moment – the symbolic crossing of a bridge in a biblical downpour – all of my anxieties and insecurities about what I was about to do rose to the surface in one hot flush. I was already sick with nerves and lack of sleep after my first evening with Mike. The primal fear of the unknown, the stomach-turning loneliness of suddenly living away from home, the irreversible jeopardy into which I had placed all my existing friendships left me close to tears and gasping for air. Though I momentarily felt like throwing myself in the dirty old Thames, to put a painless halt to this new-life, new-school, new-town, new-friends, new-room, new-address, where-are-you-from madness, and entertained the prospect of quitting, in a split second I had dismissed it. Gathering my portfolio under my inadequate dad-jacket, I ran like hell to the other side of the bridge, with the others, past the auction place, past the old man's pub,

he first of Fulham's many antique shops and down
gon Road. My destiny awaited. And some paper towels.
Perhaps in a parallel universe, I gave up on that bridge, my
dad came and took me back to Northampton and now I'm
an aisle manager at Sainsbury's.

There are 27 of us on the course. All shapes, all sizes, all fash-
ions, one or two suspiciously mature-looking. Dave, our
course tutor, all patchy beard and South London bonhomie,
gets us all to introduce ourselves to the rest of the group. I
can't think of anything funny to say so I stick to Andy Collins
from Northampton. The smell is of damp coats.

The fact that we're in an infants school takes me swimming back to the original day one of the rest of my life at
Abington Vale Primary.

It is 1970 and things aren't going very well. I'm five years
old, bowl haircut, second teeth, tan sandals and frankly
making a meal of the transition from civilian to conscript.

Mrs Carter – hard platinum perm, mysterious support
bandage on one knee – and Mrs Sutton – short hair, short
woman, no visible dressings – have formed a benign coalition, currently engaged in a pincer movement, prising me
from my mum's leg.

'Come on, Andrew!'

'Come on, don't be silly,' choruses my mum.

She's been here before. I wasn't much keen on letting go
of her leg at the threshold of playschool either, despite the
promise of a curriculum based exclusively, as its name gently
hints, around play.

Through hot tears I scan the classroom I am determined

not to enter, Clarks heels dug into the rubber dust mat. It's full of kids just like me, from streets just like mine, getting on with things, none of which appears to be too taxing. There's a sandpit in a raised plastic tub on legs; an aquatic equivalent in which splashing around with sleeves rolled up and dad-shirts worn backwards as smocks is apparently encouraged; a modest library in the corner; a nature table with a calcified old starfish in pride of place among the bark and leaves; a fish tank possibly containing some death-row tadpoles; easels; poster paints; coat hooks with pictures above them for identification ... what harm could possibly befall me here? What was I making such a fuss about?

'What are you making such a fuss about?' asks Mum, a note of despair now creeping into her voice. She wants to go home. Unfortunately so do I.

No, I wasn't exactly a brave soldier at five. At home I was every inch the show-off – something of a handful in fact – but put me outside, unaccompanied, and I went to pieces. Whether this outdoor timidity was because an older boy called Nicholas once hit me with a stick, unprovoked, near the allotments and taught me a lesson about the cruel unpredictability of the wider world, or simply because Mum and Dad made 6 Winsford Way such a safe and happy place it seemed insane to venture very far from it without a hand to hold, I don't know.

Simon and I played outside together before school, but we didn't stray much further than the end of Milverton Crescent – near the allotments – finding plenty enough to do (plenty of places to hide and seek) in the garage or the back garden. School was a voyage into the unknown and I could do without those. I knew what I liked: assembling

Wacky Races jigsaws at home, playing Action Man at home, and riding the toy tractor at home.

Eventually, the first-day tears dry up and the crushing inevitability of submission becomes too great for me to resist. It's clear that I'm not going home to ride the tractor down Winsford Way's gentle incline. I'm staying here. All day apparently, which seems a bit extreme. I let go of Mum. It's something of a blur, but she seems to recede into the distance behind me as if on a Travelator while I am led into the belly of the classroom – she's clearly making a break for it before I change my mind. There are no emotional farewells.

'Now, what do you want to do?' asks the maternal Mrs Carter, indicating with a sweep of her hand the various activities being played out before my sore eyes.

'Some drawing,' I snivel. 'Want to do some drawing.'

She sits me at a table and furnishes me with all a boy could need: rough, off-white cartridge paper and wax crayons. They're different from the crayons *at home* – these ones are tapered like lipsticks and don't have little jackets – but they seem to work. The paper's different too – I'm used to drawing on the headed pads Dad brings home from the office – but it'll do.

I speak to no one, keep my head down and methodically draw a picture. Of a boy. Blue trousers, red and purple shirt with black buttons, dark hair, solid black floor and he seems to be standing in an orange doorway, emerging from it, you might say. When it's finished Mrs Carter writes 'boy' on it in grown-up felt pen. I'm moderately pleased with my work, the first picture of the rest of my life.

It seems self-evident to me now that the crayon 'boy' is me, aged five. Not quite a blank canvas, obviously, but neatly coloured in and facing the world, arms outstretched, ready to be shaped by things to come.

If I'd drawn a semi-autobiographical picture of a boy on 24 September 1984, he wouldn't be wearing a purple shirt with black buttons, he would be wearing a second-hand evening jacket with the sleeves pushed up and an untucked lumberjack shirt. His army trousers would be rolled up to the calf, to reveal sailing pumps and no socks. His hair would be a backcombed black explosion, wilting slightly from the rain. Yet despite the veneer of style and self-knowledge and the determination to do some drawing, he is in truth no better prepared for transition than the small boy in 1970.

The radiators came on magically yesterday. After two nights of Ice Station Zebra that seemed symbolic (fuck it, everything seems symbolic this week: bridges, the rain, the lyrics of Everything But The Girl). I used the communal shaver socket in the toilets for the first time during a Gold Run before breakfast, secure in the knowledge that the buzz would block out any unsavoury unisex splashing sounds emanating from within the cubicles. I even ventured for a quick stroll, not quite a Chelsea one, more of a suspicious scurry, but I found Ralph West's nearest postbox, the object of my mission. Just knowing where it was made me feel closer and more connected to Northampton, which has become paramount in keeping my homesickness at a containable level.

In the afternoon, with Stephen, who's even further from home and more wide-eyed about London than me, I walk the length of the famous King's Road, which is actually in real Chelsea – just across Albert Bridge from the halls. We make the most of a dry spell to troop from what used to be Malcolm McLaren's sex shop all the way to Sloane Square. Even though nobody seems to have so much as a back garden round here in the Royal Borough of Kensington and Chelsea, they're all dressed for the country. One look at the impressive Georgian vistas tells me that I could never afford to live here. For me, it's high-rise Battersea. Yet at this unexpectedly vulnerable stage in my development these touristy boulevards north of the river make me feel curiously safe, if a little impoverished. They make Stephen feel aspirational. We're both in our coolest second-hand clobber. It has been our first day on the catwalk and we felt less out of place than by rights a boy from Morpeth and a boy from Northampton ought to.

I can't help wishing Kevin was here to see all these clothes shops and the real punks with foot-high Mohicans. Or maybe I just wish I was back there and Chelsea was an exotic break, now over and done – mapped out, described in my diary and put safe behind cellophane with the rest of my happy holiday snaps.

'What's the food like?'

Trust Mum to want to know what the food's like.

'It's fine.' (Actually, I should talk it up a bit.) 'It's lovely. We have fish fingers for breakfast!'

'Breakfast?'

Mum pulls the corners of her mouth downwards, as if to say, 'You and your fancy London ways!' as she brings out my tea: fish fingers.

'Not like these though. They're a bit dry. Nice – but dry. I have them on toast with a fried egg. It's a great way to start the day. And it's free.' (It's not strictly free: staying in the halls costs grant money, but once you've paid at the start of each term, it sort of feels like it's free.)

It's Friday night and I'm back in Northampton, just like I said I would be, back at the family dining table, a visitor in my old life. I've only been away a week but it feels like a month. I now understand what it's like for Simon when he's home on army leave, except I have no tattoos to show. Dad's not home from work yet but Mum's made me an early tea because I think she assumes I won't have eaten properly since last Sunday's send off. It's 2,000 light years from Battersea and yet I'm expected to call Kestrel Close home. It's confusing all right. I tuck into Mum's proper Birds Eye fish fingers, moist, crispy, delicious, and tell her my war stories.

'What about the toilets?'

'You get used to them.'

'I expect it's the same for everybody. How are the showers?'

'Fine.'

I haven't been in the showers – I've been washing my armpits in the sink. For a week.

'Have you spoken to Valeria?'

'Not yet. I was going to phone from here if that's OK?'

Valeria. The girl I am in love with.

Yes, in love. Unconditionally. When did this happen? Where else but in Jersey, three weeks before leaving home. You might use the term 'holiday romance' with a knowing sneer but that's how this one started and look where it ended up –

with my head over my heels. It was no Paula from High Wycombe. Simon may have hit the jackpot in the shallows of the Merton ballroom in week one with a long-limbed girl called Louisa. But when she went back to Blackpool, it was I who struck gold in week two. Looking only for a snog and the balm of conquest I found true romance and something in my eye.

Valeria, who rather recklessly and unconvincingly told me she was 20 when she was actually only fifteen, was a vision. Petite, toned and bronzed, long, wavy, sun-bleached hair, blue eyes, glossy lips, big white teeth and a cut-glass voice that suggested elocution lessons, Valeria even had a name that marked her out from the crowd. She was something else.

She was also an orphan.

Both her parents had died and she lived with her grandmother in Hove. She was, although she kept it hidden beneath her sunny exterior, a tragic figure, an accident waiting to happen. Despite the voice and the stern airs and graces of her grandmother, there can't have been that much money there or what were they doing on holiday in a cheap-and-cheerful hotel like the Merton? That said, I was instantly seduced by the heady aroma of sophistication around Valeria – the way she whistled the words 'fresssh fisssh' and clipped the 't' in 'shut up', something she said often, half playful, half regal. I had, it's fair to say, never met anyone like her.

We met in the hotel bar on the Saturday. With wicker chairs around low, glass-topped tables and the Rose Wilson Trio providing the background music, the bar itself, manned by moustachioed Portuguese smoothies in red waistcoats, was largely bereft of young people. That made homing in a lot less complicated than at home. It was a race between us and the waiters for anyone with a skirt and a pulse. Some girls on holiday will always go for the waiters. But not Valeria. She was flanked by her two female cousins, both older, clearly a cut above chasing the servants, maybe even a cut above the likes of us. The numbers were good: there were three of them and I was with Simon and a Liverpudlian sailor we'd met at the hotel called Barrie (two servicemen and a conscientious objector). Simon made the initial approach – that's the infantryman in him – and we put two tables together and made six. For the rest of the evening we drank Bacardi and Cokes, let Barrie do most of the talking, and Valeria and I sort of paired off.

By the Sunday I was her panting lapdog, and had enthusiastically adopted her twin affectations of chewing medicinal-tasting Hollydent gum and putting in Optrex eye drops for fun and cosmetic effect. Our eyes glistened all week. We spent every waking hour together, developing catchphrases, acting soppy, learning loads about me but less about her, and we kissed for the first time in the TV room on Tuesday, having been forewarned in the *Sun* horoscope of 'a wonderfully romantic evening when your pulse will be racing'.

Physical advancement was kept in check by Valeria's oldest cousin Janet, who played guardian and literally prised her from my arms in the TV room on the Wednesday. We slept together, and I mean slept together, on towels by the pool in the daytime and that's as far as it went, which, of course, only made our bond stronger.

Mum and Dad watched sagely from afar as the week moved inexorably on. They'd seen holiday romances in the Merton before: Paula, Lynn, Judy. They knew how these things panned out. What they'd never seen was their eldest son cry his heart out in the car on the way back to the airport.

'Stop crying now,' says Mum in the front seat. Her eyes are glazing over too. It's infectious, like the smell of car-sick.

'I don't want to,' I sob.

'Don't be silly, Andrew,' says Dad without taking his eye off the road, embarrassed to the very marrow of his stoicism. Dad's probably thinking: *How on earth is this bawling poofter going to survive in London?*

'He's not silly!' says Melissa, weeping too out of sympathy. A car full of crying girls.

'You can always write,' offers Mum.

'I don't want to write!' I insist. 'I want to see her!' Another wave of convulsions prevent me from continuing the discussion.

'You'll get over it.' Dad again, reassuring only himself. 'You'll forget all about her.'

'John!'

The hire car hugs another corner as we head to Jersey Airport where British Midland are going to take us home.

These were not the first tears. By the time of our parting on the Saturday, Valeria and I had become so attached we couldn't bear the idea of being separated. Her eyes glistened first, unassisted by Optrex, and mine followed as we said our last goodbyes in the foyer, surrounded by the labelled luggage of those taking the courtesy coach. On Saturdays the Merton lobby is a clearing house, with each down-hearted, skin-peeling departure replaced by a travel-worn, optimistic arrival. The grumpy Irish porters do their damnedest for only very sporadic tips. I certainly never saw Dad give them anything.

It took me by surprise. I had never cried for Sally. In fact, I hadn't cried since childhood, since starting the new upper school and finding myself with no friends in my class. These were adult tears: unselfconscious, unforced, unstoppable. My body was actually seizing with grief in the back of the car. I hugged Melissa for comfort, something else I'd never done. I had to keep my fake plastic Ray-Bans on for self-preservation when I boarded the plane. I cried for a second time 32,000 feet over the Channel.

Bearing in mind that I was three weeks away from leaving home for ever, it could be argued I was crying not for Valeria, but for myself and the family life I was about to leave behind.

No, scratch that. I was crying because I had fallen in love with a little orphan with big white teeth and blue eyes who said fresssh fisssh. In seven days flat. These things happen. And now I was living in London. Which is closer to Hove than Northampton. Closer to *her*.

Dry your eyes, Morrissey.

six

Auf
Wiedersehen

Jumper Mike referred to today's vegetable lasagne as 'the old veggie laz'. Rob – OK, so I was wrong about Rob – does a spot-on impression of Mike when he's not around, shortening the names of the individual members of Queen in his ongoing verbal quest to reduce everything down to mere syllables, to save time.

Stephen is in hysterics at it, doubled over, just stopping short of getting down on his knees to slap the ground. Stephen's never met anyone like Rob before. I've never met anyone like Rob or Stephen before. In fact, all three of us have only ever met people like ourselves before. We have each come from different corners of Britain, each drawn by semi-focused dreams of London.

It may not look much – three teenagers mucking about and taking photos in their Sunday best in Battersea Park on a crisp autumn morning – but this is a tipping point for me:

the first full weekend I've spent in London since moving. The veggie laz was my first Sunday lunch at Ralph West. The three of us have only known each other a few weeks but already we go everywhere together – our shared dislocation giving the bond a new intensity. I don't need Mike any more and, thankfully, he doesn't need me.

Actually, Stephen's no longer a teenager. He turned twenty on Tuesday. To mark this important juncture we ventured forth and tried out the pub on the corner, the Prince Albert. After a jolly evening in there, during which Stephen dipped more than once into the fat envelope of money he received from his parents, we christened it our local. Like arriving at a half-built resort without a pool we soon learnt that Chelsea – unlike most self-respecting colleges – doesn't have a union bar. To top off the evening, we spotted a famous character actor drinking in the pub. At least, Rob did.

'At the bar,' he says, between gritted teeth.

'Where?' shouts Stephen, standing up and knocking his stool over in his haste. Rob and I dip our heads in shame. 'I can't see anyone famous.'

As he sits down again, Rob and I explain that the shortish bloke with dark hair, slightly balding, was in *Auf Wiedersehen, Pet*.

Stephen stands up again to look, his Geordie radar now twitching.

'He was never in *Auf Wiedersehen, Pet*, man!' Stephen sounds like he was.

'The second series!' I clarify.

'Ah, I never watched the second series,' says Stephen. He

was probably too busy out buying clothes to watch the second series of anything.

'He played the plumber who liked country and western.'

'He's been in loads of those cop programmes,' hisses Rob. Stephen looks blankly back at us.

To be fair, if you'd just walked into the pub, you might suspect that Stephen was the minor star. He certainly makes an effort, which is more than can be said for our character actor. At a statuesque six foot, Stephen is a right trendy. He's into Brylcreem and zoot suits and braces and 1940s ties and wears a weird, plasticky-looking yellow watch. But as we have observed in the pub, his poised, *Face*-reading, Zippo-flicking, clothes-horse cool is as delicate as the skin on a cup of coffee, barely disguising the clod-hopping Geordie oaf beneath. Stephen reminds me of all those Spandau Ballet interviews in which they explained away their silly attire as an escape route: commoners in their pomp. The working classes and the aristocracy have always been the best dressed, they said. It's middle-class kids like me who look like tramps.

Sitting as I often do on his bed in his room drinking coffee and powdered milk with a skin on, I can't help but marvel at Stephen's rituals. After he's washed his peroxide-tinted hair, he covers it with grease, slicks it back and then puts a black woolly hat over it, to set it. He smells like my grandad. He smells like home.

My first weekend in Battersea is significant because it's the first without homesickness. But it took a trip back to Northampton to understand that home was no longer there.

Feeling at a low ebb – and low on pants – I'd sloped home for the weekend to rekindle the old days with Kevin.

We drive down town in the afternoon, park the Metro in the multi-storey, mooch around the usual shops, say hello to Goz in Habitat and buy some hairspray and Dextrasol in Boots. But all at once the place seems tired: full of shop girls and kids who are all going to get married and die here. I keep this new feeling to myself. I buy an album in Our Price and we have a strip of photos taken in the Photo-Me booth at the bus station. I tell Kevin about the punks on the King's Road and that some German tourists had asked me if they could take my picture outside Sloane Square tube.

I play my record when we get back to Mum and Dad's: ABC's rather over-the-top *Beauty Stab*, which Stephen got me into, playing it at such booming volume I only had to leave my door ajar to listen to it, along with the rest of the third floor. Kevin doesn't like it. I decide not to mention the Small Faces or the Byrds either, two bands Rob's getting me into against all the rules of the raincoat.

We get a Saturday night lift into town with Vorn – the old friend with whom Kevin has partnered up since my departure – park in a new spot, go to the latest hang-out, the Bantam. I try to look excited yet I feel like a stranger as they enthuse about the new band they've formed. There are plenty of familiar faces in there, including Sally, who at least seems interested in hearing all about London. But she soon rejoins her latest tall boyfriend with a job. Kevin, Vorn and I drive off in search of a house party and end up at a bonfire do, where we symbolically watch the embers die.

Kevin and Vorn's new band uses a drum machine. Replaced by a box that you plug into the wall – they don't need me any more. And frankly I'm beginning to care less and less with each passing hour. Steeled by a few Fosters I'm starting to relish my new-found life.

'See this, Northampton? It's a fucking student railcard. It cost £12 and it means the world is my oyster.'

Well, off-peak at least.

Rob Mills knows all about how to squeeze every last drop out of a travelcard. He may sound posh, but to Rob every penny counts. He is something of a rarefied creature, having been, as he relishes putting it, 'creamed off' at school – that is, taken out of the top stream at comp and turned into a non-fee-paying 'day boy' at Cranbrook, a posh grammar school. He is the milky-white, cherubic-looking son of a greetings card salesman and a housewife. He hails from the Kent equivalent of Winsford Way (Wheatfield Lea), and yet dresses like an Eton nob, permanently buttoned up: school trousers, school shoes, never without a tie. He even swaps the tie for a dicky-bow on occasion. What would Kevin think?

My earliest recollection of Rob is that of a mild irritant. I remember glimpsing him across the canteen in a jacket and tie on that uneasy first night in halls. His clipped, arrogant voice cut through the general tentative hubbub of cutlery and introductions. I presumed he had been misinformed and dressed for dinner, but at breakfast the next morning he dressed just the same. Mike and I exchanged an amused glance.

God, I hope he's not on my course, I thought to myself.

Inevitably, he was. Still, at least he knew which bus to catch.

It took only a few days for Rob to make his mark at Chelsea: confident, irascible, slightly unreal, as if perhaps his entire personality was an act. Permanently acid-tongued and quite prepared to wrap Sellotape around his own face for laughs, he seemed to give not a flying fig if anyone actually liked him or not.

At the end of the first week at Chelsea, with all those new names to learn, everybody in the first year knew Rob's. Some hated his loud, cocky guts and the way he rubbed his hands together and said, 'Just the job,' like someone's dad (his own, in fact). But I loved him. I had thought Kevin irreplaceable but I was wrong. We all replace people. Friendship abhors a vacuum. I have Rob and Stephen now; Kevin has Vorn – and a drum machine.

I'd never met anyone like Rob in Northampton either. There had been no posh schools or day boys or creaming-off – not in my orbit anyway. The class system there is just front garden or no front garden. Auntie Sue speaks nicely, but she's not posh, she lives in a house like ours. Uncle Allen and Auntie Janice live in a big house with a full-size snooker table and drive around in a Jag, but he's a builder and she works in Sainsbury's. That's money, but it's not class. I've seen evidence of wealth in my otherwise sheltered life – the occasional double garage, talk of a boat – but never the ingrained, brattish, world-owes-me-a-living confidence of Rob. Or Valeria.

Oh, Valeria.

I think I want to die.

In the split second that it happened I tried to imagine a

more embarrassing scenario than your own grandparents catching you in your parents' bed with a fifteen-year-old girl – but nothing came to me.

You have to hand it to Nan and Pap: they kept their cool at what might have been, for some grandparents, a difficult time.

It was 6pm on the dot, the prearranged time at which they would arrive here to give Valeria and me a lift to the train station after our awayday weekend in Northampton. We were, at that prearranged moment, out like a light under the double duvet in Mum and Dad's bed, having spent the night there and eaten breakfast there and taken photos there and drunk Bacardi and Coke there and fallen tipsily asleep in the middle of the afternoon there. Mum and Dad are in Amsterdam, blissfully unaware.

We didn't hear Nan and Pap let themselves in the front door.

'Andrew!'

We didn't hear them call as they came up the stairs.

'Andrew!'

We didn't even hear them open the bedroom door ...

'Andr ... ooh!'

I met Valeria at Victoria Station in London on Friday evening, showed her the halls, introduced her to my new friends Stephen and Rob and then brought her to Northampton for the weekend. Valeria and I have been spending most of our weekends together since I started college – being near to her has helped me through my onset homesickness and doubled my chances of finding a letter in the Ralph West pigeonholes of a morning as we queue groggily for our shrivelled fish fingers. Hers are always in blue envelopes, the colour of the Optrex logo. But our time together has not been a breeze. Her grandmother has never approved of a funny-looking and undistinguished nineteen-year-old art student wooing her fifteen-year-old charge and when I am on the south coast I have to stay on the sofa of Valeria's tolerant elder sister Melinda in Brighton.

Valeria has recently moved in with a foster family. They remind me of Tom and Linda in *Reggie Perrin*: pine kitchen table, kids call them by their first names, crack open the nettle wine and quiche at the first opportunity. Nice, modern people, quite unlike the sort of parents you get in Northampton. Even though this removes Valeria's all-seeing granny from the equation, I still can't stay overnight with her (for self-evident reasons) and spend much of my time down there tramping from one place to another, essentially baseless and incumbent on the kindness of slightly posh people I don't know especially well. It's actually bloody exciting.

But this is the conversation that took place at Mum and Dad's on Friday evening when the two of us arrived, young and glistening and in love. I was taken to one side while Valeria finished her fish fingers.

'I've had a phone call,' says Dad, with a serious look on his face.

'Not her grandmother,' I groan.

'No, her guardians.'

'Who?'

'Tom and Linda. It was Tom I spoke to. He seems like a decent chap.'

'He is. They have wine with every meal.'

'He's a bit concerned.'

'About what? They know she's here.'

'He asked me if your mum and I were going to be here. I couldn't very well lie to him.'

'Oh Dad –'

'She is only fifteen.'

'She's a mature fifteen.'

'It doesn't alter the fact she's underage.'

This next bit is obviously very embarrassing for Dad to say, but he's quoting Tom.

'Valeria's guardians don't want you to see her without her clothes on.'

I am dumbstruck. I know they're very modern and eat quiche but I can't believe Tom and Linda would say such a frank thing to my mum and dad who they've never even met. They don't want me to see their foster-daughter without her clothes on. God, why not just come right out and say the words?

Dad soldiers on. 'They asked me for my assurance that this wouldn't happen. I gave it to them.'

'But how can you stop us if you're in Amsterdam?'

I wish I hadn't said that – it sounds as if I'm baiting him when I'm not.

'I can't stop you. But she's our responsibility while she's under this roof, whether we're here or not. You're not to have sex with her. What if she got pregnant? You'd be breaking the law and so would we be for allowing it to happen.'

Well, this is a conversation I never thought I'd be having with my dad. Put it right up there with the Abigail Transcripts.

'I want you to promise me you'll be sensible, Andrew.'

'I promise.'

The killing joke is, at that point, in all the weeks we'd

been betrothed, I'd never seen Valeria without her clothes on. A swimsuit, yes, a vest top, yes, but nothing that anyone else holidaying in Jersey hadn't seen, never intimate nakedness. Our quality time had amounted to little more than hand-holding and cuddling in a Brighton wine bar called Crusts and snogging like schoolchildren on benches and sofas and the back seat of her cousin's car whenever we had a fleeting private moment. Of course, she was bound to snog like a schoolchild; she *was* a schoolchild. Our love had been about beating the odds, avoiding her gran and writing soppy letters, not taking off clothes.

That said, we did have the house to ourselves that Saturday night.

And we had waited two months.

Well, my grandparents have certainly popped that particular bubble of unwedded bliss. Valeria and I are now running around like fools, getting clothed, making ourselves presentable and packing our bags in time for Pap's diplomatic return at seven o'clock for a later train. There is a modicum of wicked irony in the fact that Valeria and I have spent the last eight weeks on the run from *her* grandmother and now *mine* have caught us with our pants down.

I'd be lying if I said that all my weekends were as eventful and surreal as that one, but the fact remains: I didn't spend a single Saturday or Sunday in my new home in London until November. I was either in Brighton or Portsmouth (where her cousins lived) or Northampton. I lived, on paper, in SW11 and yet I left every Friday and went somewhere else on a train, to reluctantly return on the Sunday evening with tales to tell Stephen and Rob and, if I'd stayed with Mum and Dad, Ritz crackers and clean underwear to put away. For this we must blame the power of love. A force from above. A skyscraping dove.

Love was certainly tearing the arse out of my £12 student railcard.

Loving Sally had been easy. Too easy. Cosy, convenient, local. Loving Valeria was like *The Krypton Factor*. Not only did we have to resist temptation and save ourselves for each other throughout the week, when we did reunite at the weekend, it was always at someone else's hospitality and privacy was near impossible to come by. Because it was difficult to use the payphone (one situated on every other floor of Ralph West) without an eavesdropping queue forming behind you, Valeria and I were able to communicate our undying love only through letters, written and read two days apart, even by first class.

Which is why our undying love started, well, dying.

Until the bi-weekly blue envelope arrived *telling me* that she loved me, boyfriend-paranoia would set in and I would start to assume she didn't; that some good-looking member of a Brighton psychobilly group had swept her off her feet at Crusts while I was drinking a pint with Stephen and Rob at the Prince Albert, talking about but not writing our first essays.

Adversity held us together. Then in November the letter arrived that began, 'I really don't know how to start ...' which meant she really didn't know how to finish. Together we found a way. If I'm brutally honest with myself, Valeria's undying love had done its work by November. For those crucial months she had given me something to fixate upon while I worked through the first dose of homesickness and readjusted to London time. I can't have been anything like as useful for her. A surrogate parent? I wasn't mature enough for that. Perhaps, as she insisted, she really did like my funny Northampton voice.

'Go on, say style!'

'Stoil.'

Big kiss.

Patronising cow. The eye drops went into a drawer.

Plenty of students start college with a girlfriend or boyfriend 'from home' and spend that first term battling the inevitable: a grant-maintained Canute feeding money into the payphone after dark in the hope of turning back the tide with 10 pence pieces. This natural deselection is a fact of early college life. You write, of course, but gaps start to widen between letters. Hidden meanings appear between the lines. You convince yourself that it'll be fine and we'll all be home by Christmas, but girlfriends and boyfriends on the home front are living on borrowed time while you live in your borrowed town. The worst part is when the meter runs out and you both know it. At the sound of the beeps, instead of putting more coins in, you think, 'That'll go towards a pint,' and say you've got to dash, your money's running out and there's a queue behind you. It's the first big lie.

Every civilian relationship survives a couple of weeks of firefighting – the 'off' letter, the panic phone call about the 'off' letter, the over-compensatory post-phone-call letter, the resumption of normal service, the weekend visit, the last, desperate shag. And it's here in bed that the truth finally has no place to hide.

My girlfriend from home was a little different, of course. She wasn't from home, not mine anyway. I harboured lofty, romantic ambitions for Valeria and me – not that she would become my beautiful wife in a beautiful house, but that somehow we would carry on seeing each other at weekends for ever and ever and not mind sleeping on sofas and in the backs of cars, fully clothed, eyes wet, constantly anticipating capture.

It ended, officially, at Victoria Station.

SCENES FROM A PRETEND MARRIAGE (1)

Victoria Coach Station, London. December. It's difficult to think of a less romantic setting than the dark, noisy, fume-filled bus garage at Victoria where Valeria and I have agreed to meet. Like the lobby of the Merton Hotel at the other end of our romance, it is a place of comings and goings, hello-goodbye.

Think *Brief Encounter* remade by Mike Leigh. You'd need eye drops after spending any time in here. She is passing through London and wants her coat back. We exchanged coats at the giddy height of our love affair one weekend in Hove. It felt like exchanging rings or vows. I'd only ever given one item of my clothing away to a girl before (a checked shirt to Sally), but this was no ordinary item, it was my persona-defining blue Oxfam mac. That's love. I am wearing hers now, for the last time: a beige zip-up jacket with roomy sleeves and elasticated cuffs, not my 'stoil' at all but that's also love. Or was. The coats have turned to alimony.

Valeria emerges from the exhaled smoke of a coach exhaust, not wearing my mac but carrying it in a plastic bag.

She calls over. 'Hello.'

She sounds brusque and clipped and less elocuted, the

sunlight in her voice has gone. It has been two weeks since the decisive ending-it letter. I remove her beige jacket in readiness as Valeria marches towards me. Suddenly her forthright manner strikes me not as charming but as ugly and brattish. I can't wait to get this over with. Neither, it seems, can she.

'Hi,' I say, attempting to sound businesslike. 'Here's your jacket.'

'Thanks. Here's your coat.'

She hands me the bag. It's a Boots bag. I wish I'd brought hers in a bag.

'Which way are you going?'

'That way. I'm meeting one of my friends.'

'Right. Well, I've got to get back to my essay. So …'

'Thanks for coming out to meet me.'

'It's all right. It's not that far.'

'See you then.'

An awkward split second where I almost move to kiss her but reconsider. We head in opposite directions, me to the tube, she God knows where. I get my beloved mac out of the Boots bag and put it on. She's rolled the sleeves up way too high, which irritates me as I unroll them, and it smells of her: body spray and the beach.

seven

Four Lovers Entwined

Well, somebody was bound to leave me a voodoo doll eventually.

It was waiting for me on the floor outside the door of Room 317 when I came home from college this afternoon. A five-inch-high black figure made from soft material, sitting there dressed in a little black-hooded coat, with a safety pin prised open to form a vicious spear and thrust portentously into its belly. No note, no clues, nothing. Just this gloomy, monkish effigy.

I'll be honest, I was spooked all through dinner. What had I done to deserve this macabre scare?

I sort of knew.

My decisive second term had, since Valentine's Day, 1985, been loaded with incident, much of it romantic, most of it complicated. A Ray Cooney farce played out with trousers around ankles between floors and now, of course, a *Bergerac*-style mystery with me playing both John Nettles and the murder victim. If the first term had been about wiring up speakers and putting things away, the second was about painting the halls red and notching the bedpost. Getting things out.

There was something about the New Year. Just as I'd excommunicated myself from the town that had raised me, I was forced back there for three weeks at Christmas as some form of humiliating penance. (The halls turfed us all out during holidays, enabling them to power down the generator, rest the laundry service, lower the canteen shutters and recharge Ralph's batteries.) Exile in Northampton simply served to galvanise my conviction that I just wasn't made for this town. Not any more. And I couldn't wait to get back to London.

I was able to affect the detached tourist around the old haunts, the Berni and the Bantam and the Black Lion and the Bold. The old magic was gone and I felt like Banquo's ghost at someone else's table. It wasn't just me who felt disenchanted about the place. The latest craze among my old set – those who'd stayed behind – was to head off in convoys to Nottingham's Rock City to get their kicks. I saw no need to feel guilty for wanting to get out of town if they did too. Life for all of us had moved on.

I resented being back with Mum and Dad for three weeks, living under what I regarded as their Chilean jurisdiction of repression, regularity and rules. I saw not a shred of irony in the fact that mealtimes at the halls were far more regimented, and that after lights out the Ralph West night porter roamed the corridors to tell us to keep the noise down. Dad had written me a benignly threatening letter in early December which in précis said, 'Get a haircut or you won't get a Christmas.' I didn't fully appreciate the portent of this proposal at the time, but once through the front door, with a reflexive, put-upon sigh, I booked myself in for the afternoon at Catz in town and had the worst excesses of my first term at Chelsea artfully lopped off for the sake of peace on earth and goodwill to Mumkind.

'Happy now?' I said, as I walked in the front door.

Actually, they did seem to be happy. In return, they gave me a car.

They gave me a *car.*

I had yet to become belligerently and intractably left wing, so the perfect Christmas gift came wrapped with not a whiff of middle-class guilt. That followed later. By the time the *NME* and Sir Keith Joseph had turned me into a belli-cose, barricade-storming socialist in the summer term, I felt self-conscious about having my own set of wheels. I would make much of the fact that my parents hadn't actually *given* me a car – it was merely my Mum's old Metro handed down when she upgraded to a Vauxhall Nova – but there was no talking round the fact that a student with a car is a rare thing indeed. You only had to look at the size of Ralph West's car park to know that.

Maybe I could give people a lift to the barricades.

I christened my second-hand car 'Shake' – in honour of the Cure song 'Shake Dog Shake' and the fact that it did just that on the M1 over 40 miles an hour, as if it was perhaps, in *Star Trek* argot, 'breaking up' – and I glued cut-out letters announcing its name on the blue sunstrip Simon had bought me for Christmas along with a furry steering wheel cover.

So I travelled back to London in January not by cut-price rail but by hazardous, icy road, my portable tape player on the front seat stoked with the Art of Noise and Lloyd Cole & the Commotions (Kevin's opinion of whom I don't think I need to relate), plenty of Ritz crackers and clean underpants in the hatchback, and at least one sexual misadventure to regale Rob with when I got there. A regrettable quickie with a girl I met in the Bold on New Year's Eve called Sandy who said I looked like Tom Bailey out of the Thompson Twins (this was deemed a compliment) and from whom I never heard again.

I joined the AA on Sunday, 6 January 1985, a deceptively mundane act of form-filling that was loaded with significance – I was a big boy now. To borrow the association's own tagline: *It's great to know you belong*. It's also great to be able to charge your friends petrol money for a lift to college every day: 20p each (which worked out at almost £2 a week, the price of a gallon of four-star in 1985). This entrepreneurial spirit, which went down well with my dad and would have earned me a proud pat on the head from Norman Tebbitt, was no doubt stimulated by the experience of my first freelance cartoon work, which a former Ralph West boy turned art director David Williams had been putting my way since our shared Northampton roots had caused us to cross paths, thus preventing me from becoming a drain on my parents' finances and in a roundabout way paying them back for the car.

I should have been pretty pleased with myself as the new term unfolded. Outwardly mobile, financially independent, socially established. Rob and I had gelled into some kind of double act, with he the raconteur ('Come on, Rob, tell that story about your Dad again!', 'I'm not a jukebox!'), and I the louche, moody, scruffbag diarist. We had been to see The Smiths at Brixton Academy and afterwards pushed our way out of the steaming, cardiganned throng into the tense, urban night and hopped nonchalantly on the back of a 45 bus which took us all the way to Battersea, feeling like real Londoners. He and I began a course of weekend jaunts in Shake, picking a direction and just driving, connecting up the capital's labyrinthine streets, from West Hampstead to East Ham, making the city ours. Rob shot a surreal, self-congratulatory cine film of me standing in the street and chucking my *London A-Z* over a fence: not needed on a voyage of discovery.

I should have been on top of the world. But I wasn't. That's not the student way – you live a heavily subsidised life within institutions designed to shield you from the harsher realties of the working world and your parents give you food and postage stamps even though you no longer live with them, and yet your response to all this good fortune is to place the back of a hand to your lavender-scented brow and wail, 'Woe is me! I have an essay on the role of women in advertising to write by May! I found an Elastoplast in a cheese roll at the canteen! And I had to call the AA out under their excellent Home Start scheme this morning to charge my battery! Why me?'

Of course, all this self-pity would have evaporated if I'd had a girlfriend.

In truth, the girlfriend-shaped hole in my life was the source of all my angst, the void into which all corresponding joy was violently sucked. I lived in what was tantamount to a hotel, whose young female guests outnumbered the males by a ratio of 3:1 and yet I couldn't get a single girl – or indeed an unsingle one – to sleep with me. Unless you've been a nineteen-year-old boy during a drought you won't understand the ache, the longing, the self-flagellation. And so much awful poetry to write. My chances of affronting or riling a girl sufficient for her to go to the trouble of making and leaving me a voodoo doll were as good as nil. Sandy didn't even know where I lived.

In late February, desperate, I devised an ingenious form of martyrdom. Having collected my new sheets and pillow-cases as per usual from the laundry room on a Tuesday morning, I took the bold step of not putting them on my bed. I would leave my bed melodramatically unmade. That would show them! If no one will lie in it with me, I declared, what's the point of making it?

That night I slept on top of the bare mattress with just the brown bedcover over me, the fresh sheets folded in a pile on the floor. It was chilly and itchy and stupid. For my penance the gods of Ralph West sent me a girl.

Catherine is, frankly, astride me. I can't believe my good fortune. Bloody hell, the jumper's coming off. This certainly makes up for news in the *NME* today that the Cocteau Twins have cancelled their GLC benefit gig.

Catherine is from the middle of nowhere in Scotland – a Ralph West resident and painter. Her father is a sculptor. You might have heard of him; I haven't, but then I've only heard of two sculptors. Three if you count Rodin but I don't even know his first name and it's hard to focus on such matters when a girl is taking her jumper off in your room.

Catherine has finely sculpted features; unlike many female art students who disguise their shape under shapeless clothes for fear of objectifying their own gender and thus undermining their artistic integrity, she favours long skirts and tight black jumpers that hug her windswept Scottish curves. She has long, straight, mousy hair, a ruddy, make-up-free complexion, and often goes barefoot at breakfast which is a turn-on in itself. On top of all this, she is the only girl I've met since becoming a student who seems happy to sit on top of me in my room.

I'm already calling her my highland fling.

It's Auguste. Auguste Rodin.

Catherine slept in her own bed that night and who can blame her – mine didn't have any sheets on it. She was also worried about what her sixth-floor neighbour Debbie might think if there was no answer when she knocked on her door at breakfast. Catherine was no dirty stop-out and in the halls of residence reputations must be preserved. Still, we certainly connected that evening, and although the relationship – if we may call it that and I think in the circumstances we must – lasted just eight days from introduction to termination, nobody got hurt. What I mean is, I didn't get hurt.

The social calendar dictated our premature coming-out at a Chelsea-organised party. Catherine and I sat together at a rotten nightclub called the Embassy in Piccadilly less than 24 hours after jumper removal. We canoodled together on the night bus and repaired this time to *her* room to spice things up a little, although I recall it being slightly less romantic due to all the lights being on. I was already beginning to get that nagging, tied-down feeling in my bones. It was Thursday.

By their very nature, first-year halls romances play out in time-lapse, like a badly written Mills & Boon novel flicked through in the shop. Unlike training-bra relationships forged at school – in other words at Mum and Dad's pleasure – these couplings are no longer restricted by access or privacy or a lift home. Military planning is no longer required in order to facilitate a hand up a skirt. No thought need be spared for how you'll get home after your bit of slap and tickle. You *are* home. Even if she kicks you out at two in the morning during a cold snap, you can creep back to your room in your socks. Which is why the spring term transforms Ralph West Halls from an Inner London Education Authority hostel into a South London pastiche of the Playboy Mansion. Not because all 19–20-year-olds are insatiable, amoral sex maniacs – although many are – but because at that time of life it seems ungrateful to do otherwise. Whizzing hormones and biologically programmed opportunism clearly play their part in this circus, but it's more than just sexual gratification. I was away from home for the first time, displaced from familial love, and clearly a part of me was trying to fill that void – clean sheets, hot food and emptied bins do not replace family life, they merely parody it. But was I really looking for love that term or simply reassurance that after Sally and Valeria I could mean something to another girl? And another. And another.

By Friday, Catherine and I were having awkward conversations about 'obligation' and 'doing exactly what we want'. On Saturday I tipsily declared my love to a St Martins girl with a bob called Jo at an ad hoc third-floor lift-lobby party, thus drawing a line under the highland fling.

'I'll leave you to it,' said Catherine, as I sprawled on the carpet with a bottle of Cinzano gazing rheumily into Jo's saucer eyes. Catherine returned barefoot to the sixth floor to announce tearfully to Debbie that I was just like all the others. Which I was. And so was she. And so was Jo.

Even though nothing happened between me and Jo, I felt guilty the next day and spent much of the afternoon making Catherine a torn-paper collage of a map of Scotland because I knew she missed the highlands. More to the point, Jo already had a London boyfriend. (And a mini-fridge in her room, which put my car into the shade.) I tiptoed up to the sixth floor and Blu-tacked my peace offering to Catherine's door. Would it heal the wound? It would have to pretty quickly, as I was starting to have impure thoughts about Lara.

I can with confidence rule Lara out of the voodoo doll investigation. Principally because she doesn't live in halls, nor would she have the imagination to perpetrate such a hex. Or the skill to make a doll. A supremely ungifted Sunday painter on my course, she has a flat of her own in Pimlico, just behind the Tate Gallery, which is handy for an art student you must admit. When I say flat, it's actually an apartment; an apartment in a block where guests are buzzed in by a doorman who then phones upstairs. She effectively has a receptionist. Inside, it's like a photograph in an interiors magazine: new wooden furniture, scatter cushions, a green oven.

I more or less wasted three whole weeks of my life on Lara – weeks in which I could have been wooing girls much closer to home (in terms of proximity and class). But it took me that long to work out that she was so far out of my league she may as well have been royalty. Lara was quite the poshest girl I had ever met. She actually said 'yah' instead of 'yes' – just like Princess Di – and wore pearls and stripy shirts with upturned collars under navy round-neck jumpers. And flat shoes. Rob called her a Sloaney and wrote her off as the type who treated art college as finishing school – slumming it with the students for three years. Having moved among the privileged at Cranbrook – and picked up the finer points of their accent – Rob was a lot wiser on these delicate matters than me. I just thought she liked wearing her collar up.

Learning curve.

It was an infatuation heightened by the challenge, and when everything in your life's in flux, anything seems possible. I ladled lots of attention on Lara at college. Observing that she smoked Rothmans International, I bought her a packet of 20 from the newsagent as a token of my affection. Never having been a smoker, I was anything but conversant with the coded nature of cigarette brands, but these Rothmans came in a fancy blue box with gold trim and a royal crest, and inside the fags were divided into two compartments of ten, which was very cool. Were they the cigarette of the aristocracy or was Lara slumming it? I waited until she was down to her last Rothman and presented them to her and she called me 'sweet' and somehow held back from kissing me patronisingly on the head. It was all the encouragement I needed. I gave her a lift back to her flat one lunchtime to pick up some keys and she uttered these words:

'I don't know what I'd do without you.'

I started to wonder what shape she was under those unflattering jumpers. Lara invited me round for what she called supper, which turned out not to be a sandwich and a hot drink before bed but a kind of late dinner. Not expecting a full meal, I ate my normal dinner at halls before driving over the river to Pimlico. This actually turned out for the best as she served up pasta with hardly any sauce on it, just oil really, as if it was half finished. I wish I could tell you that supper turned to wine and dimmed lights and the removal of that jumper, but we were not alone. Lara had also invited our friend Jane Chipchase from college, who comes from Basingstoke and is as unused to all this finery as I am.

We chatted about the course and the tutors and briefs and crits and then Lara's flatmate turned up. She was called Mouse and that was a bit weird. She looked identical to Lara and I noticed that they both have these red cheeks and when Lara said, 'I really do,' it sounded to me like she said, 'I rarely do', which means the opposite and that's confusing. Then she put on a Eurythmics tape and the scales fell from my eyes.

Looking back on it, I don't know what came over me. It was clear from the photographs of Lara riding her horse that she'd no sooner go out with me than the doorman. I invited her to a halls party and she never turned up. The Eurythmics!

Filled with gloom, I was forced to invite a catatonic, big-haired shop-assistant ex-girlfriend called Geeena (her spelling) up from Northampton to stay the weekend. She hardly said a word between being picked up from Victoria Coach Station on Saturday and being deposited back at Victoria Coach Station on Sunday. Of course I felt dirty and opportunistic, but at least she didn't have a horse or a receptionist or a flatmate named after an animal, and, to quote my new Killing Joke 12-inch, 'the act is done'.

Next suspect: Teri from Portsmouth. Fashion student. Black clothes, staggeringly long auburn hair, small breasts and a long-term boyfriend back home, though she didn't regard this as a barrier to halls romance, so neither did I.

'Can I take my clothes off?'

Now there's a question.

Rob's gone back to Kent for the weekend, so I feel duty bound to get off with someone new and unexpected, just to piss him off and live up to what is now his snake-like caricature of me, but no girl has ever asked me if she can take her clothes off before.

It seems so stupid to have to say yes.

'Umm, yes.'

I met Teri through Catherine, which was awkward. Catherine and I had gone for a drink in the Prince Albert the previous night and she'd brought along three of her friends from halls: Vicky, Tracey and Teri. I'd seen all three of them around socially – by which I mean in the dinner queue, the laundry queue and the phone queue – but never actually met them. I liked Teri immediately. I think I liked the fact that she had this boyfriend at home in Portsmouth. The boyfriend acted as a kind of insurance. He meant that Teri and I could dally without difficult questions arising. It's clear to me now that it wasn't love I was after, but a largely self-gratifying, method-acting version thereof. Perfect for the unreal pantomime of our student world. Because grown-up sexual intimacy was involved, albeit still achieved in teenage haste, the stakes were higher, the potential for hurt and heartbreak increased. But it was still a game.

After last orders, the five of us retired to Teri's room on the first floor, which, all draped in black fabric and netting, was more like a Gothic tomb. Where had this girl *been* all my life? And that's when we decided to be students and stay up all night. If there had been a telephone box, we'd have all tried to squeeze into it.

The others dropped out one by one, first Tracey, then Vicky, then – after a determined effort to stay the course and stop me sleeping with her friend – Catherine. It was with a heavy heart and sore eyelids that she threw in the towel at 4am, knowing that she was unable to avert the inevitable. Teri and I had certainly worked hard to find ourselves alone, and the gently probing conversation that followed was interrupted by purposeful bursts of getting up and walking around in order to stay awake. We eventually dozed off – she on the bed, me on the mat – at 5.30am, which is the precise time at which all students who try and stay up all night doze off.

I tiptoed out of her room at eight and went straight to breakfast, feeling understandably delicate. I sat with Stephen, but decided against telling him where I'd spent the night, even though I hadn't laid a finger on Teri. Catherine shot me dark, disapproving looks across the fish fingers, having made her assumptions and cast me as the villain, like it was any business of hers. I'd made her a collage of Scotland – what more did she want?

While Teri sensibly slept, undisturbed, for the rest of Saturday, I gathered up all the strength in my spare tank and honoured a commitment I'd made to Stephen for our

Rob-free weekend: to go clothes shopping. This meant getting dressed up in second-hand suits we *could* afford, and trotting off down the King's Road and South Molton Street to look at first-hand ones we *couldn't*. Stephen's constant refrain while perusing the racks: 'Fuckin' lovely, that!'

It was probably the lack of sleep, but I kept thinking that perhaps last night had never happened and in fact I'd never been to Teri's tomb and drunk bad wine and instant coffee until 5.30am. Everyday noises like ringing tills and pelican crossings seemed unnaturally amplified and I thought I could hear my own blood being pumped around my head. At one stage I felt like I might pass out in the oppressive, stuffy heat of a boutique which only seemed to be selling three different jumpers, two pairs of shoes and a range of military cap badges. Thankfully, I kept it together. Wouldn't want to embarrass Stephen in his imagined natural habitat. We bought a crêpe from the crêpe stall on the way home and saw Tom Selleck filming a London-based episode of *Magnum P.I.* on Albert Bridge. This lifted my tired spirits.

And now Teri's in my room and she's asking me a question and I'm saying yes and she's doing what she just asked me if she could do. I think I'm in love, but I don't know what sort of collage of Portsmouth I can do at the other end.

Teri and I were not built to last. Because of the boyfriend, we never really went public. She would leave me notes in empty Silk Cut packets outside my door. Sometimes she just left empty Silk Cut packets, meaning she'd dropped by when I was out. Sometimes she left a packet when I was clearly in, which was a little more spooky. I got off on the intrigue though, and loved the fact that she wore men's pyjamas. Then one time when I ventured down to her room after lights out, I heard a low, male voice behind her locked door and made a swift exit up the fire escape. The boyfriend had dropped in unannounced. My enthusiasm for the relationship waned after that. He was fine as a concept but not as a physical threat.

One evening, with nothing better to do, I watched *Falling in Love*, that night's rented video in the hall coffee bar and, in characteristic style, I found consolation and omen in what was really just a boring film about Molly and Frank, two middle-class suburbanites having an affair after a chance meeting.

'I'm very married,' says Meryl Streep, before embarking on the fling.

'I am too,' replies Robert De Niro.

When all was said and done, Teri was very married and I was playing with fire. The Silk Cut packets soon packed up and I was free to fall in love again.

Her name says it all: Dawn. It's late May. The weather has turned prematurely hot and the roof of Ralph West is the place to be. Dawn has broken, like the first dawn, flooding light and magic across my grey, post-Portsmouth existence. She is a dishevelled and buxom illustrator from Central School of Art and Design, larger than life and twice as colourful, with her Medusa-like orange hair and the messiest, paintiest room in halls. It's like a work in progress: wherever you stand or sit or recline, there's a tube of paint or a bottle of ink or a felt-tip pen within easy reach – in case inspiration strikes. Paint without a top, ink without a lid, pens without caps. Dawn gives the impression of being dizzy, although it might be an act; her outfits look as if she coordinates them using a lottery system and she ties up random fistfuls of her voluminous Kia-Ora hair depending on the day. I find her fascinating, although I think what clinched it was the spooky black-and-white childhood photograph she has on her pinboard. In it, aged about five, she is being hugged by a man in a horribly realistic polar bear suit. It's winter, there's snow on the ground, other people are skating on a frozen pond, while Dawn beams winningly for the camera – despite the fact that she is being attacked by a bear. I fell in love with the girl in this picture. Though in real life she dwarfs me, I want to protect her from the polar bear.

Protection was, in fact, the one thing missing from our rapid, dizzying halls affair. After a couple of weeks of intensive negotiations, forever rolling onto dirty paint palettes and laughing like idiots, Dawn went home for the weekend – somewhere and nowhere like Farnham, to attend a ball. I missed her, like you might a regular girlfriend. Then she returned and informed me that she was late for her period and she was never late. It stole the sun from our hearts.

Dawn and I lived the next week in mutual terror, one nail-biting day at a time. Life at Chelsea tried to go on, but everything was loaded with significance. I worked therapeutically hard on our latest project, a calendar. Mine was based, with typical lack of adventure, on lyrics by The Cure, each couplet illustrated with a painterly smudge over some photocopies. I dedicated one month to Dawn using a Xerox of her polar bear picture. Months and the crossing off of dates suddenly held added melodrama.

A few of us attended a mixed-media performance of Mayakovsky's pre-revolutionary Russian poem *War and the World*. Set in the First World War, there was a lot of blood in it, which of course spoke directly to me. And then Rob and I drove to Rotherhithe in pre-revolutionary Docklands to research another college project and had Shake broken into and stolen by joyriders. This, at least, took my mind off Dawn and the fact that she was going to have my child.

Up in her bomb-blast room on the fourth floor, Dawn started obsessively painting pictures of a girl using lots of red paint. I didn't even need to ask any more; just pop my head round her door and smile hopefully, at which she would gently shake her head.

Then, the day after the car theft – the day Rob and I went back to Rotherhithe to collect the windowless, abused Metro from the Metropolitan police car pound – Dawn came through with the good news. A shadow lifted from our lives and I withdrew. Something I should have thought of a lot sooner.

Of my spring-term dalliances, Dawn lasted the longest. I was finally tiring of the endless game of chase and yearned for something with a longer shelf life than a fortnight. Of the three, Dawn was also the most fun – the most like a mate as well as a mate. And not forgetting we were for a while almost mum and dad – a textbook teenage pause for thought. We shared something during that scare, something more intimate than student sex, something proper couples experience – co-joined woe. Though Dawn and I never walked up the road arm in arm or carved our initials inside a love-heart under the desk, we went to the next level (which is entirely different from getting to next base). And then, released from biological bondage, we ran to the hills.

Exit, pursued by a bear.

* * *

So who out of our three real suspects wishes me dead or in agonising pain? Who left the hex on my door this Tuesday afternoon? Who's the black magician?

My desire to remain on amiable terms with all three of my new ex-girlfriends is, I think, noble and heartfelt. There is, I admit, a measure of self-preservation in this – four lovers entwined, domestically at least, all living in the same building. Indeed, at one potentially sticky point, I had Catherine, Teri and Dawn all in my room at the same time. I detected no animosity though and fondly imagined them happy to be members of a select halls cult. Perhaps they could organise coffee mornings to swap experiences. *It's great to know you belong.*

But I was wrong. One of them has unfinished business with me. Bad business. She wants me to suffer and by leaving an evil spell outside my door she has her wish. I'm lying on my bed trying to write a late-night letter to Mum and Dad but my eyes are repeatedly drawn to the little black doll sitting propped against the biscuit tin of Pantone markers on my drawing desk. I remove the pin, bend it back into shape and throw it away but I feel compelled to keep the figure until I figure out who left it and why. I don't believe in evil spirits, but I am scared of the skeletons in the trees, and the secrets hidden within that black cowl have infected the room with unease. What really worries me is not that the voodoo will actually work and cause searing pain in my stomach – how can it now that I've pulled the pin? – but that one of my recent relationships is spinning out of my control and coming back to haunt me. I like to keep a lid on these things.

Is that a scratching at the door? It certainly isn't a knock. Nah. Imagined it.

There it is again, scritch-scratch, like a windblown twig on a window. I turn the volume down on the now disturbingly other-worldly Cocteau Twins.

'Hello?'

No answer. I leap off the bed and open the door wide, expecting to find another effigy at my feet. In fact, it's a full-size girl.

'Hi, did you get my——?' She spies the doll on my desk and answers her own question. And mine.

'Did you like it?'

'Was I supposed to like it?' I ask, not unreasonably.

We keep our voices down as it's after lights-out, but I'm not inviting her in.

'It's a peace offering,' Teri reveals, sweetly. 'I made it at college when the teachers weren't looking.'

'What's the pin for?'

'Pin?'

'It had a pin through the middle.'

'No, it didn't. It's supposed to be me, that's why it's in black.'

'Well somebody stuck a pin in it.'

She wrinkles her nose. 'That's really horrible. God.'

It dawns on her that her peace offering has backfired. 'I just wanted to show that there's no hard feelings. I know things were all a bit funny when it ended and I know it freaked you out when Mark turned up.'

'Not as much as it freaked me out when a voodoo doll turned up.'

We both smile. Amiably, like friends. The doll looks like a doll. A soft, cuddly Teri doll thoughtfully run up on a fashion course out of off-cuts and college thread. I want to kiss

Teri and invite her in and revisit old times but that's wrong and I don't. Instead I thank her kindly for the offering and say, 'See you around,' and she spirits away.

I lock the door again. (We always lock our doors. There are some funny people in the halls.) Turning the Cocteau Twins back up to a level that won't alert Lenny the night porter but will erase the silence, I put my Basildon Bond pad away and recline on my bed, single but no longer singled out for revenge. I begin to drift off and sink beneath the waves of undulating, chiming guitar. The spell is broken when the needle hits the run-out groove. Then I shake myself just sufficiently awake to get out of my clothes.

The unlikely phrase, 'Can I take my clothes off?' echoes through my head. I think perhaps it always will. Then another question: if Teri left the doll, who stuck the pin through it?

eight

Such Bloody Awful Poetry

I'd written poetry before leaving Northampton and starting college, but always under the cover of song lyrics for whichever band I was in at the time. I'd like to tell you that A-level Tennyson, Arnold and Hopkins fed into my work at this time, but they didn't. While they wrote about faith and doubt in the age of Darwinism, I wrote about the sad truncated life of James Dean – 'Born in 1931, he left in '55/The rebel never found his cause/But the Giant is still alive' – and the coming apocalypse – 'No one got time to arrange a party/Tomorrow don't mean a lot.' And I shall never forget the haunting first line of 'Lime', inspired, I might add, by the colour and not the fruit:

'Lime, lime, lost in time …'

Though not all as memorable as that, my poetry generally hit the same note of meaninglessness and juvenility, always patted into a neat ABCB or ABAB rhyming scheme – easier to sing that way – and with a catchy chorus. Robert Smith had more to answer for than T.S. Eliot.

I'd also like to tell you that cutting myself loose from parental hegemony and standing on my own two feet in the big city improved my poetic licks. But all it did really was increase my productivity by an alarming margin. Such bloody awful poetry, and such a lot of it! Like any angst-ridden late teenager with hormones coursing round my body and the worries of the world ricocheting around my head, you would all too often find me in poetic mood. On my bed, alone except for The Smiths or the Sisters of Mercy, hunched over an A5 pad, dredging up words from the very pit of my soul, my Pentel giving voice to a running buffet of conflicting emotions and feelings: fear, regret, ambition, lust, trepidation, self-pity, anger, lust, envy, sorrow, loss, happy, bashful, sleepy …

I started to build up quite a body of work once I'd moved into halls. I even gave each new volume a title or pithy quote to distinguish it from the last – 'Something always goes wrong when things are going right' (not Matthew Arnold, but Matthew Johnson, otherwise known as The The). The shite poured out of me; something about the heightened melodrama of the place, and the Benny Hill speed with which comings and goings came and went. That and being cruelly separated from my true inspiration, Valeria. What a catalyst she turned out to be.

I never wrote any poems about or to Sally, but that's because she was right there next to me the whole time, outside of school hours at any rate. My feelings for Sally were conveyed through the love-innuendo in my diary. But Valeria and I were a prepackaged Greek tragedy thrown together then rent asunder within days of meeting. I was also filled in those dying summer days with a sense of doom and not-knowing about leaving home and starting Chelsea. As you can imagine it was something of an inspiration overload.

The immediate inevitable result was an epic poem in six parts called 'Eye Drops'. Finding my first legitimate, original piece of symbolism in the Optrex that represented my long-distance girlfriend and the tears we had shed in the lobby of the Merton, I threw all caution to the wind and went third-person:

> *One by one the seconds torture*
> *Making wounds*
> *Exposed to air that's cold and negative and empty*
> *By her side*
> *He feels so safe*
> *Yet holding her in time like water*
> *Waiting for the final signal*
> *Nothing matters*
> *Such is life*

That's just part one. By part six he's 'scratching at maps and clawing at air'. When a young man can convince himself that time is like water *and* makes wounds, he's really up and running, poetrywise. You can't convince a student who will happily drink snakebite out of a plastic glass not to mix metaphors.

You see, there comes a point in every boy's life when expression must take one of two forms: poetry or football. Only one man has managed to combine the two, but since Eric Cantona was still shouting at goalkeepers and throwing his shirt into the crowd at Auxerre and Martigues at this time, he need not trouble us here. I was never any great shakes at sport so it was perhaps inevitable, especially in the lavender hothouse atmosphere of art school, that I would come to release existential and romantic tension through words. Let's be frank and call it literary masturbation. It builds up inside of you until it must eventually be released, preferably alone and behind a locked door, although if you can get a girl to help, even better. And, just like an onanistic emission, once externalised the poem should be discarded. The very act of producing it is sufficient; the means and, if you will, the end.

Of course I kept all mine (except 'Lime', which is lost). I'm looking at a fat folder full of them right now, about seventy written over three years, some dated, others not (but all of them *dated*, in the other sense). All written in Pentel, some on loose scraps of paper, others gathered in pads – sorry, volumes. Christ, they're bad.

I'd say that 99 per cent are inspired by girls. This is probably just as well, because when I attempt to essay the bigger picture, the results are even more embarrassing. What, in May 1985, compelled me to write the poem 'Culture', I don't know, but I'd like to think I was the first to articulate the fact that 'the marketplace streams with mass-produced dreams' and that 'the printing press bleeds for the mass who can't read'. Apparently an 'elitist confusion' unties 'the plantation worker' too. Anyway, back to getting a shag …

The feeble attempts of a few miles to
Push and pull
And create a negligible strain on that certain special 'something'
In vain
That certain uncertainty

The uncertainty of the next chapter in a screenplay
Written in advance

Entitled, enigmatically, 'Something', this early poem commemorates the decisive wobble in my relationship with Valeria, hence reference to the 'push and pull' of 'a few miles' (London to Brighton). The fact that the word 'strain' is an anagram of 'trains' (our sole mode of transport) may just be coincidental but note the subtle play on words in the negative use of 'vain' – deliberately back-referencing the author's vanity. Seeing my life as a film was a recurring and distinctly unoriginal motif. I watched a lot of films, albeit not enough to know that screenplays don't have chapters.

It's key I think that a later stanza in 'Something' is nicked wholesale and uncredited from the David Bowie song 'Sons of the Silent Age' (*"Heroes"*, 1977). For this, we may lay the blame squarely at the doorstep of Mr T.S. Eliot, or at least in the staff pigeonhole of Mr Gilbert, my English teacher at Weston Favell, who so brilliantly untangled the metatextual references in *The Waste Land* at A level. I figured if TS can lift quotes from Baudelaire, Webster and *The Tempest* and leave it to Brody's Notes to supply the annotation, who's to stop me? So it is that lines and phrases from The Cure and Talking Heads and Stephen King and *Apocalypse Now* constantly find their way into the warp and weft of what we'll call my Ralph West Period.

This is because all teenage poets secretly want to be discovered and published and for Mr Brody to disseminate their work, seeking out and identifying the samples. 'The Sky and the Impossible', a surreal piece from late '84 in which peasants levitate and 'the focal point is a hacked-off joint', takes its name from a line in a Cure song called

'Strange Day', as any student of the band's *Pornography* album will know ('and the sky and the impossible explode') – in other words, it's my gift to future generations of English scholars. As ghastly as this sounds, I truly believed I was writing these poems for others to read. Which is like keeping spent hankies around the room.

> *Hanging*
> *Waiting*
> *The next shot is yours*
> *Another way of saying OURS without the WHY*

As Valeria faded from my work, new sensations inspired me. Again, taking my cue from my record collection – this time Echo & the Bunnymen's 'Villiers Terrace' (*Crocodiles*, 1980) – I came up with a poem called 'Skeletons' in early '85, about Bacchanalian excess.

> *Alcoholic evenings*
> *Biting tongues*
> *And sniffing carpets*
> *Getting mad at really nobody*
> *And dying for a cause*
> *And dying for another*
> *Will you pass your friend*
> *And stop*
> *To see*
> *The skeletons in the trees*
> *It's me*
> *Alone and almost at home*
> *Within the confines of this loop*

Written in the first weeks of the new term, 'Skeletons' is emblematic of my slide into Cinzano hedonism, suffused with macabre imagery, strong drink, fictional debauchery and a touch of self-flagellation. I'm very much 'in character': the tortured artist, the neglected bachelor, the hardened Londoner. My study bedroom has become a prison cell-cum-boudoir. The influence of Morrissey – his celibate self-pity rather than his wry northern English humour – comes into its own.

The pivotal image of the poem, the skeletons of the title, came directly from a fine art student from Manchester called Julie and her account of taking acid. She'd had a bad trip and, among other things, saw skeletons in the trees. Because I had yet to really cross paths with illegal drugs at this point, even from a spectator's position, they retain a mythic hold on my imagination. At Nene College, Paul Garner revealed that a punk friend of his called Jon had dropped acid and listened to the *Apocalypse Now* soundtrack album on headphones: he'd 'been to Vietnam'. Far out. I was filled with jealous but fearful awe. Now, thanks to Manchester Julie, I had another vivid image of what hallucinogens could do and it scared me further, especially with all those trees in Battersea Park just outside my window at the halls.

But who needs psychedelic drugs when your imagination is so clearly working at full pelt? It had to be, as the cold, hard, mundane reality of my existence was nothing like as colourful as the one presented in my bloody awful poetry, where death is around every corner, every rejection is blown up into a shot through the heart and blood flows both metaphorically and bloodily.

Two hours until my next meal
And what will I do?
Feel my tongue
Pace my room
Check the time
Forget people's birthdays
Count the crackles in my music
Bite my tongue
WISH
Search for the sound I'm after
Tangle my hair and
Cut my face in a few places
Count my blemishes
PLAN

Nothing worse than having to wait two hours for your next meal to be cooked and served up to you in a subsidised canteen among your peers. Is it any wonder I was so miserable?

An acoustic atmosphere, red and real
Evening glasses
How do I feel
About discussing the execution with the condemned?

Just for the record, I never actually executed anyone while living at Ralph West Hall.

What's happening, blood?
Why do you seep from inside of me?
Why do you show yourself?
Let me sleep and I promise I'll dream only thoughts

Of contentment and routine
I know I ask too much of myself
But please please bleed from somebody else

The pain of cutting yourself shaving there.

What do you want?
What the fuck do you want?
Is it me or am I carving our names on the wrong tree?

Actually, that's not bad.

If virginity's fashionable, the masses are square
From our vocabulary, who took 'care'?
Loose-fit covers on footloose girls
Laughing intently, the embryo uncurls

That's quite enough of that.

As we leave the teenage poet, he's currently struggling with a poem called 'New Life'. It's about losing a red pen. Well, we've done the apocalypse and the sky and the impossible.

I've mislaid my red pen (but that's irrelevant;
And it's not that surprising – I live in a bag
And out of one too – what a week I've had
That's another poem
Shit. That's another book
I want an existence where I don't have to cook
Until then I'll freeze – a week on my knees
Be your guest
Somewhere to rest

I'm a travelling man and I hope you're impressed
So back to my pen …)
I've mislaid my pen

The mislaying of the red Pentel, though literal (I had actually lost my pen), also hints at the precarious nature of life between A and B, London and Brighton, London and Northampton, and at our more general overdependence on material things. Losing items of stationery is a hazard when constantly in transit and who on a grant can afford to spend money on pens that go missing? The red pen represents security and the loss thereof. Perhaps a search of the hatchback would have yielded results.

Or perhaps, like lime, it was lost in time.

nine

Get Fresh

NEW PAD FOR SARAH
*Princess Margaret has treated her 21-year-old art
student daughter Lady Sarah Armstrong-Jones to
a £300,000 Georgian home on the borders of
Chelsea and Kensington. Sarah has been looking
for a London base for some time.*

Newspaper cutting, 19 September 1985

It was Stephen who stuck the pin through the voodoo doll,
with not a thought for the consequences of his actions.
That's Stephen all over. I have forgiven him. He was in a
foul, vindictive mood because he'd come off his bike on the
King's Road while ogling a fashionable woman outside
American Classics. Came home, saw the doll, improved it,
forgot about it.

'I've absolutely fucked it, man!' were his precise words
as he told the sorry tale of his high-profile crash. He meant
the mangled bike-frame but he might equally have been

referring to his cool – a precarious commodity in his grace-less hands.

Stephen, lovable Geordie oaf with sausage fingers, a bent crossbar and an exotic-looking scar above his left eyebrow, perfectly embodies the dangers of distraction in a town that's full of them. This is a boy who's had his head turned. We all have, to varying degrees. As we arrive back in London for our decisive second year at Chelsea – one step closer to our varying degrees – and contemplate life away from the cotton wool and the invisible force-field of halls, it's evident that we've changed beyond recognition in a year.

Stephen used to change beyond recognition three or four times before he was ready for a Saturday afternoon catwalk up the King's Road. Once, having gathered up the courage over a course of days, he went out wearing a quilted jacket, a black polo-neck, a brooch, baseball boots and a sarong. Well, he told us it was a sarong – it looked suspiciously like a skirt to our untrained eyes, but we don't read *i-D* as closely as he does. Another time he fashioned a poncho out of an old ethnic bed-throw, threw it over the top of his crumpled beige jacket and a pair of plus-fours and added a wide-brimmed hat and a satchel. Even north of Albert Bridge, where the Sloaneys and the models are, he elicited a few second glances.

'I've always dreamed of looking stupid on the King's Road,' he told us, over a pint.

Rob and I might laugh – and we did, loudly and often – but there's something very London about believing your own hype, making your own luck and living your own dream, even if that dream is of looking stupid in a street of prohibi-tively expensive clothes shops.

It was while parading on Sloane Square in some egregious church-bazaar get-up that Stephen was approached by a man. It was bound to happen eventually.

'Excuse me,' the man said, stopping him in mid-stride. Stephen assumed he was being picked up, which he was. 'Have you ever done any modelling?'

'Nah,' replied Stephen.

The man handed Stephen a business card and said, 'Why don't you give us a bell? I scout for the *Tatler*.' This sounded like a euphemism but it turned out not to be. He really did scout for the *Tatler*.

Less than a week later, Stephen, aged 20 from Morpeth in Northumberland, whose eyebrow scar was self-inflicted with a lino-cutter in print-making week, was dressed in real designer clothes and draped all over an amazing-looking woman in her knickers outside a disused wharf for a big magazine shoot. He was now taking a year out of college so that he could travel the world as a model for the Marco Rasala agency.

'It's fucking incredible, man!' were his precise words when he struck the deal.

As I wrote to my parents, 'This never happens in Leeds.'

While Stephen was jetting off to Milan and Tokyo, and Lady Sarah Armstrong-Jones was unpacking sugar cubes and speaker wires in her £300,000 Georgian pad, I was homeless.

All right, homeless with a car. And a government grant. But this didn't alter the fact that as the second year began I was, as the Goodies used to be, of no fixed abode. Rob had moved in to a tiny rented hovel in Putney (no overnight guests allowed, by order of Mrs Reed) and the rest of the old halls gang were smeared across London, lining the pockets of unscrupulous landlords of every race and creed. Meanwhile Ralph West was refilled from top to bottom with bright-eyed, bushy-tailed, sharpened-pencil first-years – each one the very image of me, exactly one year ago, with expectant, box-carrying dad and packet-fresh Blu-tack, pushing open the window to air their brand new study bedroom, blissfully unaware of the subterfuge, carnality and heart-break that had probably occurred on that very mattress, behind those very orange curtains. But love didn't live there any more. And I didn't live anywhere.

This was my own sorry fault. I had, with blind optimism, applied to get back into the halls, even though the place is designed for first-years. With some inevitability, I received a letter as early as mid-July telling me my application had been unsuccessful. What to do next? Well, September felt a long way off in mid-July so I postponed worrying about it and, rather shamefully, got on with my summer holiday: ten restless, fidgety, clock-watching weeks of telly, navel contemplation and supplementary benefit in Northampton (without even Kevin to entertain me by day as he had a nine-to-five job).

When the time came in mid-August, after a certain amount of anxious prompting by Mum and Dad, I threw all my eggs into one basket and wrote meekly to Mr Hartnell the warden at Ralph West Hall to ask to be put on the waiting list for the new term. Throwing myself at his mercy, I promised him – a young, beardy Asian social-worker type who called you 'mate' – that I would become an active member of the halls committee if he let me back in. It was bit like putting a shawl around your shoulders and pretending to be a woman in order to claim a lifeboat seat on the *Titanic*. It was low, cowardly and humiliating – and it meant that I would have to attend meetings about the jelly snakes running low in the halls coffee bar – but it might nonetheless save my skin. And when the ship goes down, you'd better be ready.

Mr Hartnell wrote back, informing me that I was now officially number 21 on the waiting list, mate. The utter shame. Standing in line for a first-year's room. By the start of September I was up to number 11. This meant that ten first-years had to move out of halls before I moved in. Why on earth would ten first-years choose to leave a place that served two hot meals a day, did your sheets and held Valentine's parties? Were they insane?

Still, my apathy made these odds my best bet. In the meantime, once term started, I would sleep in the car.

I hoped I wouldn't have to, of course – the car was just my last resort. Every self-respecting London vagrant needs a fall-back option. Although mine was more of a hatchback option. What I actually did as 22 September dawned was less dignified and self-respecting than kipping on the back seat of a Metro: I begged.

On my first Sunday back in London, following some preliminary pleading, I found myself on my back in Simon's old sleeping bag on the floor of a chic basement flat in leafy Highgate, North London. I was the guest of David Williams, who responded favourably and with his usual generous, urbane nonchalance when I just came straight out with it and *asked*.

* * *

It seemed fitting that David should be my first host. Since I'd started at Chelsea a year ago, he'd always been there in the background, putting odd bits of freelance illustration work my way and occupying a role somewhere between foster-parent and Professor Higgins.

He was 24 but he may as well have been as old as 28. David was from Northampton, he'd even been to the same school as me. Thanks to a mutual acquaintance just before I left home for London I found myself showing my portfolio not to a bunch of bearded tutors but to an art director from a fancy design firm in London. A smooth operator with a chocolatey voice and big round tinted spectacles in blue frames, David was charm personified. He 'interviewed' me in the front room at Kestrel Close, tall and groomed and wearing an expensive-looking leather jacket, and then casually dropped into the conversation a prospective freelance illustration job worth 'a couple of hundred'. (A couple of hundred!) It felt like something real and significant, which was a welcome distraction from the nebulous ache of my Valeria-longing and Chelsea-dread, an opening into the shiny world of professional graphic design.

The company he worked for was called Imagination, based in Covent Garden – all chrome railings, doors with circular windows and corporate livery in grey and 'Imagination blue'. I knew it was a pretty state-of-the-art outfit as I'd already seen their business card and it had a telex number on it. This was the first office I'd been into since visiting my dad's as a kid. But now I wasn't a shy guest, I was part of the team. I felt I had seen my own future, and it wore round, blue-framed spectacles, carried a number of credit cards and drove a Vauxhall Chevette.

A year on and David was still very much my benefactor and kindly offered me a floor to sleep on – as a student he'd lived at Ralph West and knew the lie of the land. Unfortunately, at his flat, I found myself sleeping between two farting rugby players whom he was also putting up for the night. I was grateful for the roof, but not for the finer points of this ripe, overcrowded arrangement, so I tiptoed out of there early the next morning, threw my overnight bag in the car and drove away with the milk floats. Actually, nobody seemed to get milk delivered in London, but you get the idea. The pre-rush-hour drive through Central London flushed the farts and night-sweat out of my clothes. With the windows down and Prefab Sprout up, gliding like a bachelor in a building society advert past the Telecom Tower, Nelson's Column, the Houses of Parliament and Albert Bridge, it felt like I had the keys to the city – if not to a room I could call my own.

That night, after a day at college spent mostly finding out where people were living now and generating bags of sympathy for my vagabond status, I was instinctively drawn back to Ralph West Hall – except now, keyless, I had to wait for someone to enter or leave through the front door before I could slide in. It was demeaning having to skulk. I justified the visit by dropping in on Mr Hartnell in the office to see what condition my admission was in. With some relief, I discovered that some first-years simply hadn't turned up – the result being, I was now a manageable four places from the top of the waiting list.

My vagrant status made me feel closer than ever to the place and I loitered with imagined impunity for the rest of the evening, Shake nestling in the tiny car park just in case.

My friend Jane, the one who had accompanied me to supper at Lara's last term, had just moved in, but she wouldn't let me stay in her room because, she said, she was 'feeling a bit monthly'. I made a few fruitless calls from the payphone and ended up sitting around the fourth-floor lift lobby, seeing who came along. I fell into conversation with a first-year I'd noticed at Chelsea called Duncan and sweet-talked him into letting me stay on his mat. I like to think that I'd have done the same for a poor, homeless second-year if the roles had been reversed a year ago.

It hardly needs stating that overnight visitors are not permitted in halls of residence. As a result, everybody has overnight visitors, every night, sometimes two or three to a room, sleeping in the wardrobe if they have to. It's a Marx Brothers film with so many people in the hotel room they're spilling out of the door. If students didn't entertain overnight visitors in halls, the streets of London would be lined with steamed-up hatchbacks.

On Tuesday I had run low on sweet-talk so I drove all the way 'home' to Northampton after college, there to feel the benefit of a soft, warm bed beneath my back. Despite the best efforts of a contraflow near Luton, I was back in London in time for an art history lecture the next morning at 11am. I was all of a sudden a commuter, which was not my idea of fun, so I readied myself for another night of basement flatulence in Highgate. Before driving north though I donned the shawl and cajoled a dinner from the Ralph West canteen. David had only ever offered bed and breakfast.

I then made my way across London up to Highgate: Albert Bridge, Parliament, Lord Nelson, Telecom Tower. But when I got there, the lights were off and nobody was home.

He was probably working late at Imagination, something I stupidly hadn't imagined. So I did what any bright person would have done in the circumstances: I hung around David's front door for an hour in the cold like a burglar, wishing I had change left for the phone box. It was getting late. Shake seemed to be smiling at me seductively from the kerbside, but sleeping in the car was like paying for sex: only in emergencies. In a panic I drove all the way back to Battersea – Telecom, Nelson, Parliament, Albert – to loiter by the phone at Ralph West again.

Not having the heart to knock on Duncan's door, I managed instead to strike up a jolly conversation with another Chelsea fresher, a young fogey called Rory, who turned out to be hospitality personified and let me unroll my rank sleeping bag on his floor. Not only that but he introduced me to a couple of his friends, also at Chelsea, one of whom rashly offered me *their* floor for Thursday. Things were looking up.

It was then that I started to run out of sympathy for London's genuine homeless. It's not so bad! A bit of driving around and sweet-talk in the lift lobby. Oh, and did I mention that Rory's friend was a girl? That *was* my idea of fun.

'Where did you pick *him* up?'

Susan's friend, who is confusingly also called Susan, seems surprised that Susan has pulled so early in the evening. I'm not 100 per cent sure I like the disdainful emphasis on the word *him*.

'This is Andy. He's a second-year at Chelsea.'

It's official then: I've been picked up and I'm a second-year.

More importantly, a second-year at the 1985 Chelsea School of Art Freshers' Party: free entry for first-years, £2 admission for the rest of us. It's not a freshers' ball – Chelsea's too petite and fashionable to throw balls – but it is an opportunity, in the fine tradition of such events, for first-years to get roaring drunk, break the ice, have indiscriminate sex with second-years and then regret it for the rest of the year. I've heard it called Fuck A Fresher Week, but I refuse to entertain such crude, debasing terminology.

Where did Susan pick me up? In Rory's room last night when she and a friend of hers called Georgina came down for a cup of coffee. They'd seen me at college over the previous three days but were surprised to find me being entertained by unassuming Rory. I called it healthy integration between years.

I was also able to impart some ancient halls wisdom to all three of them for nothing: if you prefer fresh milk to Five Pints (and who doesn't?), simply place your carton in a plastic bag and hang it out of your window by the handle. Then close the window, keeping the heat in and the milk out. That way it stays refrigerated in the winter. I could tell they were impressed and grateful – no doubt they felt as rootless and apprehensive as I'd done a year ago. Like some wise Buddha sipping my coffee there in Rory's room, for the first time in my life I felt like I knew something others had yet to learn. Was this the complex glow of approaching maturity that I was feeling, or simply lust for Susan? She was a bit chubby and with buck teeth but she had a glint in her eyes, and you had to admire someone who'd offer a virtual stranger a room for the night on the basis of refrigeration advice. I had high hopes for the new term in that very moment.

'Who's that girl you're with?' asks Jane at the bar with a raised eyebrow. Susan is already blearily propped against a pillar, experiencing the socialising effects of crap wine gulped from plastic pints. The freshers party started at the provocative hour of 6.30. It's only 7.30 now, but people are already dancing and shouting and getting off. Rob's holding court and telling preposterous tales of Mrs Reed. Rory has joined the other Susan and Georgina in gently interrogating Susan in my absence. (*My* Susan.) They're probably asking her if she's all right, meaning: 'Are you sure you know what you're doing?' Hopefully she's telling them she's fine, meaning: 'I know exactly what I'm doing.'

'She's a first-year,' I explain to Jane, refraining from using the f-word. No need for first names – don't want to get too attached.

'Well done, Andy!' says Jane, archly, not really meaning well done. Actually meaning: 'You snake.' She punches me in the arm as she walks away, still feeling a bit monthly obviously. I return to Susan's side with another wine for her, feeling a little altered myself on that fine student cocktail of grape and grain. Am I really a snake? After all, she picked *me* up. And it is freshers' week.

An hour later, we have stumbled back across the river to halls and fallen asleep in Susan's bed, adding another story to the silent, degenerate history of its mattress. There's a likelihood that the act was done, but we only have fleeting excerpts in the wrong kind of soft focus. First-year and second-year successfully integrated and at least I'm not sleeping in the car.

* * *

Look at me passed out there like a straw-haired corpse, face down in a patch of my own liebfraumilch drool on Susan's pillow, our inert, hot limbs covered by regulation brown bedspread, dreaming of dark and troubling things, breathing as heavily as a phone pest. Andy Kollins, aged 20, Chelsea School of Art, no fixed morals. Unable to leave the playground of Ralph West.

Was I really any wiser behind the façade of graduation to second-year?

Would I really do anything for a room?

If those freshers sat me down and really pumped me for information about surviving the first year, what would I tell them? To avoid the veggie laz. To automatically discount the first friend you make, especially if he likes Queen. Make your bed no matter how poetic you're feeling. Terminate that relationship 'from home' before Christmas. Don't let the crits grind you down. Carry an umbrella or find a friend with a car. Remain on friendly terms with everyone you sleep with – after all, Ralph West Hall might seem like a big place, but it shrinks with casual sex. Avoid the Ethelburga estate at night, but the little Londis mini-mart is a godsend if you run out of milk or crackers. Place your carton of milk in … no, we've done that one. If you enjoy your first year at halls so much that you can't bear to move out, get your application in early and don't be put off by the waiting list. Take a year out to become a male model. Get fresh with a fresher in your first week back.

I lie there still, under bedclothes, face down in a pillow that's still slick from my dribble. My trousers are in a heap and so is my head. The freshers' party comes flooding back. Literally so for poor Susan, who's bent over her sink, noisily recycling wine and little else. Like the gentleman I am, without even lifting my head I ask her if she's OK. She replies with a guttural moan and says she wants to die. That's not quite the reaction I had hoped for by spending the night with her, but she has a point. Regret is a dish best regurgitated warm. Out of respect for Susan, I crawl out of her bed and curl up on the floor under the brown bedspread. I even turn the pillow over for her. I manage to prop my head against my overnight bag in such a way as to block out the sounds of her profuse vomiting. I will be asleep again before I even have time to wonder if we did or didn't. It will take quite some time to get fresh again.

Mercifully, I only had to rough it for two weeks. During a long weekend tactical retreat to Northampton the good news came by phone: in his hand Mr Hartnell the warden had a piece of paper and it was my application form. I had risen without trace to the top of the waiting list and he was able to offer me a room of my own, mate. I jumped for joy in Mum and Dad's lounge even though my back was still killing me after all that floor sleeping. Whether Mr Hartnell had actually noticed that I'd been sleeping under his roof pretty much every night since term began I don't know. I was indebted to David and Duncan and Rory and Susan and a Welsh rockabilly called Vaun, who actually went out for the evening and left me his keys. And to the terrifying Mrs Reed for graciously allowing me, for one night only, to kip at Rob's.

I grew used to the comfort of strangers in that insecure fortnight, but it made me grateful for the simple pleasures and perhaps made me a more humble human being. As if to mock how very far I hadn't come, I was restored to an identical berth just four doors down from my old room. In acknowledgement of this divine joke, I wired up my stereo and stuck on Talking Heads – 'This Must Be The Place'.

Which, I'm fairly certain, happens all the time in Leeds.

ten

I Mean, Lenin's Dead

'Can you tell me what you're demonstrating against here today?'

The TV news reporter thrusts his microphone under Rob's nose. It's a media scrum. The bearded bloke shouldering the camera the size of a Korean airliner reminds me of John Harper without the roll-up – though what we're doing here today is far more important than a silly performance art project. Unaccustomed as he isn't to showing off in public, Rob lets rip in his very best grammar school accent against the real tools of the fascist dictatorship. He's good.

'The Inner London Education Authority want to merge all five of the main London art schools under the London Institute umbrella …'

Go, Rob! Points for 'umbrella'!

'We're Chelsea students and what we're concerned about is the loss of identity. Each of the five colleges is very different, and by amalgamating them you destroy that individuality.'

'Thank you!' says the reporter briskly, whipping the *Thames News* logo away and moving on down the line of colourfully dressed demonstrators. I hope I was in shot, nodding furiously in my distinctive checky shirt and brandishing a placard reading SAVE OUR SCHOOL.

I'll be honest, it's the first placard I have ever brandished. This is my first ever demo – likewise Rob's – and truly exhilarating it is too. There are art students and tutors in hats and coats and army bags as far as the eye can see. Even one or two bored-looking coppers wishing they'd been bussed up to Orgreave for some serious overtime. Considering we're all doing art, our placards are a bit ropey, but the sheer size of our hair seems to swell the numbers and it's a nice day for it. A noisy picket at County Hall on the South Bank of the Thames on the day of the Authority's decisive tea-and-biscuits meeting, followed by a shapeless march across Westminster Bridge to Leicester Square for some more chanting and brandishing. Hard on the feet (especially if you're dim enough to wear sailing pumps) and hands (all those splinters), but a chance to feel relevant, impassioned and engaged. It's also a legitimate day off college. Perhaps if a few more of these lazy bastards actually bothered to attend college on a regular basis – instead of staying in bed and waiting for the muse – the plea to SAVE THEIR SCHOOLS would carry more weight.

At last, student life has awakened my inner Trotsky.

London seems on the face of it a good advert for Labour councils: Ken Livingstone's Fares Fair scheme means reasonable tube and bus prices for all, and thanks to the GLC we almost saw the Cocteau Twins. But the GLC is supposed to be about keeping things local and devolving power and giving grants to lesbian unicycling co-ops, not about amalgam-ation and centralisation and umbrellas, which is why the London Institute has aroused our collective ire. *That's* what we're demonstrating against here today, Thames News.

I guess my conversion to the Loony Left began before Christmas when Education Secretary Sir Keith Joseph, with his wiry hair and his big ears, announced plans to make us – well, our parents actually – pay an extra £520 a year in teach-ing fees. Mine are already expected to provide the shortfall in the minimum grant after means-testing. Dad, who'd enthusiastically voted the Tories in and plays golf and every-thing, was also enraged by Sir Keith's plans and wrote a bitter diatribe to Michael Morris, his local MP – who, like Rob, wears a dicky-bow. There was a student demo in protest at Sir Keith's plans in London, but I didn't go on that one, an act of apathy I regretted much more acutely than I expected. Marching is after all a traditional student pursuit, like collecting traffic cones and threatening to kidnap people unless they buy a rag mag. Actually, Chelsea doesn't have a rag mag, or indeed a rag week. It's too cool.

The bill was rejected by Conservative back-benchers and Sir Keith was forced to back down, but it polarised my feel-ings. The Thatcher government were the enemy within.

I wasn't much of a political animal growing up in Northampton. I hated views; views caused arguments; argu-ments got in the way of dancing and snogging. However, I'd been horrified by the sight of ships getting torpedoed in the Falklands War, especially with my brother joining the army, and lived each day with the certain knowledge that there could be a nuclear holocaust at any minute – or at any four minutes. Should it happen, this catastrophe would be the doing of cracked actor-cum-world leader Ronald Reagan. Imminent Armageddon informed so much popular culture, from *Not the Nine O'Clock News* to '99 Red Balloons', it was impossible not to feel involved.

That said, I felt it best not to worry unduly and saw only self-congratulatory folly in wearing a CND badge. What protection would a button offer if Reagan pressed his? Anyway in Northampton it looked like only ugly girls wore CND badges.

What I now see as this rather trite and sexist worldview was never going to survive at *college* college. Not at *this* self-consciously plural, libertarian, Mayakovsky-reading seat of learning, which I described rather drolly in my diary last week as 'Chelsea School of Anti-Racism, Anti-Sexism, Anti-Classism, Anti-Institute, Anti-Septic, Anti-Dote, Ant-Eater, Auntie-Janice and Ain't-That-Peculiar'. A hard dose of reality – even the two-meals-a-day, clean-sheets-on-Tuesday kind – has knocked some sense into me. And now politics has arrived squarely on my doorstep, complete with further pantomime villains to add to Thatcher, Reagan and Chernencko, namely ILEA's grey, soulless, Orwellian pen-pushers, hell-bent on sucking the life out of *my* art college! Save our school! Save our school!

The best part about today's demo, the thing that really gets my blood racing and makes me feel part of a greater struggle, is the fact that it's completely pointless. We're picketing a foregone conclusion. The London Institute is but a few raised hands away from resolution and there's nothing a bunch of chanting art students can do about it. Just as the GLC is ultimately doomed, so the Institute's illustrious success is preordained. Chelsea School of Art will soon be a cog in a bigger, better-oiled machine.

We tried though. We tried and we failed.

In the week before the County Hall demo, Rob and I were selected for an important revolutionary task by Chelsea's head of illustration Susan Einzig. A wearily charismatic, bra-less old woman who apparently fled Nazi Germany as a girl in the 1930s, she hated my work and had recently described me in front of everybody as a 'sausage machine'. However, I had a car, and might prove useful for the cause. We were to drive into Central London and collect up all the save-our-school petitions, left in politically strategic places like the Serpentine Gallery and an art bookshop on the Charing Cross Road.

'Would you be a couple of darlings and do that for me?' Susan implored in her Anglicised German singsong. 'For Chelsea.'

Sensing a plated opportunity to (a) get in with one of the senior lecturers, and (b) have the afternoon off college, we pledged allegiance and agreed on the spot. It would be an adventure in terms of both politics and parking. We pulled into the forecourt of no less than the Royal Academy of Art on Piccadilly and left the car in a blatantly unauthorised space with a note under the windscreen wiper saying, 'Urgent business with the president.' Exactly how convincing this must have seemed beneath a blue visor strip bearing the letters S, H, A, K and E, who knows, but it was true! And we got away with it. Again, believing your own hype pays off.

That day, Rob and I were close to fainting with the excitement of being chosen for this revolutionary quest. Even though many of the petitions were less than half full – notably the one the Cork Street Gallery had helpfully concealed under a stack of pamphlets for a Mantis Dance

Company event at the ICA – it actually felt like we were work-ing for a dangerous underground cause, plotting the over-throw of some tsarist regime with our reckless parking and Xeroxed forms.

We weren't. We were pissing into the wind of change.

Still, at least we made it on to *Thames News*. Collectively, at any rate. There's no footage of Rob orating and me nodding, much to our chagrin as we sit and watch the evening bulletin in the Ralph West TV lounge, our feet still killing us. I'm pretty sure I can see my distinctive checky shirt ('Where?' 'There!' 'Point at it!' 'It's gone now!'), but it's not about indi-viduals, it's about the massed ranks of checky shirts.

The revolutionary spirit infects the halls and we start planning an illegal party on the lift lobby of the third floor. The right time to crack open the conciliatory Martini. I think perhaps Rosso tonight, comrades.

I was, it's fair to say, a complex little socialist in 1985. There was nothing rehearsed or black and white about my views. For instance, on the issue of Northern Ireland I was caught between a reflexive instinct towards troops-out and an under-lying sense of unease about Ken inviting Sinn Fein to tea while the IRA were still targeting London. (Targeting London both-ered me less when I lived in Northampton.) My feelings were further clouded by the fact that my own eighteen-year-old brother did more than one tour of duty in South Armagh and sent me letters whose *Apocalypse Now* bravado barely concealed genuine fear of having his legs blown off. I wanted troops out because I wanted Simon out.

My stance on the issue of gender politics would also

pinball between gut reaction and ideology. While I was in Northampton for the summer holidays, I asked Nan to save me her copies of the *Sun* and she'd bring round a week's worth every Thursday. I keenly followed the exploits of Axa the Amazonian warrior on the comic strips page, also George and Lynne. But there was a more serious motive for stockpiling copies of the tabloid: I used to cut out topless models from Page Three and Pritt-stick them into my diary under the heading 'IRRELEVANT SEXIST EXPLOITATION'.

What precisely was I doing? I even knew some of the irrelevant ladies' first names – judging from my 1985 diary I think you'll find that Tracey, Lu and Anelise were all conspicuously in gainful employment with News International that year. You may glibly conclude that despite the postmodern context I was in fact simply ogling the top halves of Tracey, Lu and Anelise like any other red-blooded *Sun* reader – especially the one where Anelise, 36-22-34, is pouring water down herself from a conch shell. And you would be right.

In my own defence, it was a confusing decade. All that glamour and yet so much guilt. The contradictions were everywhere. If I gazed out of the lift-lobby window on the ninth floor across the Ethelburga estate I would see new instances of stone cladding on recently purchased council houses. Miners from as far as Yorkshire and South Wales were regularly seen shaking buckets at well-heeled commuters on the Embankment. While one Labour council in Liverpool sent redundancy notices round in taxis, ours rubber-stamped amalgamations like the Institute. The London Docklands Development Council tore up what Rob and I had seen to be the arsehole of the capital and was yet accused in great graffiti daubs of destroying communities. There were nude ladies in the *Sun*, and there were nude women in *The Face*, one politically unacceptable, the other deemed artistic.

The battle for my political soul would ultimately be fought over women. I loved women. But did I respect them? They were the natural object of my young affection but not objects – I swear. Yet with all that flushed sexual adrenalin sluicing round how could I be sure? All I can say is I had been in love with art school girls since the day I stepped foot through Nene's doors and saw that sea of baggy dungarees. And now I lived in a building that was full of them; in fact I moved in circles where men were practically an endangered species.

Halls provided a constant, fascinating parade of bewitching girls in dad-shirts, leggings and impractical earrings. And they divided neatly into two types. (OK so I'm objectifying a little.) On the one hand you had your Fashion Victims – alabaster-skinned creatures on textile courses who ran up their own flamboyant outfits every day and, as such, always turned up late to breakfast. On the other you had your Fine Artists – fetchingly unkempt, nocturnal spirits smudged with charcoal and content just to stab a pencil into the ad hoc bun of hair on top of their head to keep it out of their dinner. Fine Artists either wore boots or went barefoot and took the little packets of cheese and biscuits back to their rooms to nibble on at night. The rest of us just scoffed them.

It wasn't a complete sweetshop; the law of averages saw to it that there would also be some Tomboys, perhaps ceramics students or graphic designers. These, short-haired and trousered, would usually hang around with a Fashion Victim and a Fine Artist, as if to complete some kind of

GLC-approved triumvirate. Life was certainly simpler in goth-on-goth Northampton, but the possibilities for cross-pollination here were heady.

The tightrope was desperately seeking sex without being sexist. The best I could hope for was to communicate my confusion through my art.

After the wall of indifference and disdain I came up against at college for my People At Work project – a puppet theatre based on the Ralph West canteen, subtly suggesting that People At Work are being 'operated' by unseen hands – I regrouped artistically and gathered my thoughts. I'll show them. The next brief was Famous People: simply, to 'explore' a famous person. It was, as they liked to call it in the illustration department, an 'open brief', meaning you could do what you liked. The tutors supplied us with a list of potential subjects – Darwin, Freud, Mozart, Trotsky, Luther – but granted us the freedom to go off-list, which was just as well. I chose to explore Madonna, who, a year on from *Like a Virgin*, had taken over the world with her bras and her beauty spot. *Penthouse* had recently published the hairy-armpit early nude shots, which I was able to acquire in the name of research.

I threw my heart and soul into this project, producing pages and pages of sketches and notes and research. But what I imagined to be my *pièce de résistance* was a huge portrait of Madonna exploding. The theory was, we'd seen so much of her, the next logical stage of exposure would be to see her insides. Thus did I justify a rather brutal depiction of Madonna in her pomp, showering an audience with offal, detritus and glitter from the approximate direction of her vagina. This unsettling image was met with a certain amount of *résistance* from the feminists in the group (i.e. all of them – except Lara, who was too much of a deb to give gender politics much thought). However, I deftly explained this grotesque image away as a comment *on* sexism, not sexism itself. Yes, it was a painting of a woman's uterine lining in mid-air but its graphic nature was surely no more offensive than a pop singer encouraging twelve-year-old girls in Colchester and Caenarvon to expose their belly-buttons and wear little more than lingerie in the street.

Against all odds … they bought it! I silenced their unease with a robust ideological defence. Susan Einzig couldn't bring herself to say that she *liked* my pictures, but she admired my guts, if not Madonna's, and conceded that it was a 'lively response' to the brief.

Then I went home to closely re-examine the *Penthouse* pictures. I repeat: a confusing decade.

My political transformation from sheltered, suburban naïf to cynical, metropolitan lefty was incremental and slow. Influence came from many quarters and change was absorbed gradually. It would be nice to think that my ever-evolving hairstyle reflected this change. At the end of year one it was a multi-hued haystack, graduating from blond at the sides through various shades of orange into a deep burgundy at the parched, split tips. It was decadent and unplanned; anti-establishment, for sure, but unfocused and, frankly, to the outside world, a mess, a bit like Ken Livingstone's dream of a rainbow coalition.

At the start of the second year, just in time for my new NUS card, it was completely blond – except for the obligatory short brown patches above the ears – and as high and as wide and as long at the back as anyone on stage at Live Aid. In October, sick of all this artifice and angling for a place on the committee, I decided to become electable and had my hair chopped short and spiky by a girl called Lucy on the ninth floor and then dyed it utility brown. A convoluted return to my roots. (It was even called 'Natural Brown' on the box of Nice'n'Easy chemicals – a paradox that was not lost on me.) With shorter, less ridiculous hair, I began to wear my Breton fisherman's cap on a daily basis, a nod to proletarian resistance workwear which was *de rigueur* for the young socialist. That, a pair of dungarees and a hillbilly undershirt and I could almost pass myself off as someone who tilled the land. Even though, in actual fact, I drew pictures and got my sheets washed.

There was something noble and unionised about being an official Ralph West committee member. I'd had little choice but to apply, having used it as a lever to get back into halls. Handily, for the nine committee places, only nine residents applied. We all got in. At our first meeting in the Prince Albert on 23 October, refraining from calling one another comrade, we appointed a chair, treasurer and secretary, agreed that the halls should establish better links with the student liaison officers and voted against having fireworks at a forthcoming party. My lofty position within the halls council didn't, however, stop the domestic bursar leaving me a brusque note telling me off about the brown hair dye splashes around my sink area. I scrubbed and scrubbed like Lady Macbeth.

Some time over the summer, I had wiped the pretentious 'K' from my surname and reverted back to Collins. But far from normalised, I then made it my life's work to get every-body to call me Boone. This was chiefly so that Rob and I would sound like a double act: Mills and Boone. Also, it's the kind of thing you can do at college as you rattle along the conveyor belt: change your hair colour, change your style, change your name. I started signing my pictures and the notes on my door as Boone. It being the mid-Eighties, I spaced the letters out. All the trendy designers were doing this.

Sadly, only Carl, a first-year from Bedford, actually called me Boone. And Rob, a bit, mainly in notes left on my door. But it kept me occupied and, more importantly, gave me a pseudonym for my cartoons like Vicky or Trog. One of our more significant new first-year friends was called Run. His actual name was John Wrake, but so established was this childhood nickname he actually succeeded in getting every-one to call him Run. From day one. Even the tutors. No surname, just Run. Cool as anything. Though he was in the year below, he was a year older due to some circuitous route through higher education, and we soon secretly worshipped him. He was much better at being a lefty than me. His credentials included wearing an earring, having the sides of his head completely shaved up to about two inches above the ear, and understanding the situation in Nicaragua.

Rob, Run and I eventually joined forces and started a fanzine. When I say started, we produced one issue and made our friends buy it. Not quite in the same league as legends of the Sixties underground student press like the *Berkeley Barb*, ours was printed up by Dennis and Dick in the Chelsea print room with the full blessing of louche head-of-course Peter Donnelly. Which is not to say it wasn't subversive. It was called *Seventy-One Per Cent*. Not some heavy statistic – the percentage of 'disappeared' Chilean activists still unaccounted for by Amnesty International since the military coup in 1973 – it was the mark all three of us had coincidentally been awarded at the end of the first term, and the most often used reduction ratio on the photocopier (A3 to A4).

A cursory skim through the first and only issue of *Seventy-One Per Cent* gives a snapshot of where our heads were at. There are lots of deliberately grainy second- and third-generation photocopies for what can only be described as that Xeroxy fanzine look: one of Rob's tiny ear pressed flush against the college copier, another of Jimmy Durante and a succession of Eadweard Muybridge photos of a really, really fat woman. There are articles, if that's not too strong a word: three perspectives of the same June Brides gig at the Harp Club in New Cross; an overview of Cocteau Twins interviews in *Sounds, Melody Maker* and *Jamming*; memories of four days' work experience at *i-D* magazine; a look at the burgeoning London cabaret circuit; an insider's view of what it's like to grow a beard; an appraisal of Tony Hancock; a vicious parody of *The Face* called – alert the side doctors! – *The Faece*; a drawing of Robert Elms being hung by the neck; and, very much the meat and potatoes of the magazine, a real seven-page interview with John Peel by Run, which he blagged, organised and conducted all off his own back. Now you can see why we were so in awe of him. While we fawned over professional illustrators, he went out and bagged a broadcasting legend.

In this extract from the *Seventy-One Per Cent* interview, Run asks Peel to elucidate on his notion that political revolution is self-gratification:

'People striking attitudes, shouting slogans, adopting postures and so on, I really think in their heart of hearts they know that it has no effect at all beyond satisfying themselves,' opines Peel. 'It also provides, as I do at Radio One, a function of the establishment. I mean, these people never actually say what it is they want. People say so much about what they don't want.'

Run counters, 'Yes, but at the moment I think people are just so pissed off with Thatcher that any alternative would be desirable.'

'Yes, but people then go beyond that,' Peel parries. 'I mean you read the *NME* and it's full of anti-Kinnock stuff and so on, but who are they going to vote for? I mean, Lenin's dead.'

He was right of course. Older and wiser than three mollycoddled student revolutionaries – Peel had probably *read* the *Berkeley Barb* – he'd hit the nail on the head. We were just striking attitudes and shouting slogans – SAVE OUR SCHOOL. But the words of an old man weren't going to stop us. We would continue to fight the power by photocopying things in the belief that we were seizing back the means of production from the bourgeoisie, going to New Cross and shaving the sides of our heads.

It had happened without me noticing of course, but I had actually turned into Rik off *The Young Ones*.

eleven

Gone to Forever

These are consecutive, unedited extracts from the notepad stuck to my door, Room 313, autumn term, 1985. They speak, in rough-hewn haiku form, of the ongoing soap opera that was Ralph West Hall. The messages in bold are my own.

- **Gone to college forever**
- **Gone to forever forever!**
- Seeing as you fell asleep on yer best mate I fucked off home on the N14 – Rob
- Turn it down!
- **Writing witty anonymous remarks is very clever. I wish I was that subtle**
- I'm in 114, girls
- No I'm not any more
- Remember the towels, brownhead
- **Goodnight**
- Thanks for the Pentel
- FIRE FIRE FIRE FIRE FIRE DEAD!
- I love you

'The Cocteau Twins might be there!'

Those were my exact words at dinner tonight before Rob and I hopped aboard the 22 bus into Central London. I was half joking.

'Do you really think so?' Rob asked, almost daring himself to believe it.

'You never know ...'

He snaps out of his reverie.

'Fuck off!'

It's endemic of London life and its heady possibilities that Rob and I could convince ourselves over dry canteen food that the godlike Cocteau Twins might just turn up at a show-case gig for three other bands on their record label; a gig we had tickets for. Why not? On our last jaunt up the King's Road, we spotted Mike Score from A Flock of Seagulls, Jill Gascoine off ITV's *The Gentle Touch* and George Best (who, to be fair, does live locally but for extra points was carrying a bulging laundry bag). Run interviewed John Peel. Rob worked at *i-D* magazine for four whole days. So why ever not?

It's been a good day. At the crit, Susan Einzig made some right-on quip about part-time tutor Anne Howeson wearing a Benetton jumper, and her response was a curt and unprece-dented, 'Oh *fuck* off!' And someone anonymously left the message 'I love you' on the little notepad I have now stuck to my door at halls. Six little words in total – oh *fuck* off, I love you – but symptomatic, you must admit, of a good day. And now me and Rob and a new platonic pal of ours called Victoria are walking with our hands freshly stamped into the brightly lit bar of the University of London Union, here to see – in reverse order of billing – Dif Juz, Xymox and the Wolfgang Press, collectively the more obscure end of 4AD's roster.

The place should, we feel, be fuller on a gala night like this, but you can't beat a union bar, even someone else's, for feeling at home. Chelsea's lack of a union bar means the idea of dirt-cheap beer in plastic glasses thrills us to our very penny-pinching marrow. And look over there, it's the Cocteau Twins.

Elizabeth Fraser and Robin Guthrie, two-thirds of the band who have eclipsed The Smiths in our universe, just standing there, in old coats, like an ill-matched couple drinking the same dirt-cheap beer out of the same plastic glasses as the rest of us. Why are they not being mobbed or carried shoulder-high by an adoring throng or at least being given a spontaneous round of applause just for being the Cocteau Twins? Because nobody else here recognises them. Do these ULU types not read the *NME* from cover to cover and pore over every photo caption? Or perhaps they're all just too nervous, awestruck and cool to approach them. I am suddenly all three of those things.

'They're here,' I mutter under my breath, facing away from the Cocteau Twins so that they can't lip-read me.

'Who?' asks Rob.

'Where?' shouts Victoria, little round teapot of a girl.

'Don't look!' I hiss. 'Liz Fraser and Robin Guthrie, just standing over there.'

Victoria as good as puts her hand to her forehead like a ship's lookout as she scans the bar for our quarry. She's northern. She has no tact. I position myself between her and them. We don't want to appear gauche. After all, nobody else here is taking a blind bit of notice.

'Oh my fucking Lord,' mutters Rob.

He blushes.

'Am I blushing?'

We both nod.

'Have I got food in my teeth?'

We both shake our heads.

What to do now? It was enough that we *saw* Jill Gascoine and George Best; there was no need to take it any further, we're not Americans, we're not autograph-hunters, we're not fans. But these two people make the very music that excites our skin and inspires our hearts and has us up all night listening over and over to a tape of one song recorded off John Peel and trying in vain to make out the right words. So what's our strategy?

Dif Juz are onstage. We all troop into the hall to take in their gently undulating instrumental soundscapes. By 'we' I mean us, the Cocteau Twins and a couple of hundred other gig-goers. Rob, Victoria and I engineer it so that we're standing quite near them but not creepily close. We occasionally watch Dif Juz too. Then it's back into the bar. We repeat the ritual for Xymox, who are German, noisy and the sort of band Kevin would like. Then back into the bar. We try and convince ourselves that just seeing the Cocteau Twins in the flesh and under harsh strip lighting is worth the £3.50 admission. But it's also our big chance. They're here, we're here, nobody else has recognised them – how to take this a stage further while retaining our iridescent, rococo 4AD poise?

I search my memory for a precedent. Once, when I came to London on a Nene College day-trip round the museums and galleries we were ambling through Hyde Park and spotted David Rappaport – lead dwarf from *The Time Bandits* and bit-player in *The Young Ones*. He was perched on a bench, on his own, so we plucked up the courage and went over to him. We told him how much we liked him and his work and he was really chatty and it was a happy occasion, but … we were tourists then. That's the kind of uncool thing holidaymakers do: go up to people. Me and Rob and Victoria live here. We—

Victoria has gone straight up to them.

'What's she doing?'

She walks over, taps Robin on the shoulder and starts talking to them, bold as northern brass.

'What's she saying?'

Rob and I are mortified – that the teapot has blown our cool and is probably asking them idiotic questions or telling Liz that we fancy her – which we do, in a non-sexual, put-her-in-a-glass-case kind of way. Also, that *we're* not talking to them at all because we are cunts. We opt to loiter a few steps nearer.

Victoria eyes us over Liz's shoulder, knowing full well that we are itching to join her. She beckons us over with a jerk of her head. It's time.

Rob gathers all of his creamed-off Cranbrook arrogance about him and marches up to Liz with his gambit.

'Excuse me, Elizabeth …' the full name is a nice touch, it's a pity he's addressing her like a ticket inspector on a train. 'Can you tell me why you've released two EPs rather than putting out an LP?'

Her response is immediate and strangely familiar.

'Oh *fuck* off!'

This at least gives me the 'in' of joining the laughter. Rob is already too red to redden any further. Robin grins silently into his beer. It is a wonderful moment. Elizabeth Fraser, her words so indistinct, angelic and ethereal on disc, has just told my friend Rob to fuck off in a broad Scottish oil-rigger's accent. The ice is broken.

My moment comes when I remember that I still have my ticket for the Cocteaus' cancelled GLC gig in my wallet, between my NUS card and a photo-booth shot of me and Kevin. I could have taken it back, as instructed, to Room 1a at County Hall and had my £1.50 refunded but I chose instead to keep it as a memento, never imaging I would ever show it to the Cocteau Twins. I ask them about the gig-that-never-was and produce the evidence. They seem baffled.

'I don't remember agreeing to do any GLC gig,' says Liz, wide-eyed.

I express my shock at the precarious façade of the music business and the sheer gall of Ken Livingstone. She takes my ticket to examine it. Liz Fraser is handling my ticket!

'We were never told about it,' Robin snuffles dismissively.

'But the *NME* said you cancelled due to ill-health.'

'That's the *NME*,' she replies. 'I'm fine.' She certainly is, if a little downy around the face up close. Rob's jealous that I'm now doing better than he thanks to my ticket coup, but that's life – he's the one who went to Room 1a for his £1.50 back.

Our intimate tête-à-tête is cut short by the telltale sound of an intro tape, at which we actually accompany the Cocteau Twins back into the hall. The five of us, momentarily together, as if in a dream. I want to whisper those other three little words as Liz sways along to the Wolfgang Press:

I love you.

Oh *fuck* off!

* * *

- Dear Andy, Had to go, 'cos meeting friend at 7.30, going to Covent Gdn, the Punch & Judy pub (top entrance) at 8.45. If you're desperate, I'll buy you a drink (so will Tracey) – love, Sue x
- **Gone to Union Bar, back at some earthly hour**
- **I'm on the phone**
- Not coming to the pub
- **Well fuck you then**
- I'd rather you didn't
- Andy Pandy!
- **At a meeting**
- **I'm on the phone, then the queue**
- Postin' a letter
- **Fiona, I've gone to the Prince Albert so come if you want to – Andy**
- Rob's here

OK I can't exactly stand up and say with my hand on my heart that my second year at college was an uninterrupted string of demos, protests and acts of civil disobedience. I continued to wrestle with my conscience over Page Three, I studiously lapped up the more donkey-jacketed rhetoric in the *NME*, I visited galleries and museums and expanded my mind, and my general anti-war feelings were fanned by reading books about Vietnam like *Dispatches* and *The Short Timers*. But one ideology, one 'ism', underpinned my every move and my every thought, more than socialism, pacifism, even humanism, and that was hedonism. I wanted to have a good time, all the time. The notepad on my door became a sort of collective social diary.

After my brief period of rootlessness I had landed on my feet again. I was a second-year living in halls with all the swagger and influence that comes with the position. I could give out jelly snakes at the snack bar to girls I fancied, loaded with symbolism of course. I had no plans to return to Northampton until the holidays forced me to. I lived down 'the girls' end' of the corridor. There was no such thing on paper, but happy circumstance saw to it that I was the only bloke between the lift and the fire escape. I liked those odds.

'And to the right, inappropriately enough, is Red Ken's home, County Hall, a huge, fuck-off building, designed by Ralph Knott, started in 1911 although the intervention of two world wars prevented its completion until 1958.'

'We went on a demo outside there. *Thames News* interviewed Rob.'

'Really? You were on telly?'

'Nah, they edited it out. Fucking cunt-arses.'

'On your left, Victoria Embankment, Hungerford Bridge coming up, and a load of shit-arse tourists getting on at Embankment tube to travel one stop to Charing Cross, even though it's quicker to walk.'

'And cheaper.'

Since arriving in London I've been on a boat roughly once a fortnight, or so it seems. In the name of casual excess, we spend half our lives traipsing up and down wooden jetties and hopping aboard tubs called things like the *Thames Princess*. This particular pleasure cruise has been arranged by the committee at Ralph West Hall. By me. I was out-voted when it came to booking a band, so

A Cast of Thousands, of whom nobody's ever heard and nobody wishes to hear, are playing a set of indiscriminate Then Jerico-type sludge-rock on the lower deck. Everyone else is up here on the top deck, watching beautiful, twilit London go past, with Rob and I doubling as unpaid second-year tour guides.

It's a residents-only jaunt, which is why there are so many non-residents. That includes Rob – of no cleaned abode, Putney – although he spends so much time at the halls, Veronica and Sam and Brenda all assume he lives here. He certainly makes himself at home. The pair of us are never short of a willing audience, or at least one too bamboozled to complain, and the latest comprises three first-years from the sixth, eighth and ninth floors, one Northern Irish, two Scots, all three a long way from home. The Scots are Sam, the very definition of a don't-fancy-me Tomboy in trousers and hairshirt, with a cigarette tucked workmanlike behind her ear, and Brenda, who's short and round and square, if you see what I mean, and has a squeaky Scottish voice reminiscent of the man who used to read out the Little Nose stories on *Jackanory* when I was a kid. And then Veronica – a Thames princess who has casually kicked away my sea legs. She's also a classic Fashion Victim: a student on foundation who's taken the name of the course literally and plastered herself with it. An enigma wrapped up in a puzzle wrapped up in an assortment of black, grey and purple layers.

My round: 'Does anybody want another one?'

I don't. I've been 'getting in the mood' with a bottle of Hock since six o'clock and, at one stage, having danced naked round my room – solo – to Magazine's *The Correct Use of Soap*, I found myself recklessly shaving the sides of my head with a Bic razor. The bald patches are not level, but we are on a rocking boat so who's going to notice?

'I'm fine,' says Brenda, abstemiously. She's not the type to dance round her room, or even be naked in the first place.

'I'll have another bitter,' says Sam, bluntly, her blue eyes glazed like the pots I imagine she regularly slides out of the college kiln on one of those frying pan things. The sides of her head are already shaved with a Bic razor. Presumably a ladies' one, although you can never tell with Tomboys.

Veronica just looks at me with those big, painted, Irish eyes from under meticulously tousled bangs of dark hair, teased out – possibly with sterilised tweezers – from under a turban-style headband so as to look as if they've just decadently fallen out during a tropical storm or torrid clinch. Not for her the vulgar commitment of saying yes or no. I decide to get her a wine anyway, just in case it increases my chances with her later.

– We're having a party so SHUT THE FUCK UP!
– Dear Shitey, I (Rob) will be in the Hand & Flower (pub along King's Road past World's End, on left as you go towards Fulham) about 7–7.30pm. Killer Rabbits. Free food and makin' a video, so make sure you look good. Bus: 11 or 22. Love Rob xxx
– **I've gone to bed. Knock only if it's important or you're someone special**
– **I am in**

- To Andy, I'm sorry I've had your knife so long but ta anyway – love Fiona
- Come up and see me sometime x

I never did get off with Veronica that night; never did muck up her immaculate hair, but I kept trying. My merry dance around this unattainable girl was a microcosm of student romance, with its rituals and codes and seemingly endless permutations for physical interaction. You begin with a large group – your year at college, say, the inventory of Ralph West Hall, a boat full of partygoers – and your task is to gradually pare that number down into smaller and more manageable sub-sets until you're left with the requisite two. The magic number. What you mustn't do is end up with one. The tragic number. This holds true for social interaction in any circle, but the whole process is caricatured by the neverland of higher education and more viciously again by halls, where the very lack of anything more pressing to worry about than running out of instant coffee or a knock on the door from Lenny throws the procedure into sharp relief. The pursuit of happiness turns into an ongoing maths puzzle. You wake up in the morning thinking about the numbers and go to sleep at night still doing the sums. Five's a party, four's a crowd and three into two won't go.

- **Andy's gone to Putney**
- **And he's back**
- Is it all right for me to get a lift?
- **Yes**

- **Write something you bastards**
- **Out as hell**
- **Back like anything**
- And still the biggest piss artist as ever
- + The noisiest
- **Me and Rob are at the pub and that's as official as anything**
- **If, by some chance, you get here while I'm gone, Rob, I am restocking the coffee bar with coffee and I will be the tiniest amount of time, so wait, matey**
- Andy you look rather ill – have an early night, luv, Georgina and Sarah K

Still haven't and it's two weeks now since our first encounter. Longer. Am I losing my touch? Fireworks night has been and gone and nothing went off. I want the one I can't have and it's driving me mad. Oh yes.

Like all the best fashion girls, Veronica likes to play the victim. She has her troubles. I haven't yet quite worked out what they are, but I'm certainly putting the man-hours in. The more I can't have her, the more I want her.

A pattern in my masochistic wooing of Veronica Immaculate has emerged. It feels like going round in circles and happens pretty much every night. Rob turns up at the halls in his tartan tie for a visitor's meal, announcing his arrival by saying something loud and rude about someone in the queue; after eating we call on Veronica, who without exception will already have Brenda in her room and some-times but less often Sam, who is a bit of a loner. It's as if Veronica employs them as chaperones, her own insecurity guards, always putting up a barrier. We all trot off to the Prince Albert, Rob just happy to be away from the spectre of Mrs Reed and his one-ring hob. Veronica barely speaks all evening except to put down Rob with some barb, which he respects. She laughs, but in such a way that says, 'You are fortunate to enjoy the brief patronage of my amusement.' Wrapped up in her black, grey and white layers, I mentally unpeel her. I find myself mesmerised by her eyes. Occasionally she'll catch me at it, and stare me out. She always wins. The rest is babble.

Brenda talks about this and that and how much she loves and misses her mum and dad. Sam simply looks like she has a lot on her mind. A tricky bit of ceramics perhaps? A squeaky potter's wheel? Why do students from Scotland feel the need to come so far south when it obviously pains them so? Ralph West is brimful of homesick, near-suicidal Scots.

The fun transfers to one of our rooms, usually mine (I can be persuasive like that), and never Sam's (who might have a body in there for all we know). Rob and I do our best to keep the party entertained until he's forced to go off in search of a night bus and tiptoe up the stairs of his hovel without waking Mrs Reed. He'll often call in on Fiona or Sue or Sarah before leaving the halls, but that's another story.

Brenda and Sam outstay their welcome while Veronica arranges herself on the bed with not an eyelash out of place, like she owns the room and we're her guests. I run around making coffee, offering warm German wine and Waitrose almond biscuits and flipping the Prefab Sprout LP over and over until Brenda and Sam finally head for their beds. After something like five hours of painfully measured, Jane Austen-style courtship, Veronica and I are finally left alone.

I take the opportunity to switch to 'mood lighting' – which means turning the bedside lamp off and the one above the sink on, deftly sliding the wardrobe door over the sink area to reduce illumination to a thin ribbon. If I'm feeling really brave, I'll sit on the end of the bed and Veronica and I will actually exchange words.

These are our Little Talks, or don't-talks for Veronica. She'll throw in something noncommittal and tantalising like:

'I've got one or two things suspended in mid-air back at home.'

This is supposed to explain why she doesn't feel she can get off with me, and why, in fact, she prefers to torture me by staying in my room until 3am and lying on my bed but, contrary to the rules of engagement, not inviting me to lie next to her.

I'll tell her everything I can think of to tell her about my life up to and including yesterday and she'll drink it all in like a poker-faced journalist and then she'll go and pronounce Prefab Sprout as Prefab Sprote, winning in an instant my undying love and devotion for another 24 hours. Because there's promise in those eyes. At three she'll make her excuses and leave and thank me for a lovely evening and for the wine and biscuits and she'll disappear. In another instant, the magic number turns tragic and even though I've done the maths again and again it still doesn't add up.

I wish I fancied Brenda instead but she's too round and high-pitched and buttoned up, and Sam … well, Sam's not for fancying – she's for making up an odd number.

* * *

- **Whoever nicked my pen is obviously morally deficient and socially a big fat bad time. Don't you dare steal this one**
- Andy I am writing this in the dark but please can I borrow your crimpers in the morning, I'm not going to college 'till 10.00. PS If I can't it's okay
- **Gone to Putney forever**
- **Gone to the pub forever**
- Dear 'Funny Feelings' – I'm wearing your smile today, *muchas gracias,* Veronica

See? There she is, at it again. Leaving me a clandestine note calling me Funny Feelings – I recklessly revealed to her that she gave me 'funny feelings' – and telling me she's 'wearing my smile'. She's even signed it.

- **I am just bloody useless and ill and weak and wobbly and I'm not moving out of this bed all day. I will empty my bin myself, when I can summon up the energy. Thank you. Let me sleep**
- Dear Andy I hope you feel better soon, and get lots of sleep. In case you feel really rotten, here's two paracetamol that may make you feel better. Lots of luv, Addi
- Hope you're well soon, Sue x
- **Try 114**
- **Now I'm in**
- Morning Andrew + thank you for waking me up
- **Gone to town again**

- Andy my sweet – the party (Jenny's) has moved to the Coffee Bar (woweee) – then to my room (probably) see ya! Love Victoria (Plum) xx
- **A couple of aspirins and an early night and _____ is all I need. Bye**
- I love you

We're drunk. Rob's spinning wildly to 'The Boy With The Thorn In His Side' on the dance floor which isn't a dance floor but the floor of the canteen (parties that don't take place on boats or in lift lobbies or Victoria's room are always in canteens). It's Christmas. The Ralph West party. I'm drunk and I'm over Veronica.

Rob's all over Brenda. There's a glint in his eye, brought on by half a bottle of Croft Original in my room before dinner and two pints in the Prince Albert. In a moment the pair of them will be having a 'well it *is* Christmas' snog. It isn't Christmas, it's 11 December, but term ends in two days and Ralph West closes down and we'll all be in Scotland by Saturday, except the tiny handful of us who don't come from Scotland.

I'm marginally less drunk than Rob because as a committee member I had to do an hour's shift on the door, taking people's money and stamping their hands. There was a moment of electricity when it came to Veronica's hand. I held it for just a split second too long, but it passed.

The DJ follows The Smiths with 'Everything She Wants' by Wham!

'I'm not dancing to this!' I shout over the opening bars.

'I love this one!' squeaks Brenda.

Rob takes her hand and spins her around like a top. Well it *is* Christmas.

I repair to the bar which overlooks the canteen. Run and Carl are grumbling about their end-of-term assessment marks – or more accurately, about other people's. Carl is dressed in full Blues Brothers regalia, which is something he does often. You have to admire his commitment. He wore a fez into college the other day, something he'd never get away with in Bedford and he knows it.

'Cainesy? What's he done to deserve 81 per cent?' asks Carl, rhetorically, taking off his dark glasses.

'Looks trendy, says the right things at crits, gives them what they want,' grumbles Run, pulling on his fag. Run's wearing exactly what he wears every other day: jumble-sale jacket, stretched, sleeveless oatmeal cardy, home-stencilled T-shirt, torn jeans, one earring. Not for him the frivolous wholesale acceptance of social convention. Anyway, these are the clothes he met John Peel in.

'Absolutely!' declares Carl. He always says absolutely.

'Boone! My man!' he shouts at me as I amble over. He always says this by way of a greeting. He once slept on my floor at halls and kept his pork pie hat on all night. You have to marvel at that level of affectation.

'Got half a bottle of sherry in my room if you fancy some later,' I offer.

'Eurgh. Medicine,' says Run. He's a cider man.

'Does you good if that's what you mean.'

'I wouldn't say no,' offers Carl.

'All right – unless I'm getting off with someone,' I throw in as a provocative but probably empty caveat.

I order two lagers and a cider – 70p a pint, served with a smile by a cool Italian photography student called Gino.

Sam's up here, away from the dancing. She manages a scowl in my direction but she's far gone. Like Run, she's in daywear. No sense of dressing up, these people. Where's Veronica? At least she makes the effort. I'm wondering in my plastic cups whether I should make the effort to hunt her down – well, it *is* Christmas. My thoughts are interrupted when all the lights go on accompanied by an audible groan. It can't be over already?

We all gather and gaze down into what is once again our canteen. I can see Rob and Brenda amid the shell-shocked throng, red-faced from dancing and flushed from sudden exposure in the strip light. Then Mr Hartnell the warden enters dressed as Santa Claus, ho-ho-ho-ing and wishing us all a merry one. Lenny the night porter is right behind him wearing cardboard reindeer antlers. Even Run manages a smile at this.

'It's like being at school,' he mutters. Of course it is.

After a short speech and a 'See you all next term!' Mr Hartnell departs, the houselights go off and the disco lights resume. 'Relax' by Frankie Goes to Hollywood comes on. *Bam-bam-bam-bam-bam-bam*. It's a bit last year but who cares, it's better than Wham! and Carl and I race downstairs to stomp about with the rest of them. Run tightens his grip on the bar, stares implacably and lights another Marlboro.

It's one of those celebratory, joyous physical moments: a canteen full of pissed students, off-duty dinner ladies and a night porter in horns joined together for a fleeting instant, dropping all our daily personal worries and free from the harsh realities of the world beyond.

At times likes these, anything feels possible. Never mind that it's only a Wednesday. What if we harnessed the sheer hamster-wheel power of this hedonism? What if all the students in all the world currently leaping about to Frankie Goes to Hollywood in decorated canteens got together – couldn't we make some serious changes to the way things are run? Ban the bomb! Kick the CIA out of Nicaragua! Dismantle the London Institute before it's started! Seize the means of production! Feed the world! Troops out! Choose life! Relax! Don't do it! When you wanna go to it! Maggie, Maggie, Maggie, out, out, out!

Alternatively, we could just disperse into the building when the party winds down at the stroke of midnight and drink ourselves closer to oblivion on Black Tower and sherry with our wardrobe doors deftly slid over our sink areas.

Knock! Knock!

No, it's not Lenny. I think Lenny's turning a deaf ear to the after-hours festivities tonight. It's Mills and Boone! We're head-spinningly pissed and knocking on random doors in search of brand new friends at 2.45am.

'Evening, ladeeez!' Rob slurs.

Room 205: a small gathering of three fashion girls, one called Holly, plus northern Richard, who's a kind of honorary lady. Enough reason to burst in and hand round our full-size bottle of Bacardi. At its best, halls really can be like living in a vertical village.

'We're drunk as anything!' I explain, unnecessarily. Some foghorn banter and then we're off to the next random room to spread Christmas cheer.

We call the lift, which bears the hallmark 'Express Lifts Ltd: Northampton,' something I never cease to point out to strangers during conversational lulls between floors. ('That's where I come from!') The lift doors part to reveal a slumped but contended-looking Carl, his Blues Brothers hat only slightly askew.

'Mills and Boone! My men!'

He's been sitting in here for about half an hour now, travelling up and down, up and down. You have to marvel at that level of affectation.

We hop in, offer him some white rum and decide, randomly, to go to the sixth floor. When I say randomly, it's Veronica's floor, although the last time I saw her, she was having an intimate-looking conversation with Gino in the emptying bar. Part of me doesn't dare knock on her door.

Hearing music and voices coming through the door of Room 617, three floors above my first-year room at Ralph West, we try it for luck. No idea who lives here.

'Hi,' says a bleary-eyed hippy I think's called Gary. You don't see many beards at art school. Don't recognise the music. It sounds a bit Indian. Others are crashed out on bed and floor behind Gary and there's the sweet smell of dope.

'Just wishing people a merry Christmas,' falters Rob. We bid the hippies farewell and move on. It's getting late – or early – and we are forced to admit that our door-to-door gatecrashing act is running naturally out of steam. And Bacardi.

A couple more random doors and then I say it:

'We might as well try Veronica.'

Rob's already marching in the direction of 605. What if she is in there getting off with Gino?

The last, days-old, note on her door reads: 'Goodbye, cruel world.' Typical of Veronica to flirt with suicidal imagery when in fact all she meant to convey was, 'I've gone to bed early.' Underneath, though, is a new message, scrawled in what looks like blood but must be red ink: 'I've had enough. Don't bother to come up.' It's not Veronica's writing. I look at Rob, suddenly serious. He looks at me. We take the stairs.

We bang on her door.

'Sam? Are you all right?'

I'm crouched down peering through the keyhole. The lights are on but I can't see her. There's no key in the lock, so I rattle the handle. It's open.

'Sam? It's Andy and Rob.'

Again no answer, so I pop my head round an unintrusive crack in the door. She's standing at her sink area looking oddly serene, as if perhaps washing her socks or preparing to shave the sides of her head. She says nothing, just looks at us with mute eyes as we tumble through her door.

We've come to ask if that's her note on Veronica's door. She doesn't need to answer.

'Fucking Christ,' says Rob.

Nothing in my seven terms of higher education and personal development has prepared me for the sight that greets us as we enter the room. Sam's sink area looks like it has been painted red.

In a moment of measured sensitivity – utterly out of character but demanded by the situation – Rob gently takes the knife from Sam's right hand as if trained to do so. She offers no resistance. I don't even know how she's still standing. It's not even a scalpel or something surgical, but what looks like a dirty old model knife, with which Sam has been literally digging holes in her soft, white Scottish wrists.

It's amazing how all squeamishness leaves you at the moment of truth. Rob sits Sam down on her bed and wraps handkerchiefs tightly around her wrists, which seem somehow to have stopped bleeding. Perhaps there's no more blood left in her veins. Like the alcohol in our bodies, it has all but drained away.

I've no idea why but it suddenly strikes me as imperative that I remove all evidence of this act from Sam's sink area. I must cleanse. While Rob tends to her wounds, I wash down every inch of the walls and sink and mirror, swilling her gored toothpaste tube and soap under the tap, transfixed at the already-clotted viscosity of the blood. How long's she been at this act of self-excavation? While everyone else has been rolling their joints and draining their lager, Sam has noiselessly and methodically and seemingly for the benefit of Veronica – her immaculate, desirable, alabaster friend – been killing herself.

Rob gently walks Sam down the fire escape and out to the car park while I dash back to the third floor for my car keys and some shoes and socks, stopping by at 605 and taking down the note – more evidence removal. It's about three o'clock now; we've been drinking for nine hours, but I feel alert and awake and attuned enough to walk a tightrope. Despite the icy temperature, the car turns over first time. Over Albert Bridge in total silence except for Rob's unnecessary, 'Are you sure you're all right to drive?' and we're there. We park in the first space we find at St Stephen's Hospital on the Fulham Road and hurry inside casualty. This is an emergency, albeit no accident. After a brief, wordless wait, Sam is taken away.

Rob and I pace up and down in the paper-chained waiting room like expectant parents, as sober as judges although probably not smelling that way to the night staff. But nothing they haven't seen, or smelt, before.

After an age, a doctor comes out and asks us a lot of probing questions about Sam as if we are perhaps next of kin – and in vast, lonely London we might as well be. It's then that we truly and shamefully realise how little we know about her. Scottish. Ceramics. Smoker. Despite our proximity, we hardly know her.

A nurse eventually brings her out looking forlorn and about ten years old with her wrists stitched up and dressed and a prescription for some antibiotics in the pocket of her coat. The coat Rob dressed her in like a parent. She smiles apologetically.

Hardly a word is spoken on the drive back across Albert Bridge, its fairy lights still twinkling with possibility. It's Christmas every day on this bridge. We accompany Sam back to her room and with a promise that she'll be all right, we leave her to the safety of sleep.

Something has finally shut me and Rob up, and put the whole shallow, hedonistic cabaret into perspective.

twelve

The Prisoner

January. It's windy today. Really windy. Battersea Park won't shut up. The glass in the windows feels like it might blow in. It's no day for going out. Undeterred, me and Ingrid have wrapped up warm and are battling the elements. In coats and scarves we walk arm in arm through the Ethelburga to the little chemist to buy some Lemsip for her next-door neighbour Cathy, who's feeling under the weather. We, meanwhile, are on top of the world. When a walk in a gale to the chemist is fun I'd say you're into something good.

I met Ingrid just before Christmas on the night of the party; the night of Sam. She and Cathy were in one of the random, mood-lit, smoke-filled rooms Rob and I barged in on; two Chelsea foundation girls who we'd seen around but never put a name to. They received us generously even though it was late and we were uninvited and one of us was Rob. So smitten was I that even in the short time we were in what turned out to be Ingrid's fetchingly messy room, I began to take solace from the fact that there were no boys in there.

Rob inspected the work on Ingrid's wall.

'Some nice marks,' he boomed, the very thing a Chelsea tutor might say in a crit, as he peered at a large, Christ-like charcoal life drawing on her pinboard. Christ-like save for the fact that it was headless.

'You're in the second year?' Ingrid enquired, exhaling with poise.

'Yep.'

'You're at Bagley's Road?'

'Mmm-hmm.'

She looked as beautiful close up as she did from the other side of the canteen. A picture-book representation of beauty: bee-sting lips, pert nose, big eyes, fluttering eyelashes, all framed by a luxurious wild mane of dark brown hair. She was wearing dungarees. Grey and black chequered clown ones; the sort it would be hard for just anyone to look good in. We were too drunk to have a sensible conversation so Rob and I moved on. But beyond the Bacardi, I had felt something. And now we're crossing the road together, arm in arm. Her hair's all over the place but she still looks like someone I'd do anything for.

It's been a long time since I had someone I could safely call a girlfriend. Two years and four months since Sally; sixteen months since Valeria, if you can count Valeria. But those relationships suddenly seem pedestrian compared to Ingrid. She's a dream girl with a slightly unreal, almost fictional quality to her. She comes from Jersey which is, to me, a fond idyll of sand and sea. There's a sense of destiny, even though I don't believe in it. It's just been different with Ingrid. I knew it was special as we didn't get off with each other the first night we met, and we didn't sleep with each other the first night we got off with each other. This was her decision, admittedly, but I have managed to post-rationalise high romantic intent into the initial abstention.

The year did actually begin with a bang, but the wrong kind, the *old* kind, the pre-Ingrid kind. Kate was a sixth-form friend who'd gone to study art at Bath. But it wasn't Kate. She invited me to her 21st birthday party in the first week of the new term and I drove there, giving a lift to Jill, another sixth-former who was studying something sensible at Hatfield Poly. Jill was the kind of close-circle friend I'd perhaps find myself snogging on New Year's Eve in the Bold, but nothing more meaningful, possibly because she was so tall we looked comical together. But height difference evaporates when you're horizontal and we foolishly slept together that night in Kate's front room, drunk, on a mattress, in the pitch black, oblivious to the fact that others were crashed out around us. A regrettable act for both of us, but it wasn't wholly without purpose: it marked the end of my old life. I decided to wave goodbye to the old Andy.

Within a fortnight I was with, but not sleeping with, Ingrid. At the end of the letter I wrote to Mum and Dad mentioning my new relationship, I wrote the words: 'I'm changing into a nicer person.'

A good chance to test the Pretentious Bollocks alarm now: in the spring of '86 I composed an opera. I can't remember the exact wording of the brief at college. It certainly wasn't 'compose an opera', but this was my chosen solution. I locked myself away in my room at the halls for a couple of weeks and, using my trusty Hitachi stereo, two external tape decks, a lot of cable and jack plugs, and selections from my entire record collection including Kate Bush, Pink Floyd, ABC, Tony Hancock and the *Apocalypse Now* soundtrack, I built what can only be described as a multifaceted audio collage of words, music and sound effects. I also produced a neatly handwritten libretto and copious costume design sketches. The title page of the booklet announced that it was called, with some precedent, '*Red Light and Sunshine*: An Opera in Eight Acts by Andrew Collins.'

Yes, *Andrew* Collins. Ingrid didn't like Andy, so for the first time since punk came to Northampton in 1979 I was called Andrew. That's the power of love. It comes from above.

I trouble you with this opera only because of its plot, which has certain subtle autobiographical resonance the scholars among you may be able to divine.

The hero's name is Boone, a brown-haired angel who wears fingerless gloves, a white vest, an old M&S cardy and huge cartoon wings. He has been sent to earth to deliver the opera's heroine Angharad to her destination: heaven itself. First, he must rescue her from Ex Isle, a remote island set, according to the notes, in 'a splash of ultramarine'.

Act 1 opens with Angharad locked in a tall tower by the sea. On the tape, gentle scene-setting seaside sound effects are interrupted by a discordant, percussive track called 'The Prisoner' by Tears For Fears.

Here, behind my wall I feel so small
Breathing but not perceiving

We are invited to imagine that her words are echoed by a chorus of Diseased Decadent Junkie Surfers, who, in the costume-design sketches, are pictured as sunburned muscle-men with blond flat-tops whose surfboards double as trays bearing all manner of pills, potions and spirits, labelled things like 'Dreams', 'Temporary Relief' and '100% Escapism'.

It is hardly a leap of conceptual faith to read this apparently fictional tale as an extrapolated, self-serving fantasy of my own life at the beginning of 1986. Boone, we may with some confidence assume, is me. Angharad, we may also boldly assume, is Ingrid (geddit?). The 'splash of ultra-marine' is lifted from the copy in the Jersey tourist board ads of the time. The Diseased Decadent Junkie Surfers reflect my somewhat jaundiced view of the kind of boy Ingrid had left behind in the Channel Islands. Such inspired sledge-hammer parallels persist throughout the work.

In Act 2, the action moves to Metropolis, 'the centre of business, trade, capitalism, extremism and noise', and more specifically to the Bohemian Community, 'a paradise which lies on the banks of the Great River – a never-ending party to which artists and poets are drawn from all around'. Scene 2 opens with a gatekeeper character called Mr Hartfelt 'flinging open the foyer doors' to reveal an orgy of drink and smoke. Why didn't I just call it Rolf West Hall and be done with it?

On its behalf, I sincerely and profusely apologise. But for all its weapons-grade pretence, *Red Light and Sunshine* is nonetheless a useful snapshot of how I saw myself – and Ingrid – in the spring term, 1986. Apart from my college portfolio, no revealing documentary evidence exists for the period, because, I am ashamed to confess, I set fire to my completed diary for that year. In January 1989 I placed it in a tin waste-paper bin and put a match to it, an act of self-flagellation to end all others. I'll explain later. But first back to the opera.

To cut a long aria short, Boone and Angharad fall in love beneath a red light, her jealous friend Café tries to break them up, Angharad has a nightmare in which Boone is Satan, she flees to the Hills of the North, Boone pursues her, throws himself off a cliff, nearly drowns, is saved by Angharad, 'a natural swimmer', and they end up on a faraway beach, 'nudged into the shallows by a school of killer whales'. (Yes, I know it's a *pod* of killer whales.) The climactic clinch is accompanied by 'The Power of Love' by Frankie Goes to Hollywood intercut with 'Running Up That Hill' by Kate Bush, and the curtain drops to a sample of Tony Hancock and Hugh Lloyd:

'Life would be intolerable if we knew everything.'
'I should say it would. My goodness, yes.'

I retain dramatic rights if you're interested in putting on a production.

Ingrid is making me chew a tablet. She's in her bed, I'm sitting pathetically on the end of it, experiencing an unpleasant flashback to childhood and the Joy Rides Mum and Dad used to force down us to ward off travel sickness.

It's disgusting. I want to spit it out. But Ingrid has the moral high ground. This is my penance. I carry on grinding the bitter chalk with my teeth, willing it to dissolve in the saliva-free desert that is my mouth.

'Don't swallow it, chew!' she orders, her face fixed in a tight-lipped scowl that I have never seen before. Gone is the picture-book face I went head over heels for. This morning she looks like Linda Blair pre-exorcism.

My punishment is supposed to be my salvation; after all, the tablet has been prescribed to settle my stomach. My stomach needs settling because I passed out through drink last night, something I have never done before in all my years of student revelry. Another canteen disco. Everyone was there – Veronica, Gino, Sue, Fiona, Carl, Run, even Sam, who returned happy and refreshed after a three-week Christmas break in Scotland. (We have all three agreed never to speak of that night, and we agreed this without speaking.) Last night should have been just another Ralph West party, but two things went wrong.

Ingrid stayed up in her room. And I drank the best part of a bottle of neat Bacardi on my own.

I thought it odd that she preferred Room 611 to a party, but Ingrid is a single-minded, deep, sometimes unfathomable girl and she promised to come down later on when she'd finished a large charcoal drawing she was working on. This struck me as a perverse act, but she told me and Rob to go and enjoy ourselves, so we did.

I remember us getting to the party, finding it distinctly underpopulated and embarking on a mission to recruit more residents. There we were, doing our usual trick of banging on doors and barging in on people, but we meant well and reaped results. I remember feeling distinctly woozy by the time we found Ingrid in Cathy's room, not doing her charcoal picture at all. They were evidently having a private smoking party, and sent us on our way, which pissed me off.

In retrospect, I don't suppose I was a very good advert for myself in that instance, loud and drunk. But I *was* her boyfriend.

The rest of the party I found out about at the breakfast table this morning from a rueful Gino, who, by the way, doesn't drink, smoke or take drugs – only photographs. Apparently, after some very loose-limbed dancing I curled up into an untidy ball on the stairs leading up to the coffee bar, regurgitated my dinner and then, without even lifting my head, passed out. I was cleaned up by kindly residents and sensible Sue offered to put me to bed.

Now here's where it gets complicated: Sue had her younger sister Jackie with her – and by young I mean sixteen; a sweet, doe-faced girl who seems at least two years older than that. The two of them heroically manhandled me up to my room and tucked me up, fully clothed, in bed. Jackie offered to stay with me while Sue went back to the party. She asked me if she could sleep over in my room. I have only the vaguest memory of this, but I must have said yes as she put on a pair of my tracksuit bottoms, got into bed beside me and turned off the lights. To be fair to Sue, even though Jackie was her responsibility, she was not the sort of younger sister who responded well to mollycoddling and Sue assumed she knew what she was doing. No interaction took place in that bed – we just slept. Soundly. I possibly more soundly than Jackie.

When I opened my eyes in the bright Battersea sunlight this morning, it felt like a travelling circus had been destroyed by fire in my mouth. And I found myself in the kind of novel or film where a person wakes up and finds he has slept with someone he doesn't remember sleeping with. There's a girl in my bed and she's wearing my track-suit bottoms!

Without waking her, I snuck off to breakfast to learn of the previous night's antics from Gino and by the time I got back to the scene of the accidental crime with some cold toast and a boiled egg for my overnight guest, Jackie was up and washed and happy to be there. She had even folded my tracksuit bottoms and placed them over the back of the chair. She'd also been up to see her sister, assured her she was OK and arranged for us all to go for a bracing, head-clearing walk in the park. I still wasn't able to form compli-cated sentences with my mouth so I nodded, figuring it was best to keep up appearances, endure this walk, pack Jackie back off to Barnet and hope that Ingrid never finds out. I felt like shit, looked like shit and was shit, but I still believed there was possibly a painless way out of this mess.

So what a shame it was that Ingrid had changed her mind about the party at about 10.30 last night and come down to find me. Find me she did. Tucked up in bed with a blonde schoolgirl. Rather than create a scene, Ingrid closed the door and went to her own bed, where she's been ever since.

And here we are. Welcome to the trickiest moment of my courting life since picking Sally up from school and intro-ducing her to the concept of the speculum.

'Who was she?'

'Sue's sister.'

'How old is she?'

'I don't know. Younger than Sue.'

'What was she doing in your bed?'

'Sleeping.'

'What were you doing?'

'Sleeping.'

There's a pause in which I don't know where to put myself.

'What was I supposed to think? You tucked up in bed with a *blonde* girl.' Brunettes always save up this sneery emphasis for the word blonde.

'You weren't supposed to think anything.'

'Were you going to tell me?'

'There's nothing to tell. It was a mistake. Nothing happened. We had our clothes on ... My stomach's killing me.'

'Keep chewing until it's all dissolved.'

Some relationships go on for years before getting to a melodramatic flashpoint like this: infidelity, discovery, confrontation, power games, pleading, the masochistic crunching of a tablet. Ours is just a few weeks old.

March 4, 1986. It's my 21st birthday. Gateway to manhood. It's also Tuesday, laundry day. Gateway to clean sheets. I woke up in the dirty ones with my girlfriend and we ate a hearty Ralph West breakfast of tinned grapefruit – pink *and* white, although I think they come from the same catering-sized tin – and three cups of tea. Because I was now a grown-up, I behaved accordingly and resisted opening a single card or gift until I had come back from breakfast. Also, because I was now a grown-up, most of my presents were cheques. Which is fine; students like cheques. I felt a bit guilty getting £10 from Nan and Pap Collins, who can't afford to throw their money around, but a little low-level guilt is important, especially on a selfish day like this and I was grateful for the top-up. If it wasn't for guilt I wouldn't have chewed the bitterest pill, paid the price and patched things up with Angharad – sorry, Ingrid.

A relationship needs a make-or-break moment in its first couple of weeks and that was ours. I threw myself on Ingrid's mercy and, satisfied that I had been through the emotional mill, she forgave me for what was a drunken error. Rob and Jane may call me a snake but I don't commit adultery. Not consciously at any rate. Maybe I knew, deep inside, that I was on the precipice of commitment.

Ingrid is different to all my other romances. After a week or so of preliminary wooing – during which I learned all about her past and the carefree island life she'd lived in Jersey – we got off with each other, to use the non-grown-up parlance, in my room. The seduction was going smoothly until she suddenly leapt self-consciously from the bed. Had I been pushing things too far or too fast? Was the whole thing a horrible mistake? Apparently, in the half-light of our embrace, Ingrid had suddenly seen, in mine, the face of her previous long-term boyfriend and freaked out. As misfortune would have it, he was also called Andrew. I undimmed the lights and calmed her down, as she sat there spooked under her overcoat, looking endearingly ridiculous. This certainly was different.

I know that I am serious about Ingrid because I'm already feeling anxious about the fact that, as a foundation girl, she is currently applying for degree courses, and the likelihood is she'll be in Brighton by September, her first-choice college. Now that's seven months away. Since when do I look that far into the future with a girl? It goes against all the codes and practices I've learnt in halls. What happened to a week of fumbling, some awkward breakfasts, a poem about blood and a conciliatory collage of Scotland?

To return to my 21st. I say 'just cheques', but that's the faraway relatives. Closer to home, Ingrid bought me some masking tape – a gift to be measured not in retail price but in thoughtfulness (I am currently getting through a lot of it in my artwork, it's all the rage). She also presented me with an Aero for breakfast. Addi from across the corridor, a dark-haired Jewish girl I briefly fancied when I first moved in but never followed through, gave me an *Eraserhead* poster, which is already up between *Apocalypse Now* and The Cure. Rob, whose newly dyed red hair actually now resembles Henry's from *Eraserhead*, created a lifesize photocopy of me, made by gradually enlarging sections of a photograph and sticking them all together. Gino presented me with an actual photograph he'd taken of me, stuck to some board. It is a little disconcerting being surrounded by me. Jane, her new Notting Hill flatmate Andrea and a first-year called Mark went to the bother of baking me a chocolate cake and decorating it with sticks of my favourite chewing gum – still in the wrappers. Rather less endearingly, they stuck a tampon in its applicator into the cake and attached the gift tag to the string. I bet Lady Sarah Armstrong Jones just gets expensive gifts with no thought in them whatsoever.

Addi, Fiona and Sue – who for my purposes no longer *has* a younger sister and never did – arranged for a surprise birthday spread at dinner tonight, decking out 'our' table in the canteen with a kiddies' paper tablecloth and paper cups. There was wine too, another cake with 21 candles and Fiona had personalised all the cups with our names. Sweet. Gino took the snaps. Ingrid and I played footsie under the table.

We're all reassembling at the Prince Albert now. Having been treated like an eleven-year-old all day, I am now doing what grown-ups do and buying everyone a drink.

'And one for yourself!' I say to Tony the landlord, who has been pulling us unsubsidised pints here for two years. It's the first time I have ever bought *him* a drink though. The words feel foreign in my mouth. It's the kind of pantomime Rob could always get away with, but to me it's like a rite of passage, a coming of age. 'And one for Trisha!' I add, bringing in the pub's regular barmaid. I am quite the Arthur Daley, albeit in an Oxfam mac rather than a car coat.

'Your birthday is it?' enquires Tone.

'Twenty-first.'

'Many happy returns. And cheers.'

He doesn't actually have a drink, nor does Trisha, he just sort of keeps back a specified extra amount from my tenner. This is the way the grown-up world of the pub works. I am sorely tempted to buy Slim Panatellas and hand them round, but I'm haunted by photos Rob has shown me of his old Cranbrook school chums puffing away on cigars for one of their birthdays, young, smooth-faced boys pretending to be old men. I don't want to wish the years away – I'm only 21.

'Boone! My man!'

Carl's arrived. Now he really does look like an old man in his cravat and trilby and beard.

'Happy birthday, mate!'

He presents me with a jelly, on a stainless-steel platter. 'Sorry it's a bit hard,' he says. 'I've had it in the freezer, but it'll soon thaw out.'

This detail, in an instant, delineates the halls resident from the non-halls resident. Carl lives in a rented hovel.

Nonetheless it has a fridge, with a freezer compartment, in which he can, if he so wishes, keep a raspberry jelly. I don't; I have a Waitrose bag hanging out of my window. Part of me feels drawn to the outside life, but then again, I have just been the centre of a kids' tea party and the ladies in the canteen lent me a serrated knife with which to cut my cake and a whole canteenful of students joined in the applause when my friends sang Happy Birthday. I realise my life is cosseted and cushy, but I think I've earned it. I like it here. And anyway, I have a jelly now. Given time, it may even wobble.

Mark is right behind Carl. Not first-year Mark; Big Mark. His gift is perhaps the most thoughtful of all: a copy of *Today* newspaper, Eddie Shah's much-touted new colour daily which launched, well, *today*.

'Thanks, Mark.'

I shall keep it. It speaks of optimism and colour and the future. It's been a good day and a good few weeks. I haven't written a poem for two months. Am I falling in love? Maybe. Ingrid is certainly the first girl I have ever written an opera about, you'll be glad to hear. Also, the first girl from college I have taken back to meet my parents. We have established that I am neither her ex nor Satan, and we play footsie and buy each other silly things and get a kick out of walking to the chemist in the wind. Look at her sitting in the corner there looking casually and effortlessly stunning with her snub nose and humorous check dungarees.

I'm platonic friends with Veronica. And I keep my toothbrush and toothpaste by my sink in a little personalised mug with ANDREW on it, a New Year gift from Sam. She gave one to Rob with ROBERT on. A little reminder that there's more to student life than Gold Runs, Londis and Cinzano.

thirteen

A Splash of Ultramarine

What's wrong with this picture?

At the height of the summer Andrew and Ingrid are living together in a picturesque, tumbledown cottage called Goodwood on the east coast of Jersey. Ingrid's parents are away and her sixteen-year-old sister Antonia is staying with friends, leaving them with the place to themselves. Ingrid's enjoying her last summer before going off to Brighton Poly, her first-choice college. In May, Andrew received a £700 Thames Television travelling bursary, to spend the entire two-month summer vacation in Jersey, drawing, taking photographs, keeping a kind of visual diary and assimilating himself into daily island life. This is that proposal made bronzed flesh.

Ingrid has just made him a tinned mackerel and onion sandwich, which he is enjoying in the back garden on a deckchair while seagulls drift overhead, occasionally alighting on the chimney of one of the low roofs nearby.

Earlier in the week, they drove into St Helier, Jersey's tourist-geared capital, and bought armfuls of reduced-price cakes and biscuits from the main branch of British Home Stores, which is shutting down its food hall to concentrate on clothes. So the sandwich will be followed by another sticky lattice wafer.

The family cat, Snowy, basks in the shade of the balmy early-afternoon heat. Andrew's current drawing – a view across the low roofs – is coming along nicely. Before the shadows lengthen, he plans to pack his pens and paints back into the biscuit tin and take a long Radox bath, run cooler than usual so as not to sting his sunburned shoulders. Tonight, they're off to some ultra-cool surfers' bar to meet up with Ingrid's Jersey friends, where Andrew will marvel again at the amount of change you get back from a round of drinks on this tax-free haven. He's been here for two weeks and, since paying for the ferry crossing, has barely dented his bursary.

So what *is* wrong with this picture?

First, Ingrid's parents are away on holiday. Separate holidays. He's in New York, she's in Berlin. They are currently in the throes of a difficult divorce. An act that is steadily beginning to take its toll on Andrew and Ingrid.

Secondly, Ingrid's enjoying her last summer before going off to Brighton. The clock is ticking. An unspoken air of uncertainty hangs over them like a rain cloud, even though there are no rain clouds.

Thirdly, Andrew doesn't like Ingrid's friends.

He loves Jersey – adores the place – it's where he's spent so many happy family holidays, albeit hermetically sealed inside the Merton Hotel. It should be the perfect summer: a remote island set in a splash of ultramarine. Clean sand hot under bare feet. Miles of green lanes drowsy in the sunshine. An ancient castle to heighten the imagination. Irresistible shop windows. A meal with enough flair to tempt the French across. For your perfect holiday write for full details to: Dept 109, States of Jersey Tourism, Weighbridge, St Helier, Jersey, C.I.

What they don't tell you about in the advert is the local people. To be more specific, the local young people. Not the colourful, cap-doffing itinerant Portuguese waiters and fruit-pickers; I'm talking about the arrogant, full-of-themselves, sun-kissed, cod-continental brats with their snooty attitude to holidaymakers, their soft drugs, Bermuda shorts and magnified island mentality. Jersey's not quite as wealthy as millionaire mythology surrounding the place might suggest: Ingrid's dad is a teacher who brought the family over from Yorkshire when the island hit a public-servant shortage in the Seventies. But Ingrid's friends grew up together in this unreal environment: self-absorbed, self-confident and self-pollinating.

All right, be fair, the real reason Andrew has taken against the bright young things of Jersey is that he's not one of them. To them he's driftwood. Worse, a grockle. Never mind that he's here for the whole summer courtesy of a television company, he may as well have a knotted handkerchief on his head and an unfolded map in his hand. In the cliquey eyes of her friends, always one rum and Coke away from suggesting a nude swim or a crafty spliff, he's just rolled off the ferry. He'll never assimilate. They won't let it happen, and neither will he. Like the island itself, with its current £1-million-in-the-bank entrance fee, they're a closed shop.

Mind you, the mackerel and onion sandwich is delicious.

* * *

When I first took Ingrid home to meet my parents the best thing Mum could say in her next letter was that she was 'really good-looking'. Now Ingrid was, and is, really good-looking, and I know Mum meant well, but have we really moved on so little since Sally was deemed 'really pretty' in the kitchen at Winsford Way? It's not a beauty contest. Ingrid is a girl who simply oozes possibilities. She's an artist. She's a deep thinker, a smoker and a vegetarian. She copes with a disintegrating family with admirable stoicism. Unlike other Jersey residents, she dared to spread her wings and seek her fortune on the unpredictable mainland, in nervy London where the bomb's more likely to drop. She knows what she wants and she gets it. She changed my name back to Andrew just like that. She is free and frank: she has introduced me to the concept of the contraceptive pill and to thrush (which we contracted before the summer). She has also broadened my palate and opened my eyes to the tasty addition of raw onion to a sandwich. She's a force to be reckoned with and perhaps the best thing that ever happened to me.

And she's really good-looking.

But here, at a surfer's bar called El Tico, everybody's good-looking. All of Ingrid's friends, male and female, are attractive. Can it really be the sun and sea air, or is it more to do with having no worries over and above where the next consignment of dope is coming from?

'Hi, Ing!' they all say, male and female, as we squeeze through the crowd to the little corner of the bar they've colonised. They all shorten her name to Ing. A colloquial familiarity that separates me from them. I didn't even want to come to El Tico, but what are the alternatives? Any number of other fancy-named bars with loud music and dancing licences that mean you have to pay to get in which, in turn, means you feel duty-bound to stay longer than you'd wish. Where are the pubs on this island? I don't mean the touristy ones in St Helier, I mean the locals, the Prince Alberts, the pint-of-the-usuals, somewhere I can say, 'And have one for yourself,' and actually be heard above the music.

I've been here a month now and I'm actually looking forward to Ingrid and Antonia going to France with their mum for a fortnight. The perfect holiday is starting to suffocate me.

We've been living together for the whole of that time, and although domestically it's been running quite smoothly (mackerel, cauliflower cheese, lattice wafers, wash up, feed Snowy, remember not to lock the back door in case Antonia has lost her key), we have spent an awful lot of quality time together in the garden, in the car, in our room, and as such we've covered an awful lot of ground from Ingrid's past, with reminders all around. But because the social scene is so elite and – let's face it – *finite*, these social butterflies all seem to have shared intimacies: either they've been out with each other or got off with each other or experienced a moment of Zen enlightenment getting high with one another. I know for a fact that Ingrid's been topless sunbathing and nude swimming with most of her friends, male and female, and it fills me with petty insecurity. I am burdened with knowledge. I feel all suburban and Middle-English.

Ingrid here is very different from Ingrid in halls. I don't know why I portrayed her as The Prisoner in my opera. She's free as a bird here; London's her prison, Ralph West Wing. No wonder she's been drawn to the whispering shingles and wide open spaces of bohemian Brighton for her degree. It all makes sense. I've spent enough time in Brighton to know that it'll suit her down to the ground. It's mainland Jersey. She and Valeria have a lot in common: they crave attention and boys with salt in their hair are drawn to them and their funny names like bees to honey. Ingrid was named after Ingrid Bergman because her mum loves *Casablanca*. What romance! That kind of thing doesn't happen in Northampton. We're all named after characters in the Bible there, despite the fact that nobody goes to church. I don't get the feeling that anybody goes to church here either. They worship the sun.

If I'm truthful the reason I don't want to go out all the time and mix with other people in bars is that I'm in love – and living with the one I love to boot. I want Ingrid all to myself. To be the Ingrid that I know, the Ingrid she is when we're alone. I won't share her. I've been here before. How do you keep a girl without snuffing out her flame, clipping her wings and any other repressive metaphor you care to mention? What a selfish twat I'm being.

'How are you finding it?' one of her beautiful male friends asks me.

'Brilliant,' I say. 'I used to come on holiday here.' I wish I hadn't said that.

'You should come surfing with us,' he offers, with I think some sincerity.

'I don't know how to!' I laugh. I can't swim either but they really don't need to know that.

In an attempt to make up for me being a twat, I bought Ingrid a lovely soft red jumper in Marks & Spencer yesterday, the act of which made me feel very grown-up. It's funny that a place so laid-back, sunny and French should have an M&S. I remember this being one of the island's major selling points when Nan and Pap first discovered it on behalf of our bumpkin family.

It was quite an expensive bit of knitwear, but hey, I've got £700 burning a hole in my pocket. And now I'm shoehorned into a crowded surf bar at St Ouens because I feel guilty about being a stay-at-home party pooper. I'll have one half of lager even though I feel sure that everybody else drinks and drives as a matter of course here and then I'll nurse a glass of Britvic and lemonade for the rest of the evening while Ingrid and her friends chatter excitedly about things I don't understand. The lack of drink probably doesn't help my sociability.

God, she looks beautiful in that jumper.

While Ingrid and Antonia were in France, as planned, I spent two weeks as a guest of the Merton Hotel, where I continued to draw and take photos, soaking it all up from the detached position of an observer, a chronicler. My 'holiday' fortnight crossed over with Mum, Dad and Melissa's annual vacation and it was great to see them and play at happy families, all the while secure in the knowledge that I had paid for my own bed and board and wasn't the teenage son any more.

Though I now entertained delusions of young adulthood, I'll admit it was comforting to regress slightly. I was able to forget some of my responsibilities as a boyfriend. I did my own thing during the day, usually sitting around the hotel drawing and fielding crass comments from those bold enough to approach me and gaze over my shoulder. But in the evenings I hooked up with Mum, Dad and Melissa. We ate together in the dining room where the menu was unchanged for yet another year: *soupe de jardinière* (vegetable soup), *Cassata Denise* (Neapolitan ice cream) and *Paris Brest* (a chocolate éclair). When we first came here in 1980, it was the most exotic food any of us had ever eaten, and our first time served by waiters. We thought we were in Monte Carlo.

At the end of the Merton mini-break, which had really recharged my batteries in relationship downtime, I waved my family off and checked out myself, settling up my own bill at the desk for the first time. Instead of feeling like the needy boyfriend, I was an independent adult.

'Thank you, Mr Collins, I hope you enjoyed your stay!'

Mr Collins. How about that?

Confidently taking the short route through the fruit fields, I drove back to Goodwood, expecting to find Ingrid's dad home from New York, but he wasn't. I went round to the back door, which was open, and let myself in. I had the house to myself. Peace at last. I made a mackerel sandwich and sat in the garden with Snowy, contemplating my whereabouts and wondering how I got here. How my life had turned into a holiday.

I started to think that maybe I ought to go home – wherever that was.

fourteen

Our House

'Cheers!'

Rob and I clink cans of shop-warm Special Brew in someone else's rented bedroom in Tooting, South London. He's in bed, I'm in a sleeping bag on the floor next to him. We make an unedifying pair and the Special Brew tastes disgusting, like alcoholic treacle, but there is cause for forced celebration.

'Well done, mate,' he says, generously, taking a long glug.

It is the end of a very long day. We've earned this.

The bed, and bedroom, belong to Rob's medical school friend Matthew, who's conveniently away on holiday. We've been flat-hunting, and using Matthew's room as our base, utterly against the terms of his lease no doubt. When I say 'we', the onus has very much been on Rob, as I've been living it up like a play-millionaire in Jersey all summer. I started to feel a little guilty when August turned into September, especially after Rob wrote to me at Goodwood to reveal that he was on the verge of signing up with a flat agency. It was that bad. Honour got the better of me and I booked my return ferry.

I've only been in London for a week, but it feels a lot longer, as our days have been filled with tramping from one flat to the next: Tooting Bec and Tooting Common and Tooting Broadway and Streatham Hill and Balham. It's a grinding process: buying *Loot*, scanning it for suitable places in the rough vicinity (and Tooting is a particularly rough vicinity), phoning the number, booking ourselves in for a viewing, turning up at the appointed time to join the queue of other pairs of hopeful students, nosing around the place, pointlessly tapping the partition walls, putting our names down with the unscrupulous landlord, knowing he'll never call us back and wondering just what criteria he uses to decide who to rent to. Clean hair? Girls? Accountancy students? Or is it simply the first pair to present him with a deposit and the first month's rent in cash?

So, for 60 quid each, we joined an agency called Busy Bee in leafy Clapham (a part of South London we can't afford to live in). This meant more tramping and more phone calls to achieve the same end: nowhere to live. Still, at least we would be eligible for housing benefit when we had the benefit of some housing.

The prospect of sleeping in the car was beginning to breathe down my neck. Rob was starting to wish he'd never quit Mrs Reed's to embark upon this insane Mills and Boone flatshare idea but it doesn't take an accountancy student to see the advantages of splitting costs, and one-person flats are even harder to come by in student London than twos or threes or fours. Why rent out to one when you can lash up a piece of hardboard and rent to a pair of obvious homosexuals like me and Rob? We started to think that acting like a gay couple might be more likely to get us a roof

– a couple means no girlfriends staying overnight or moving in without paying.

We awoke this morning with heavy hearts and heavy stomachs thanks to an economy set-meal takeaway of chicken-fried rice and sweet and sour pork balls from the charmingly named Dinner Box. However, the promise of Matthew's tanned return this weekend gets us out of bed and spurs us on in our quest for the homely grail. We bought *Loot* and went through the motions one more time: scanning, phoning, tramping, queuing, tapping, waiting, hoping. After a long and fruitless day, much of it actually spent stuck in the house waiting for calls back that never came, we switched to autopilot and trotted out to pick up the *South London Press* from the newsagent, not expecting much more than the usual 'Mitcham Man Falls Awkwardly' headlines. Then we saw it, under 'Flats to Rent':

STREATHAM, SW16,
2 bed 1st floor flat, f/furn,
1 bath, close to amenities,
avail now £80 pw

It was, with a bit of massaging, just within our price range. It was in South West London. It had the requisite number of bedrooms and the requisite number of bathrooms (not always a given). It was close to amenities. It was, in a word, perfect – just like every other flat we'd failed to secure in the past week. We rang the number anyway – Rob always did this, he has the best phone-voice. It was difficult to make out the name of the landlord through his accent.

'I think it's Mr Rabbit,' said Rob when he put the phone down.

It was actually Mr Rabit, pronounced Rabeet. At that hopeful stage, we liked the idea of having a landlord who sounded like a Beatrix Potter character. Perhaps Drewstead Road would be in a leafy, sun-dappled glade next to a pond with dragonflies darting about.

A finger-search through the *London A-Z* which I'd so recklessly thrown over the fence for that cine film all those moons ago revealed the perfect flat to be in Streatham Hill, not as rough a vicinity as Tooting although in something of a black hole, tubewise.

It was getting dark. We made our way over to the address and discovered it was on a one-way street right on top of a mainline railway station but boasted a couple of serviceable trees and at least the houses were Edwardian – bit of faded elegance. I thought of Ingrid, who had secured a room in a student hall on Brighton seafront, which sounded like it would be a lot nicer than this, more faded and more elegant. Perhaps I could move in with her and commute to London. Perhaps not.

There was no sign of Mr Rabbit outside at the pre-arranged time. Bad start. But at least there were no other prospective tenants huddled outside with hope in their eyes. We rang the bell. We rang all three bells. No answer. Then we heard a disembodied posh voice from the top of one of the trees.

'Are you looking for Claire?'

Rob and I stepped back from the door into the apology for a front garden and craned our necks. A dark-haired woman had her head out of the window on the top floor.

'No, we've come to see Flat 2.'

'Oh. OK.' She put her head back in and closed the window. Thanks for that. Our new neighbour. Or maybe not.

We knew that Flat 2 was the middle one and there seemed to be a light on. We rubbed our hands to generate a bit of warmth and wandered back out of the missing gate to peer up and down the street looking for Mr Rabbit, perhaps carrying a cane and pocket watch. Then a light came on in the hall and the front door opened.

'Hi.'

A girl who looked like she had hauled herself out of her sickbed was standing at the crack in the front door.

Rob went forward.

'We're supposed to be meeting Mr Rabbit?'

'*Rabeet.*' She said his name the way the poor of Nottingham in Robin Hood's time must have uttered the name of the Sheriff. 'You can come in if you like.'

This was very trusting of her, but then gay men are less threatening than heterosexuals. She was one of the outgoing tenants of Flat 2. She showed us round, which was of course Mr Rabit's job but you get a more honest appraisal from people who've lived there. She introduced us to a second pallid girl. They were student nurses, apparently unable to heal themselves. They didn't exactly sell the place.

'You've got access to the garden but it's so overgrown we've never been out there to be honest.'

'What's the central heating like?'

The nurse gave a rueful but not unkind snort. 'There are gas fires in both the fireplaces. Bit dodgy but we leave them on all evening.'

'That sounds a bit pricey,' said Rob through a sharp intake of breath, the very picture of his own dad, as usual.

'It's the only way to warm the place up.'

A perfunctory rap on the flat door as Mr Rabit entered, letting himself in as all unscrupulous landlords do. A squat, wild-eyed, moustachioed man in a cheap camel coat, he seemed most put out that the nurses had been giving us the tour. They seemed too flu-weary to be put out that he'd let himself in. But they were on their way out after all. It was these two gullible gay boys who wanted to move in.

Rabit took over and whisked us round, gently tapping the exposed pipe which led to a gas fire in the front room with his foot as if to say, 'Look! I just kicked it and we didn't blow up!'

He took care not to the kick the wall in the front room, for it was not a real wall and would have wobbled like *Crossroads* scenery, creating a relaxing wave effect from one end to the other. In order to turn a one-bed flat into a two-bed flat, Rabit – or possibly the unscrupulous landlord before him – had employed the finest master builders in London to convert the front room into a front room and bedroom with some old chipboard and a lick of paint. Rob's room, as we will soon know it, is a corridor with a single bed at one end. Easier to keep warm, we kept saying to ourselves.

I'm not saying it's the work of cowboys, but there are hoofmarks on the skirting.

So not the perfect flat after all. It's cold, grubby, badly laid out, uneven, poorly furnished, ineptly carpeted, dangerously plumbed in, and sandwiched between two other flats which means elephant footsteps above and constant fear of disturbing the people below. To the flat's advantage, some previous tenants have left a plastic traffic cone in the hallway by the phone, which at least means we won't have to go to the bother of bringing one in ourselves.

'We'll take it.'

That was an hour ago. Mr Rabit took us back to his house in Clapham – large, spacious, warm, unconverted into flats – to fill out the forms and pay him the first month's rent and a deposit of another month's rent. This we did in his office, writing out our cheques on the leather-upholstered surface of a huge, oak desk, like a doctor's. Children of various ages wandered in throughout the transaction and he shooed them away individually – Father was conducting business. Though the rhythm of his heavily accented English is sometimes difficult to catch, he is clearly a very smart and very successful landlord, with a mind like a viper.

It was gone eleven by the time we had signed our lives away. No chance of last orders, so we hightailed it back to Tooting and found an off-licence-cum-newsagent-cum-video-rental-outlet that was prepared to sell us four unrefrigerated cans of Special Brew, the fast-track to oblivion, or so the red-faced old men outside the tube station seemed to reckon.

'Better get down Lambeth and apply for housing benefit tomorrow,' says Rob, always thinking of the money.

'I can't drink any more of this,' I confess.

'Leave it by the bed and drink it in the morning.' He's joking. After all, we're no longer tramps. We are of fixed abode.

'I can't wait to phone Mum and Dad. They'll be so relieved.'

* * *

'Hello! Welcome to Streatham!'

'Hadn't there ought to be a gate there?'

It's a big day for me: having my parents round to visit my first ever home. It would be a big day for any son. They were even able to park the Cavalier right outside – well, a couple of doors down. The sun's shining, it's one of those crisp autumn Sundays that first attracted me to London for the weekend, Drewstead Road looks its best, there are leaves everywhere, covering the worst cracks and moss patches in the front yard, and, having spotted the Cavalier pull up from the front window, I was able to race down the stairs and fling wide the heavy front door to welcome them in: Mum and Dad, she with a bunch of M&S flowers and he with a bottle of M&S hock. My guests. Mum looks distinctly uncomfortable, embarrassed on my behalf, which is not the response I was hoping for. There ought indeed to be a gate there. In fact, there is just a gap in the wooden fence, but I don't quite see it as the security issue it obviously strikes Mum.

'Come on in!'

'It's nice and handy for the high street anyway,' says Dad, quick off the mark with a plus point as he wipes his feet on *my* doormat.

'It must be ever so noisy so near to the railway line,' adds Mum, not even through the door. *My* door. I give her a kiss.

'I don't even notice it,' I shrug.

Rob does. We did a deal over the rent. Because £40 each a week was higher than he'd budgeted for, I offered to pay £50, reducing his share to £30, if he took the corridor at the front of the house and I got the spacious room at the back. This is a deal between ourselves – as far as Lambeth are concerned, we're paying £40 each, which means optimum rebate. Our friendship is tough enough to handle the financial inequality: he knows I won't play the rent card. However, I've already noticed that – as predicted – my room is harder to heat, especially now that the cold nights are upon us, but I'm counting on Mum and Dad not noticing during the daytime.

They are both laden with bags containing gifts of food. You've got to love them for that. They have the family cool-box and it's loaded up with sandwiches, juice and a gateau-from-guess-where – they've bought a packed lunch! This is a big-hearted parental gesture, but it also says: we didn't want to eat anything cooked or prepared *here*. They have conveni-ently forgotten that they lived in a cramped, rented flat in Sutton when they first got married and supplemented their order from the chip shop by asking for 'batter bits', which were free.

Rob's parents have already been up. Mine come down, his come up. They drove him from Kent yesterday with his hi-fi separates professionally packed in their original boxes and polystyrene moulds in the boot. He and his dad spent most of the afternoon balancing the stylus while his mum went about the more important task of fretting – over the décor and the state of the kitchen and the safety of the gas pipe, but after the Dickensian one-room, one-ring squalor of Mrs Reed's, Flat 2 is undoubtedly a move *up* the property ladder. The first thing Mrs Mills did was open all the windows to 'let some air in'. Parents automatically do this. Rob and I have taken care to pre-empt my own mother's airing instinct this afternoon and the place is fresh and venti-lated like a wind tunnel.

Before they left, Mr and Mrs Mills took us up Streatham

High Road, for which our house is quite handy, and generously bought us a sit-down pizza from the Deep Pan Pizza Company. It was splendid, and – although I was too self-conscious to mention it – my first ever pizza in a pizza restaurant. It's amazing how spongy they are after years spent eating frozen mini-pizzas. If we could afford it, I dare say Rob and I would eat Deep Pan Pizza once a week, but we have bills to pay now.

The similarities between my own mum and dad and Rob's are uncanny. His dad found the flat solid and roomy and convenient for public transport, which it is. This is the supportive, stoic, best-of-a-bad-job paternal role. His mum found the place dour and ill-heated and noisy. The overprotective, pessimistic, nothing's-good-enough-for-my-son maternal role. If you insist on opening all the windows, the noise of the traffic and the trains is bound to intrude somewhat. Both mean well. And now my own parents are going through the same charade.

'Is this all the heating there is?' Mum asks, standing at the fireplace which once, in the time of the Duchess of Duke Street, bore a roaring coal fire, but presently houses a tragic gas fire that does an excellent job of warming up anything within a two-foot radius. The one in my bedroom can only dream of such functionality, although the orange flame-effect light bears appreciable psychological results.

'It soon warms up,' I lie.

'You wanna get rid of that police bollard,' says Dad.

'No, it looks good!' I protest. He was never a student; he can't possibly understand. But he's tactful enough not to force a discussion on the merits or otherwise of having a traffic cone in the hall.

'Right, who's for tea?' interjects Rob, rubbing his hands together.

'I'll have a cup,' says Dad, gratefully. 'We've brought some Gypsy Creams.'

'And some milk.' Mum starts to rummage in the cool box. Does she perhaps think we don't have milk in London? No, come on, it's a warm, munificent, thoughtful gesture – we can always use extra milk.

'There's a carton open,' says Rob, disappearing into the kitchen.

'Put this one in the fridge then,' says Mum. 'If there's room.'

'Of course there's room,' I say, with a smile. It's a fridge. It's the same size as your fridge. 'Why don't you sit down, take your coats off, relax and we'll make the tea.'

They both eye the settee with suspicion. Rather than actually sit on it, they just stand there and look at it, wondering if perhaps they should call someone round to 'have a look at it' before actually going anywhere near it in clean trousers. Come on, it won't bite you, I want to scream at them, but refrain, following Rob into the kitchen. Dad takes the plunge first, removing his zip-up beige jacket and just, hey, sitting down, like the first person of the day to jump into an outdoor swimming pool. Amazingly, it doesn't emit an electric shock or disturb a nesting plague of locusts. It's just a knackered old brown vinyl settee that's in dire need of some Araldite, not a death-trap or a dead animal or a portal into a parallel universe from which there is no escape.

Dad exhales, remarking, 'It's quite comfy.'

Mum looks unconvinced. She momentarily considers sitting on one of the dining chairs instead but, feeling that this would send out disloyal signals to her poor son, she takes off her coat too and sits beside Dad. 'It's seen better days,' I hear her say from within the kitchen.

'Nice of them to give us some extra milk,' I say to Rob, as complicit as any dad in this great game of making the best of a bad job.

'Yeah, we've got milk galore,' he replies, wedging the new two-pint carton in beside the one his mum and dad donated to our cause yesterday.

'Do you want to do these flowers?' I call out to Mum, trying to get her involved.

'If you like,' she calls back, up out of that settee like a shot, subconsciously brushing the backs of her legs with her hand like someone leaving a rank-looking seat on the bus or tube.

She appears at the kitchen door. 'Have you got a vase?'

She pronounces it 'vaze', just like Nan, which I'm sure quietly amuses Rob.

'There might be one under there,' I offer, pointing at one of the cupboards and realising my error too late: I have just invited my mum to inspect the kitchen cupboards. To me, they're a sign that I'm someone – my first-ever kitchen cupboards, but to her they're going to be a breeding ground for germs, full of disgusting, dust-coated old whisky tumblers and granny saucers of ill-matching shape and size. More amnesia about her own lean years living in London flatland, all memories eclipsed by what I have come to recognise as nothing less than working-class pride. Her family may have lived on a railway clerk's wages but they never had anything second-hand in their cupboards. On the contrary, every plate and cup in this flat has a history. There are no vazes either.

'Use that glass jug,' I offer, keen to get her out of *my* cupboards.

'I'd have brought you a vaze if I'd known.'

'I don't know what we have and haven't got yet.'

'Scissors?' She wants to take the stems off the carnations.

'Have a look in the cutlery drawer.'

Mum hides her dismay at the boot sale of disparate silverware in the drawer, fishes out a blunt pair of scissors and sets to work. 'This kitchen could do with a good clean top to bottom. I've got some Jif in the car and I'm sure there must be a shop on the high street that sells lining paper.'

'We've got some Jif,' I reveal, proudly. The lemon kind too. 'But you're not here to clean. We'll be fine.'

I'd love her to clean, from the very top to the very bottom, but it would shatter our new, mature parent–son relationship, the one we've been cultivating since the day Dad drove me to Battersea and helped me wire up my speakers. We've come a long way together – or a long way apart – these past two years and at last, after a lot of limbering up, I really am standing on my own two feet. Paying rent. Paying bills. Answering the door. Shopping for Jif. I don't even go on holiday with my mum and dad any more. I have my own rattan kitchen mat and my mother, a guest in my house, is standing on it.

'What's the loo like?' she asks, unable to put off the call of nature any longer. I daren't tell her.

'I don't like the look of this gas pipe,' Dad calls from the front room. I can't see him, but ten to one he's tapping it with his foot.

SCENES FROM A PRETEND MARRIAGE (1)

We're in Shake, rattling down the A23. It's October. I'm driving Ingrid back to Brighton after a weekend in London. This is now a familiar ritual. She comes up to London for the weekend and I drive her back first thing on Monday morning, early enough to beat the traffic on the A23 on the way down and just in time to catch it all on the way back. This is my penance. Having enjoyed domestic harmony with my girlfriend for the best part of a year, in and out of each other's rooms at halls and house-sharing all summer long in Jersey, I'm now back to the frustration and phone calls of a long-distance relationship, commuting between London and Brighton as if in cruel parody of the last time with V*l*r**, whose name we never speak, even though she is the reason I know Brighton like the back of my hand.

I have another year left at college, and the prospect of spending it pushed and pulled by 60 miles is not a happy one, especially not when I am forced to battle with the Surrey commuters at rush hour. Ingrid is wearing the red jumper. We are playing a tape of *The Queen is Dead*. The lyrics to 'There is a Light' – especially the bit about the ten-ton truck and dying by your side – seem achingly significant, even though they're just words.

'Did I tell you Mum's coming down to London in a few weeks?' Ingrid asks.

'What for?'

'She's doing an accountancy course.'

'She's so independent, your mum,' I respond with studied enthusiasm.

'She's got no choice.' (Slightly frosty.)

'Where's she staying?'

'My Aunt Sarah's in South Woodford. I was thinking of taking a couple of days off college and going to stay with her.'

'Where's South Woodford?'

'It's right at the end of one of the tube lines.'

'I bet she's got a washing machine.' I say before my tact surfaces.

Ingrid is not impressed. 'I can't take my dirty washing!'

'*Our* dirty washing.'

'No way.' It's her final answer. 'We're not all pushy like you are.'

I have never met a pushier person than Ingrid. It is, in part, what I love about her. I angle my head, distracted. 'Is there anything coming out of your speaker?'

She listens. 'I think so.'

I raise the volume of The Smiths to check. 'Sounds to me like it's all coming out of mine. Won't Brighton mind you taking the days off?'

'I don't care what Brighton say. It's my mum. Coming to London. On her own. It's all right for you – you can see your parents any time you like. I can't.'

'Sorr-eee.'

A pregnant pause. Ingrid sometimes does this: the 'it's all right for you' gambit. I know she's having a tough time of it at home and I tell myself to be more careful around the subject.

'I had a look,' she says, changing the subject. 'And Dan-Air do cheap flights at Christmas. Forty pounds.'

'Return?'

'Uh-huh.'

This is thin ice too. Ingrid wants us to spend Christmas in

Jersey with the wreckage of her family. I would rather spend it in Northampton. It's a tricky one. We pass the roadside café that signals the approach for the M23 turn-off, so at least we can pick up a bit of speed, make the car shake. The sign to Redhill makes me think of Bill. Lonely old Bill, pinning all his hopes on next year's holiday. I wonder whether me and Ingrid will be back in Jersey again next summer or if the miles will have ruined everything by then.

'Mum and Dad think Simon'll be disappointed if I'm not there.'

'All right,' she snips, in a huff now. 'I'll go home by myself. You go and spend it with your perfect family!'

She pointedly turns away with her arms tightly folded and looks out of the window at nothing much. Christmas is already looking like a problem. Brighton is looking like a problem. Drewstead Road is working out fine but nothing else is.

'That speaker's definitely quieter than the right-hand one,' I mutter to myself.

Not as quiet as the rest of the journey.

fifteen

Absolutely Icebox

By November, I'd settled into a happy, workable routine. In my letters to Mum and Dad – less frequent now that I was living in the real world and had things to do – I actually started detailing the contents of our utility bills.

'Got another telephone bill the other day,' I wrote. 'Rental charge for the quarter up to Jan 31 comes to £17 and my calls charge was only £4.50 for all the time we've been here. Easily covered, that one, and now my Brighton calls are no more I feel we can relax on the Telecom front. The electricity bill for the month comes to £23 but that rests on an estimated meter reading of 410 units when in reality we have only used about 200, so we have a good further 200 in credit. When all is said and done, we should be OK till Christmas.'

Then it would be on to the shopping:

'We got bean sprouts for 16p a tub from Safeway's and they've been present in salad and sandwich all week. And I love wholewheat pasta, hot or cold. Best meal of the flat so far: pasta, sprouts, celery, cottage cheese, mayonnaise and bread. We fried our own crisps last night!

'Safeway's is going mad on *lebkuchen* biscuits for Christmas. Endless varieties of spiced German gingerbread on every corner! We also have Arabic bread in the cupboard! Talking of food (as I always end up doing) we made big fat onion rings for tea this evening (twice we've had fried food in 2 days). I now have *flour* in the house. Since I've been food-buying I've really begun to understand what's expensive and what's good value. A pound of onions for 17p excites me. And all those frozen ready-meals depress me. We eat very economically, you know. Nothing goes wasted – cold mashed potato makes three days' worth of sandwiches. Just add bean sprouts, lettuce and mayonnaise and *sneer* at the college canteen price list!'

Whether they were gripped by all this home economics, I don't know, but it was important to me. Easy halls living was finally at an end.

My Brighton calls are no more. Not because Ingrid and I have split up. I admit this was my worst fear a month ago when I could suddenly see our true love worn away by the A23. In fact our calls have stopped because Ingrid no longer lives in Brighton.

After two months it became clear that she didn't like the course, didn't like the tutors, didn't like the other students, didn't like the faded, elegant seafront building she was billeted in, nor the girl she was forced to share a room with. She liked Brighton itself but that wasn't enough. So – melodramatic, impetuous, pushy soul that she is – mid-term she switched course, colleges and city – something many students think about but very few actually do.

With no help from her preoccupied parents, and certainly no strings pulled by me, Ingrid managed to get a place at Chelsea School of Art on our degree course. She's joining the new first year. What's more, Mr Hartnell tells her she's one place from the top of the Ralph West waiting list. In the meantime she's staying with us at Drewstead Road, putting money in a pot for the phone and hot water. Normal service is almost restored. The flat really feels like ours now. We cleaned the disgusting cooker last week and regularly run the hoover over the disgusting carpet. We're on more than nodding terms with the tenants above and below and Mr Rabit has only been round twice. Flatshare is working out.

There was a sticky moment when Rob's mum actually told him off on the phone for having bought the new Cocteaus album *The Moon and the Melodies*.

'But it excites my skin, Mum!'

'I don't care. You've got plenty of records.'

'All right,' he snapped. 'I'll stop phoning home, that'll save us some money.'

'You never phone us. We always phone you.'

'It's the Cocteau Twins, Mum, you wouldn't understand.'

'I understand five pounds, Robert!'

He tuts and sighs simultaneously. 'Put Dad on.'

You have to hand it to Rob. He spent the next five minutes describing the sonic intricacies of a collaboration between the Cocteau Twins and ambient composer Harold Budd, how the delicate tonal wash really showed off the bottom end of his speakers and that the rising cadences of

Elizabeth Fraser's voice sounded like ice on a window through the new stylus. At the end of it, he'd convinced his dad that *The Moon and the Melodies* was £5 well spent. Just the job.

'Explain it to Mum and I'll speak to you in the week.'

What would they think if they knew Rob and I had both bought a copy?

'Cheers!'

Rob and I clink plastic pint glasses and enjoy the maiden sip of a can of beer each, Heineken for me, Webster's for him. I can't remember which boat party we walked away with the glasses from but they are serving us well in our dream home. It's Sunday lunchtime. We recline on the vinyl settee beneath a giant poster for *The Queen Is Dead* which Rob shouldn't have bought either and settle down to watch *Weekend World* on my old black-and-white portable, mainly to mimic Brian Walden's speech impediment.

'Could be worse, couldn't it?'

'Is that poster straight?'

Ah yes, I've learnt to love this crappy place, with its thin, single-glazed, leaded windows, its dog-eared carpet and what was intended to be an ironwork telephone table bafflingly mounted at head height on the kitchen wall. I have learnt to celebrate the bastardised ragbag of kitchen equipment that lurks on every wonky shelf and inside every ill-closing cupboard, not least the green ceramic hen for keeping eggs in. We used to have one of these when I was growing up. It comforts me, even though it contains no eggs, just two lost screws and a 2p piece.

Of course Mum, a long-time evangelist of the electric hob, thinks a gas cooker is something out of the Stone Age, but I have come to appreciate what the 1970s advertisers recognised as its 'cookability', especially when boiling up wholewheat pasta and the scummy water rises. I have come to realise that there is something bracing about getting out of a steaming hot bath in a freezing cold bathroom. I look forward to padding about in my slippers of a morning and making Rob a nice cup of tea, rapping on his door to wake him up and being told not to enter. I like the way the timer switches in the communal areas feel against the palm of your hand, how you punch them in and then race up the stairs so as to get inside the flat before they click automatically off again. It's a whole new world.

I like the influence of Ingrid's vegetarianism in the kitchen. I like the three of us driving to college in the mornings and warming our hands on the car heater as we go. I like not living in the halls. I like not eating in a canteen, and not having to hang milk out of the window, and not having to man the coffee bar. I like picking my mail up off the doormat and not out of alphabetical pigeonholes. I like answering the doorbell and answering the phone and I like walking to Safeway's and the greengrocer's and the chemist for Strepsils. What I suppose I really like is roughing it a bit: the vitality of living on the breadline and comparing prices and not being able to afford to go to the pub. I'm on benefit for heaven's sake! It's certainly more real than living in a hotel.

Ingrid hates it, but she won't be living here for much longer.

* * *

Compared to the year before, Christmas '86 went off without life-changing incident, but it was none the worse for that. Rob and I threw a party in the last week of term – because we could – and the flat was filled with laughter and music and balloons. We invited both sets of neighbours as a licence to make as much festive noise as we wanted and in an attempt to be adult. A few ironically naff, hand-me-down decorations and a real tree and the living room actually looked quite presentable. Body heat and jumpers kept us warm and a jolly time was had by all. Carl wore tinsel round his hat, Rob got a snog with one of the new first-years and nobody knocked into his beloved speakers, mounted on kitchen stools, just as the manufacturers had never intended.

Rob and I dutifully returned to the bosom of our respective families for holiday week, but not before staging our own gay-couple Christmas dinner at the flat. We risked using the bottom oven for the first time and roasted a modest chicken, accompanied by good-value sprouts, carrots and potatoes. I don't even like sprouts but it seemed right and I ate them with the same pioneer spirit that I had eaten my first slice of gherkin in a London cheeseburger. We found a tablecloth with hardly any holes or scorch-marks at the bottom of a battered chest of drawers and laid the table properly. The only touch that gave us away as poverty-line benefit-scroungers was the large, undecanted tub of Saxa on the table. And the stolen plastic glasses. The leaded windows, for all their draught-letting, made the whole thing seem quite cosily Dickensian. God bless us every one.

Sadly, Ingrid also returned to the bosom of her disintegrating family for Christmas week. We could reach no compromise; our first shared yuletide was not to be. She took advantage of the Dan-Air offer while I drove up the M1. Simon came home on leave and, as predicted, appreciated my presence. The five of us enjoyed a proper family Christmas, opening presents in the morning, posing for self-timer photographs in our new items of clothing – a red M&S cardigan and some stone-washed Levis for me, an XL Cure T-shirt for Simon, new velvety boots for Melissa – and sitting down for a slap-up lunch with crackers and all the trim-mings. And German wine of course. Mum and Dad bought me a director's chair for the flat and a brand new set of plas-tic kitchen utensils – spatula, fish-slice, ladle and so on – with a nice hook to hang them on, although I doubt I'll be doing any drilling at Drewstead Road. They can go in the drawer and shame the other cutlery.

I spoke to Ingrid on the phone after lunch. She and Antonia were having a fairly awful day at Goodwood, with their parents both home. The irony wasn't lost on me. Not on Christmas Day, which for us was about unselfconscious cohesion and unity, but for Ingrid's family was about fric-tion. In her house you took sides. In ours you just took pictures. The guilt I felt about the disparity was momentary. It dissolved with the first invite to rummage in the Roses jar.

The happy snaps taken at Kestrel Close that day reveal a curious and unexpected thing: all three 'kids' are now taller than Mum and Dad, even fifteen-year-old Melissa if you count the height of her new highlighted perm. When did this happen? Were our parents perhaps shrinking? Like old people? We joked about it, of course, but there was something unsettling in the uneven row of heads; the pronounced dip. The symbolism was impossible to ignore: as their parental influence reduced, so they did they. We were literally outgrowing the frame of the traditional family snapshot, even the youngest, just over a year away from leaving school and getting a job (she fancied the bank). Simon and I had lived away from the family home for over two years; this was our third Christmas as visitors. There had been an outside chance that neither of us would make it, he because of guard duty, me because of girlfriend duty. What a depressing set of photos that would have made: Mum, Dad, Melissa. The incredible shrinking family. It was a close-run thing for a while there, or a 'near go' as my nan would say.

The nans and paps and aunties and uncles all rolled in after lunch and Mum's front room was filled with laughter and music and sherry. Yet I found the day stifling. Mum never had so much as a skylight open in her own house. The radiators – or 'rads' as they called them round here, very much in the spirit of Jumper Mike – were never off from September through to May. Now that I had my own house, I noticed these discrepancies between how I lived and how they lived. By the end of the week I was depressed. It might have been plain old post-Christmas comedown, the original cold turkey, or the fact that Simon had gone back to barracks, but I began to harbour a suspicion that it was the central heating. I'd grown used to the cold at Drewstead Road, the brittle freshness of a Sunday morning in dressing gowns, the welcome *boof* of the gas fire going on before enjoying a plate of hot toast. I once used to wear fingerless gloves to the dinner table at home as a teenage affectation, now I did it for practical reasons. Maybe it was patronising of me, and ill-founded, but in that depressurised week between Boxing Day and New Year, I cooked up a theory that the suffocating, energy-sapping fug of central heating was endemic of a greater malaise of political complacency and middle-class inertia in domestic suburbia. What Mum and Dad's house needed was airing.

I couldn't wait to get back to Streatham Hill. I vowed to spend next Christmas in Jersey.

SCENES FROM A PRETEND MARRIAGE (2)

Somewhere warm but alien in Whitby, Yorkshire. It's almost midnight, New Year's Eve, 1986. I find myself in the bosom of someone else's family. It is Ingrid's family. She and Antonia have taken a welcome break from the intractable atmosphere in Jersey and travelled to the family seat, to spend New Year with their dad's people. The house belongs to Grandma and Grandpa and is a homely riot of knick-knacks, mementos and lived-in furniture, reminiscent of my own Nan and Pap's. The extended orbit of aunties and uncles gather round the television, waiting for the count-down. Snuggled up next to Ingrid on the floor with a glass of fizzy wine, I couldn't feel more displaced. I'm glad to be with my girlfriend – and the folks seem to approve of me with my relatively small hair and red cardigan – but I'd rather be somewhere more relaxed, more conducive to snogging, and without the prospect of sharing a tiny, musty bedroom with Ingrid's dad at the end of the night. The rads are on full here too.

'Everyone got a full glass?' asks Grandpa.

The calls come back in the affirmative.

'Shoosh. We'll miss it,' says an unidentified auntie.

'Have you seen that *EastEnders* on telly?' Grandpa asks Ingrid and me.

'We sometimes watch it,' I reply.

'No word of a lie – I can't make out a word they're saying!' he chuckles. I wonder if he's joking and smile. He isn't joking.

'He can't, love,' vouches Grandma. 'Neither can I.'

'May as well be in French!'

Much laughter of recognition.

'You can understand Andrew can't you?' asks Ingrid.

'Aye,' says Grandpa. 'But he doesn't talk like them EastEnders—'

I talk more like them than I did two years ago, thanks to a lot of conscious honing of my old accent and assimilating myself in newsagents.

'Shoosh,' cuts in Antonia, 'It's Big Ben!'

BBC1 goes over live to Big Ben for the chimes. The room fills with respectful hush. Ingrid gives my arm a squeeze. She's promised me a walk after the chimes, snatch a few moments to ourselves in an otherwise overcrowded couple of days. I watch Big Ben longingly, wishing I was close enough to hear it bong in real life. The world's most famous clock strikes twelve and Ingrid's paternal family explode in good, Yorkshire cheer. They all clink glasses of Lambrusco and Ingrid and Antonia both kiss their dad, even though they say they hate him when he's not there, which they obviously don't.

'Happy New Year!'

The next morning: 1 January 1987, still in Whitby, I'm sitting by the side of a river on a bench. I'm crying. I don't know why. These are not the wracking sobs of the car to the airport, rather a burst of cathartic snivelling with deep breaths, a momentary loss of control. The sea air is a tonic. I have no time to work out exactly why this is happening, nor to truly enjoy the surprising emotional vitality of the moment, as Ingrid meekly joins me.

'I'm sorry.'

'It's not your fault,' I sniff.

'It obviously is. I make you cry.'

'I've forgotten what it's like,' I almost smile.

She sits next to me but refrains from invading my space. We both stare into the water. She too takes a deep breath. A moment ago we were in Shake, driving back from an errand in town for Grandma. Early this morning we were walking round the block in the dark, arm in arm, stopping to kiss under a lamppost, happy to be together. But that seems a long while ago. In the car on the way back to Grandma's house Ingrid started on me. It began as an innocent conversation about families, in which I'd carelessly compared hers to mine. Then came the 'it's all right for you …'

'I didn't mean to be so horrible about your family,' she says. 'I love your family.'

'I can't help it if we had a happy Christmas.'

'I know. But you have to understand—'

'I do understand. I understand that your mum and dad hate each other and you hate your dad—'

'I don't hate him.'

'You say you do.'

'I hate what he's done to my mum.'

'All I'm saying is, I can't help it if my mum and dad love each other. They just do.' Now I feel stupid for crying.

'I know.'

Until I met Ingrid, I'd never felt guilty about coming from an unbroken home.

'I just get frustrated sometimes.'

She puts an arm through mine. 'We'll be in London this time tomorrow. I'll make you a lovely dinner and we'll have a Radox bath and drink wine—'

'And watch *EastEnders*.'

A proper smile. She pulls me to her and kisses me on the cheek. 'Come on,' she says. 'Grandma will wonder where her potatoes are.'

We walk slowly back to the car. It's at times like this, almost drunk with extreme emotion, that I think: I must be in love.

'Do you have a torch-light or something like that?'

Rob and I look at each other.

'No.'

'I can't see anything up here.'

Every eventuality covered except entering the loft. We never thought we'd be going up in the loft. Rabit inelegantly descends the rickety wooden stepladder on which he has been precariously balanced, trying to get a look in the attic of Drewstead Road. Lovely high ceilings these Edwardian houses. He's wearing his camel coat, no change there, but he's also wearing a scarf wrapped round his head, like a cartoon of someone with toothache. This is his novel defence against the cold, but he looks like some refugee off the news. He should be walking alongside a donkey-drawn cart containing his furniture, although of course he'd need an articulated lorry to carry all his worldly goods. The ladder he's standing on – that's his. The loft he's been fruitlessly peering into – his. The pipes that have frozen and burst in heartless parody of the sort of thing that happens at this time of year – his.

'You could climb up there, young man,' he suggests, talking directly to me. 'But let me find a light first.'

We look at each other again as he goes off in search of illumination.

Things were going so well. Sure, we've had no running water for three days and have been boiling up snow from the garden on the stove for tea and pasta, but that's been quite exciting in its own surreal way and at least the gas heaters have been working. But that idyllic peace was shattered this morning.

When the January cold snap turned into a fully formed ice age, Rob moved into my room for shared warmth. We've been sleeping together for a week. Again, a bit like going camping, quite good fun. (I refrained from telling Mum and Dad when they phoned. They'd only worry.) When the water went off, we were a little put out. There's nothing more heart-breaking than turning a tap clockwise all the way and getting nothing but air and a sort of distant groan from somewhere deep inside the bowels of the house. Not having had to deal with frozen pipes before we made a common tactical error, and that was flushing the toilet. It flushed! Just like normal! We rejoiced! Then we realised that the cistern wasn't refilling. We had just wasted our only flush. Next time either of us finds ourselves in this situation, we'll know what to do.

Rabit, who seems to have absolutely no idea what to do, which is odd for a seasoned landlord, returns from the bedroom with a frilly bedside lamp and an extension lead. His plan is to plug it in down here in the hall and for me to take it up to the loft as a kind of Laura Ashley torch. Rob is quick to dissuade him of this course of action.

'Isn't it a bit dangerous to be taking an electrical appliance up there with water pouring through the ceiling?'

Rabit reconsiders, the pins just inches away from the moisture-flecked socket.

'All right.' He looks at me. 'Why don't you go up anyway and see what you can see?'

'Go on then,' I say, boldly, mounting the paint-aged ladder. Rabit follows me up and offers his cupped hands to push my foot against, the first time I have ever touched him. He suddenly looks small and ridiculous, not the imposing, all-powerful, oak-desked property magnate of our first meeting in October. Nevertheless he thrusts upwards and I push my body weight against his hands, and lever myself into the pitch-black attic. Adjusting my eyes to the dark and crawling towards the sound of gushing water I can make out in silhouette the point at which the pipe has split open. There's little I can do other than report back.

'There's a broken pipe,' I shout above the din. 'It's pouring out.' So, in coming up here I have been able to confirm that there's a broken pipe and that water is pouring out of it.

Rob and I heard a noise in the night. It woke us both up. A dull thud from above.

'What was that?'

'Sounded like it came from the flat above. Something must have fallen over,' muttered Rob. We pulled the quilts tighter around our bodies and dozed back off.

We awoke this morning to the sight we had hoped not to see: water building up into swollen droplets on the ceiling of my room. But still nothing major at this stage, just the odd drip emanating from a hairline crack that had appeared overnight in the plasterwork. I stood on the bed to examine it but the ceiling was too high to reach. Lovely high ceilings, these Edwardian houses. So I balanced instead on my high stool. It was good to see it getting some use. There was a time, before Christmas, when I would sit on it and draw at my draughtsman's table, but that was before it got too cold in the flat for me to actually hold a pen.

As I ran my finger over the hairline crack water ran down my hand and up the sleeve of my dressing gown. Additional junior droplets seemed to be forming along its crooked length as we watched. Rob fetched a washing-up bowl and a couple of saucepans which we carefully positioned under the more persistent drips. It placed immediate strain on the idea of this being a good game. This was now like a scene from a sitcom. We got dressed and took turns to go out into the back garden for a piss while it was still dark. We'll call this the Cold Run. We took care not to pee in the same section of snowdrift we were melting down for cooking water. All of a sudden, we were going into the garden a lot.

By the time we had eaten breakfast and warmed our hands on the toaster, a fresh inspection of the back bedroom revealed more drips and alarmingly full saucepans. Already. Fortunately the crack still wasn't raining on the bed.

'How's it coming through our ceiling?' Rob asked.

'The ice must have thawed and it's leaking out where the pipes have cracked.' Not having any experience of this type of thing, I was quite proud of my deduction.

Rob was not satisfied. 'But what about the flat above us. If it's dripping through our ceiling, it must be gushing through theirs.'

'Shit.'

The posh woman and her boyfriend are away. When the ice age came they wisely bailed out and migrated to warmer climes – her parents' house. We phoned Rabit and he came over immediately with that stupid scarf round his head, bearing the spare keys for Flat 3. First we showed him the water now cascading into the mini orchestra of cookware in my room – and the additional crack now creeping along the ceiling of the kitchen – and though it masked genuine alarm, Rabit put on a resilient, could-be-worse face.

'It's not too bad,' he said. 'Let's have a look at the upstairs.'

I couldn't help but think of the Young Ones' Russian landlord Mr Balowski, with his pidgin English and his upbeat proclamation, 'That's absolutely icebox!'

We ventured into the flat upstairs, where the noise of cold running water was louder, and using all of our forensic powers, traced the problem to its source. Our neighbours' bedroom was directly above mine. It was almost identical in layout with one small difference – their ceiling wasn't actually on the ceiling. It was on their bed. The loud thud in the night had been a six-foot square slab of sodden plaster and loosened masonry falling directly onto where they would have been sleeping. Not one of us felt the need to utter the spine-chillingly self-evident words: it's a good job they weren't here.

Above, where the ceiling used to be, water was raining

down through the exposed woodwork. It was a disaster area. It should have been cordoned off with yellow police tape: do not cross. Perhaps we ought to bring our bollard up?

Their quilt, I couldn't help but irrelevantly think, was completely ruined. Of course none of us had a number for the runaway couple, so we couldn't even alert them by phone and call them back home to pick up the pieces. And there were a lot to pick up; large pieces of damp red plaster and fistfuls of sticky white powder. They would have to wait. And we would have to go up in the loft.

Remember that episode of *Some Mothers Do 'Ave 'Em* where Frank is up in the loft in his pyjama trousers and water from the tank's gushing down onto Betty on the toilet? I wish I could stop thinking about comedies. This really did stop being funny hours ago.

Rabit called a plumber. A qualified, certified, Guild of Tradesmen-accredited master plumber no doubt, and not one of Rabit's mates. He came round and turned the water off at the stopcock, then left. The deluge turned to a trickle and the blop-blop-blop of water into pans slowed down and eventually stopped. Rob and I both wondered how long we could put off telling our parents that our living quarters had effectively ground to a halt. We philosophically boiled up a panful of snow like two Chris Bonningtons, had a cup of tea and decided to go to college. It was warm there, and they had toilets and sinks and food. Rabit promised to have the pipes in the loft repaired and lagged.

'When?'

'As soon as my plumber can get to it.'

'What do we do in the meantime? We're still without water.'

'You can buy water.'

'We can't afford to buy water.'

'This is happening everywhere in London.'

'I hope you're not going to charge us full rent this month.' (Way to go, Rob.)

'We'll have to talk about that,' said Rabit, half out of the door. 'I have many other tenants to see.'

Our very own Balowski.

'Is good joke, yes? Is earthy English humour, yes? Like seaside postcard from Leicester?'

Rob and I thought we were over the hump. On returning home from college that night, we discovered otherwise. The kitchen ceiling had fallen in. Lovely high ceilings, these Edwardian houses – perhaps you'd like a closer look at one? There was filthy, waterlogged plaster everywhere: in the sink, all over the shelves, the floor, the ironwork telephone table. The rattan mat, which was pretty rotten in the first place, was now soaked through and black. Only the screws and the 2p, safely concealed inside the hen, were safe from the deluge. What's more it stank. Civilised human beings could no longer live here.

We cleared the worst of the ceiling away, filling bin bags with plasterboard and keeping our coats on as we now did without thinking. Something – our inner dad perhaps – told us to take photos of the offending areas and the offending mess as a record of the parlous state the place was in, then we went out for chips, which we ate in my room with an inappropriate but consoling cold beer, all the while peering up at the first crack which, though drying out, had during the day quietly formed a worrying circle. A dotted line marking where the next piece of detachable ceiling would come from. There was nothing else for it.

'Hi Mum. It's me ... Not really. Listen ...'

We bailed out the next day. I drove home to Northampton – and in that blessed instance, it really did feel like home again – and Rob went to Kent by train. The donkey-drawn carts existed only in our minds, but we did feel like refugees off the news.

It was with heavy heart that we admitted defeat. There was a lot riding on the Mills and Boone flatshare experiment. After two years of pampered halls living, it was my all-important break for the border of true independence. My name in a rent book. Though it only lasted four months, my brush with Bedsitland succeeded in training me up for many important aspects of real life: it educated me about the price of bean sprouts (16p a punnet); I also knew my onions (17p a pound); it introduced me to the concept of estimated meter readings, itemised phone bills and money in a pot; it taught me the cost of everything and, at the bitter end, the value of everything too. You can't put a figure on peace of mind and basic mod cons.

I understand now that we put off telling our parents that the flat was falling down because in doing so we were finally admitting it to ourselves. They weren't the last to know – we were.

How we wanted to survive that winter, to tough it out, weather the ice age. But these are the realities of student accommodation: cut corners, cowboy conversions, mutant crockery. And no lagging. Mr Rabit was no more myopic or money-grabbing than any other unscrupulous London landlord, but he was still the worst we had ever met. Our nemesis. Through him we had tasted the tang of living in poverty, and for that we must ultimately offer thanks. It had almost made men of us. However, when the going got tough, we called our dads and they stopped it all.

And then we called Mr Hartnell, mate.

sixteen

Hubris

What are we arguing for in the middle of the road? We're rich beyond our wildest dreams.

'It's not fair on you,' insists Ingrid.

'It seems completely fair to me,' I counter.

'This puts me in a very awkward position,' squirms Rob.

Our housing benefit cheques arrived through the post today: 22 weeks in arrears at £18.05 a week – that's almost £400 each, which is a lot of Deep Pan Pizzas. Even better, courtesy of AM Hicks, whoever he or she may be, they've overpaid us for a couple of weeks when we no longer lived at Drewstead Road. We're quids in, and no less than my dad has advised us to keep schtumm, bank the money and let them work it out. 'If they ask for the difference back,' he told me on the phone, 'just act innocent and pay them. You won't have lost anything. But chances are, it'll be one of those computer errors that never gets chased up. Think of it as a gift from Lambeth.'

He'd also advised us to demand our deposit back from Rabit when we moved out, which we did, even though we'd actually broken the terms of the lease by not giving any notice. The way Dad saw it, the flat had been effectively uninhabitable for two weeks, so Rabit had broken the agreement by allowing it to get like that. Rabit gritted his teeth and wrote us a cheque for *half* the deposit each on the leather-upholstered surface of his doctor's desk. We felt it was a moral victory, took the money and ran.

And now we've scored another jackpot from Lambeth. But instead of celebrating our win, we're standing in Parkgate Road, just over the back from the halls, having a stand-up row.

'But if you hadn't been paying £50 a week you never would have been in the flat in the first place,' reasons Ingrid.

'That's irrelevant,' says Rob. 'That was an agreement between me and Andy. I realise if he hadn't paid over the odds, we wouldn't have moved in, but we would have moved in somewhere and anyway it doesn't matter what we might or might not have done, it's about what we did.'

He's trying not to raise his voice at my girlfriend of thirteen months, but you can tell he really wants to. He's indignant – after all, Ingrid has accused him of taking money off me.

'I don't want your money, Rob.'

'She's saying I owe you it.'

'You don't.'

'He bloody does!' she snarls.

Why Ingrid has taken it upon herself to represent me in this unwanted tribunal I don't know. I'm starting to feel this isn't about the money. Rob does sometimes refer to her as 'Jersey girl' in my company when she's not around, as if perhaps he can't bring himself to use her name, but she's never been a thorn in our side, or vice versa. We've been going out for over a year now, and Rob and I remain fast friends, flatmates, a double act; I had fooled myself into thinking it was all going rather well, proof indeed that two boys can get on when one of them has a girlfriend. We even lived together as a threesome for those few weeks, like *Man About the House* in reverse, and there was no friction that I was aware of. Rob was very gracious about putting her up when she was homeless, and she put money in the pot. I was hoping they'd keep each other company at Simon's imminent wedding while I go about my best man duties, but it suddenly seems very unlikely.

She firmly believes that Rob owes me a quarter of his housing benefit as he was only paying £30 out of the £80 a week rent. It had never crossed my mind. This is why Dad always said never argue about religion, politics or money.

'But as far as Lambeth are concerned we were both paying £40 a week,' pleads Rob. 'That was the con.'

'Andrew's the one who's been conned.'

'No I haven't!'

I'm being forced to take sides now. With Rob. Against Ingrid. It's painful and I'd rather not be doing it, certainly not in Parkgate Road in front of Bishop's Move Storage, but *she is wrong.*

Isn't she?

Rob takes a deep breath. 'Lambeth wouldn't have paid out if Andy had claimed on £50 a week, they'd have said it was too much for one person to pay – get a cheaper flat or we're not going to give you a rebate. By claiming on £40 each we got the maximum amount of money back. When I was at Mrs Reed's I paid £20 rent a week, which was so cheap

Hammersmith & Fulham only reimbursed me £1.80 a week. Hardly worth having. They start to pay out decent rebates from about £25 a week; £40 a week is worth £18 back, and that's why we're rolling in it now.'

'But you're rolling in *his* money.'

'All right,' he snaps. 'I'll pay him back. Andy—?'

'No. Keep your money.'

This is what my mum always used to have to say to my nan when she went for her purse of a Thursday and tried to pay for the dinner Mum had cooked her. Every week it was, 'Put your money away.' 'Take it.' 'I don't want your money.' 'I'll leave it on the side here.' 'Our Mum!'

'We're not having this discussion.'

Rob's colour is up. Ingrid's eyes are blazing. He's surprised but relieved that I took his side against hers. She's furious. Not at Rob any more, but at me.

'Let's go to the park,' she says, less a suggestion, more an order.

'I'm going back to the halls,' says Rob. He looks pleadingly at me as Ingrid marches parkwards and I scuttle off behind her. I look pleadingly back. This is one of her bad days. The bad days are becoming more frequent.

If I felt I was a coward and an impostor when I crawled back to the halls as a second-year, I was nothing less than a big fat baby for doing it in my third. But circumstances dictated a quick fix, and since Ralph West traditionally experiences a few dropouts after Christmas we knew there was every chance of getting back in. In the event, we didn't even have to go on the list. There was no list. It was perhaps even more of a Napoleonic retreat for Rob, who had been fending for himself for over a year, first under Reed then Rabit. To return to the bosom of the halls with its canteen and pigeon-holes after that long on the outside must have really rankled. Me? I don't suppose they noticed I'd been away. I'm surprised Mr Hartnell hadn't kept my room for me, just like Mum and Dad do.

On the upside, after a circuitous four-month diversion via Brighton, Whitby and Streatham Hill, Ingrid and I were back living together again. On the down, it was now clear that against all odds Mills and Boone were going to graduate from Chelsea as residents of the halls of residence. The oldest swingers in town.

'See those two with haunted eyes sitting on their own?' the new intake would whisper. 'They're third-years!'

'*Third*-years?'

The atmosphere changed at college in the third year. It wasn't exactly that people suddenly pulled their finger out, put on a serious hat and started working, but the course was infected with an air of suppressed hysteria. Like the final days of a holiday, which let's face it, they were. Some accepted that the end was near and mentally prepared for the future, others simply stayed in bed or the pub longer.

There was, however, a third way. Rob found himself among a select band at Chelsea encouraged by the tutors to consider extending their higher education for a further two years by applying for an MA course at somewhere fancy like the Royal College. Master of Arts – it had a nice ring to it, as if perhaps you got epaulettes or piping on your dungarees.

The chances of getting a grant at MA level were smaller, but there was no denying the kudos of having extra initials after your name and of course the supreme doss of doing two more years of drawing pictures. I was tempted myself to join in this jolly fantasy for about five minutes but enthusiasm quickly receded. Two reasons:

1. It was quite clear to me that my limited artistic licks needed no more fine-tuning. And the prevailing wisdom of the tutors was that I was beyond fine-tuning anyway.

2. I was becoming increasingly disillusioned with art school. Why would I want two more years of it?

Having been dismissed as a joyless sausage machine by the head of illustration and in her next Germanic breath encouraged to go for the Thames Television bursary because such awards make the college look good, I had begun to see through the gauze of pretence in which Chelsea was tastefully draped. I looked around me and realised that I was surrounded by perfectly nice but unemployable dilettantes whose egos were massaged on a daily basis by the tutors while I got on with the mucky business of earning some spare cash off David Williams with my vulgar cartoons. I was never going to be one of Susan Einzig's Artists, like delicate Tracey or smudgy Alex or painterly Ros, but as I entered the third year I reached a Zen-like state of enlightenment and accepted that I didn't give a flying fuck. Not about being an Artist.

I'd spent a whole term in a refrigerated hovel-cum-death-trap and if I was to live anywhere better come graduation I would have to find the means to pay for it. I was, after all, living in the Eighties. The job market was starting to rear its ugly head, although Susan's Artists were never going to notice from behind their giant, gouache-smeared canvasses. The institutionalised day-to-day bollocks of Chelsea School of Art had alienated me to the margins and hardened me into a commercial-minded cartooning whore. Alexei Sayle had been admitted to Chelsea because he could, as he put it, 'draw horses out of me head', and, duly misunderstood, chose to spend most of his time there *actually* out of his head rather than walk around a shopping precinct wearing a teapot. I now knew how he felt.

But people will always want sausages.

In March, in a parallel universe to Chelsea, my vulgar project about Jersey (about Ingrid) was awarded the overall prize at the Thames Bursary – a further cheque for £400 to add to the £700 I had been given for the previous summer and spent mostly on rent and food. If you'll allow me a brief gloat from my pedestal of inverted artistic snobbery: that's a bunch of annotated cartoons and snapshots of holiday-makers and houses with low roofs, deemed by the esteemed panel of Thames philistines to be better – that's *better* – than Robin Grierson from West Surrey College of Art and his photographs of Barcelona ('Roland Barthes might have called the work "a mythology" as it contradicts the dominant myth and reveals an injustice'), better than Simon Bowler of the Polytechnic of Central London and his film of a drama festival at the ancient amphitheatre of Epidauros in central Greece ('despite the various problems encountered the film remains as initially intended though unavoidably mutated and compromised'), better even than John Millar from West

Surrey College of Art and his photographs of hospital workers in Oxford and Boston ('the work is about people and with a subject this complex there is no one answer'). More worthy than all that worthiness. I had been on holiday for two months and lived with my girlfriend and fed the cat and drawn the intellectual equivalent of some horses out of me head and I had beaten every one of these pretentious, arty-farty, post-rationalising windbags. It was a quiet victory for drawings that looked like the thing they were supposed to be a drawing of.

It was also a nice day out for Mum and Dad who came down to London to attend the modest bursary-winners' exhibition and swelled with pride as I was called up to the podium to accept my prize from the MD of Thames Television. Roland Barthes might have called my victory 'a big fat two fingers' to Susan's Artists.

The merry occasion, however, was tainted by something unspoken. Ingrid and I had split up.

'I can't believe you didn't tell them!'

'What was I going to say?'

'That we've split up.'

'Have we though?'

'That's what we decided.'

'You decided.'

It was a difficult taxi ride back with Mum and Dad from Tottenham Court Road past Nelson's Column, the House of Parliament and across Albert Bridge. Ingrid had come along to the bursary exhibition because she'd been invited and we'd agreed to remain friends (and the exhibition was

about her), but the night before we'd had one of our rows
and reached an intractable position. I said I couldn't go on
like this any more. Ingrid had called my bluff and suggested
we end it. We had sad sex and it was brisk and cursory and
that seemed to draw a line under it. It was clearly meant to
be our last.

'What about the bursary?' I'd whimpered, as we lay there
impassive and not touching on my bed.

'I'll still come,' she'd said. 'Be nice to see John and
Christine. I've got no argument with them.' The very fact
that my girlfriend referred to my mum and dad by their first
names made me realise in that moment what a lot we had to
lose. We agreed to part, but to attend the bursary – me with
Mum and Dad, her with John and Christine – and enjoy the
afternoon out. I'd assumed that this meant pretend everything was hunky dory and that's how I played it. Having
parked in the Ralph West car park, Mum and Dad came up
to my room to change into their best kit and I made them a
cup of tea. When we were ready we called for Ingrid and
headed off to get a cab. She was wearing her puffball skirt
and Mum said how nice it looked, to which Ingrid pointedly
replied, 'Andrew doesn't like it.'

'Oh, it looks lovely,' Mum cooed, directed at me.

Ingrid and I had already fallen out over the puffball skirt,
so the very wearing of it was an act of defiance. It said: you're
not my boyfriend any more, you have no jurisdiction.

I should mention that John and Christine now officially
thought Ingrid was terrific. Once they'd accepted that I was
serious about her their feelings evolved beyond 'she's really
good-looking'. They found in her someone they could talk
to. They found her mature (for which read: less doll-like

than Sally and less underage than Valeria), easygoing and effusive, all of which she undoubtedly was and is. What they didn't see was the flipside.

They didn't see the girl stamping around her room because she'd lost an earring, crying and shouting, red-faced, blaming it on me, blaming it on the world, unable to think about anything else and winding herself tighter and tighter into a knot, inconsolable. Did I dare say, 'It's just an earring'? I did not. I'd already tried, 'You can buy another pair,' and had my head bitten off. I found the earring later that evening, stupid great elaborate ethnic craft-market thing, snagged on the bedspread, by which time her rage was embedded like a bee sting, barbed and immovable. She simmered for hours. I got so fed up I poured a plastic pint glass full of water over my head, partly to cool myself off, but also to draw her attention away from *her*. She was suitably wrong-footed by my self-dousing and it really did help lift the red mist.

They didn't see her roaring at me all the way home in the car after I'd made an inadvertently sexist comment about a woman driver. The comment, it has to be said, was facile, ill thought out, but ultimately disposable. It didn't merit the torrent of abuse she hurled at me.

'You are such a pig! You make me sick!'

'I've said I'm sorry!'

'It doesn't make it all right.'

'What else can I do? I can't turn back time!'

'Stop the car, I'm going to walk back.'

'No.'

'I'm going to open the door. I don't want to be in the same car as you.'

'Don't open the door!'

'Pull over, or I'll jump out.'

They didn't see her threatening to jump off the concrete ledge outside her window at the halls. It was the middle of the night and we'd had a row so she climbed out of the window in her dressing gown, leggings and pumps and sat on the ledge, with her legs swinging, three floors up. She threatened to jump if I tried to go out after her. I pleaded with her to come back in. Lenny, doing his nocturnal circuit of the ground floor, looked up and saw her. Alarmed, he made his way silently up to the third floor and rapped respectfully on the door. Without opening it, I assured him everything was all right.

'Are you sure?' he asked.

'She's coming back in, it's fine,' I said.

'OK. If you're sure ... She shouldn't be out there.'

Lenny went away, but I knew he was heading back for a vantage point in the corridor below to ensure that the girl with the long hair and the pink dressing gown had gone back in. I leaned out of the window and hissed, 'Get. Back. In. Here. Now. You. Stupid ...'

Stupid what? The possible nouns shuffled through my mind like a Rolodex: bastard, bitch, twat, fucker, fool, idiot. I settled on a loaded pause. Let her fill in the blank. 'You stupid ... Lenny'll be straight back up here.'

She came back in and I slammed the window shut behind her. She had, it seems, made her point. She had made me suffer: humiliation, fear, helplessness. Not a bad hand.

They didn't see her initiating a row with my best friend in Parkgate Road. Or making me cry by a river. Or getting up in the middle of the night and going back to her own room because of some remark I'd made and making me beg her to come back. Ingrid was an emotional fairground ride. Exhilarating, for sure, but capable of sending your heart flying into your mouth and with a propensity to induce nausea. A vivid combination of inexperience, swagger, cruelty, self-pity, want, need, melodrama, passion, destruction and hubris.

She bought a cream-coloured puffball skirt on the King's Road. The idea of this ludicrous fashion item, elasticated and doubled over to create a pleated pumpkin look, is that it can be worn pulled down like a skirt or puffed up like a full pair of incontinence pants. Thank you, Christian LaCroix. She was off out to meet some visiting Jersey pals at a wine bar in Fulham and I went up to see her and kiss her goodbye before she left. Balanced on a chair so she could see her lower half in the mirror above the sink she had the skirt puffed out and looked frankly horrendous. Worse, she was wearing cream-coloured stockings with suspenders underneath, the tops of which were exposed, making her look like a cross between a model in a Def Leppard video and an ice cream.

I'm afraid I effectively said, 'You're not going out looking like that,' thus turning without irony into my own mother, and this made Ingrid three times as determined to go out looking exactly like that. She stomped out of the room with no kiss goodbye. I had to go after her and physically coerce her back into the room by the shoulders and attempt to gently persuade her of the error of her ways.

Of course, as a man of the world, I now know what a huge relationship faux pas this was. Telling a woman, however ridiculous she looked, that she looked ridiculous, and that I knew better than her how she should dress. Ouch. All I can say is my motivations were genuinely well intended.

'Let go of me!'

'Not until you say goodbye properly.'

'Let *go* of me!'

'Just pull the skirt down a bit.'

'You're creasing my jacket.'

I had to let her go. My heart was filled with sadness and disapproval as I watched her from the sixth-floor lift lobby walking up Worfield Street looking foolish and tugging irritably at the skirt. I continued to watch as she stopped in her tracks, turned on her heels and headed back towards the halls, with a face like thunder, to change her outfit and make certain I knew it was my fault, and not Christian LaCroix's. Linda Blair was back.

So, today is the first time she's worn the puffball skirt out. Not out; pulled down a bit actually, and with tights underneath.

'It looks all right,' I said, to keep the peace.

My big mistake was not to tell Mum and Dad that Ingrid and I had agreed to split up. I told myself it was neither the time nor the place. Secretly though, I hoped we'd patch things up, because we all know what happens when a fairground ride finishes. You want to get back on. So I simply omitted that particular piece of information. I didn't lie. I never said, 'Let's go up and call on Ingrid, because she is my current girlfriend.' Mind you, neither did I say, 'Let's go and call on Ingrid, even though she is no longer my current girlfriend.' I think I just said, 'Let's go and call on Ingrid. Have you got your invites?'

The afternoon went off fine. Ingrid chatted amiably with

John and Christine and other bursary winners and politely applauded when I picked up my prize. You had to hand it to her, she coped brilliantly, when you consider that all my Jersey work was up on display, including pictures of her and her family and Goodwood, mementos of a happier period when she was still my girlfriend. If it caused her any difficulty, she hid it well. Or stored it up at any rate.

Later, as we were seeing Mum and Dad off outside the halls, Mum asked if they'd see us again before Simon's wedding. I said maybe. This was when Ingrid clicked that I hadn't told them. She hid her displeasure behind big smiles and goodbye cheek-kisses and waited until the Cavalier had turned the corner before erupting.

'I can't believe I've spent the whole afternoon talking away to them when they think nothing's wrong.'

'What's the point of upsetting them? Mum will be upset.'

'I'm upset!'

'Can we talk about this upstairs?'

'No. There's nothing more to talk about. I'm going to the shop.'

Ingrid marches off towards Albert Bridge and I follow. I must stop doing this, following her. She speeds up. Perhaps she doesn't want me to follow her. I follow her anyway – I haven't finished.

'Hey! I'm still talking.'

Silence.

'Why are we splitting up when we've had such a nice afternoon?'

Silence.

'We get on so well, and Mum and Dad like you so much …'

Silence.

'Oh, *go* then,' I give in, wearily.

'*You* had a nice afternoon,' she barks. 'I had a horrible one. You won the prize and got all the compliments and your mum and dad love each other and everybody's happy. Now piss off and let me go to the shop. I need some cigarettes.'

I let her stomp ahead, Linda Blair in a stupid confectionary skirt, utterly overdressed for a walk to the mini-mart. At least she's talking to me. There's hope yet.

seventeen

Nemesis

I've never hit a woman. I've never hit a man either, but that's beside the point. I've never laid a finger on a woman. It would be like voting Tory or expecting black people to do all the menial jobs. What would Ben say?

'Sexism in comedy and everywhere else – let's try to get together and get rid of it.'

Ben Elton is my big favourite at the moment. He's my guiding light. My moral compass. He's mobilised all the instinctive humanitarian, left-wing feelings that have been brewing up in me since leaving home and given voice to the way I feel deep down inside. I've never before been this laid bare with guilt – but good guilt, useful social guilt, practical guilt; not abstract, debilitating girlfriend-induced guilt about having a happy family or parking inconsiderately. In the space of just a few weekly stand-up routines in that crap suit, Ben has succeeded in making me feel guilty about a much broader range of stuff.

Ben Elton speaks directly to me, he speaks directly to all of us, from his pulpit on *Saturday Live*. I've never seen the halls coffee bar as packed as it now is every Saturday night at ten. Standing room only. The committee don't bother hiring a video in any more and the poor old Prince Albert empties at 9.45. One week he's exposing the folly of trying to get a double seat on a train and speaking of the repressed British character, the next he's damning Benny Hill for chasing women round the park when in fact street lighting is inadequate and women are too scared to walk through parks. On occasions we've all found ourselves clapping the TV. *Saturday Live* makes me glad I'm back in the halls.

As I was saying, I've never hit a woman. I know it's wrong. Unless it's sexist to single out women from the no-hitting rule? I expect Ben would know, but I'm not entirely sure. Let's just say I never hit. Violence after all begets violence, and how can you be against war and police brutality if you condone it on a smaller scale? Right on! Our world too!

The Tories haven't got a chance at the next election. This summer they're out. Surely. Just listen to Ben and read the *NME* and look at Red Wedge whipping up support around the country until the walls come tumbling down! It's not just about wearing Breton fishermen's caps and moaning about grants – we're the next generation and we've got something to say. We hold the reins of power. No more *Terry and June*! No more systematic dismantling of the coal industry! No more oppression of sexy women with our eyes! (Or any kind of women!)

Anyway, as I say, I have never hit a woman. But I'm about to for the first time.

She asked for it.

Thwack!

* * *

I'm pleased to say I punched the pillow instead. I'm ashamed to say the very act of not hitting her made me feel strangely alive. I could have but I didn't. A switch was thrown somewhere inside me and I hit the pillow. With that re-directed blow, that 'near go', our relationship entered a new place. I now understand why people who are in love hurt each other. No longer are we just Andrew and Ingrid, art school boyfriend and girlfriend in matching jumpers, going out with each other, playing house, pretending to be married. We are now the sort of couple who row. And not just row. Fight. We physically grab and push and restrain and, as of this moment, we just stop ourselves from hitting each other. At least, I do. I think perhaps this is what Ingrid believes a real relationship is like: fiery, raw, corporeal, bodily, antagonistic. She's trying consciously or otherwise to turn us into her parents.

As far as I know, my own parents don't do this and never have done. I could count the blazing parental rows I witnessed as a child on one soft, white hand. Mum shouted at *me* plenty, but that's different: I was an annoying twat in silly clothes. She and Dad, by and large, got on fine, even when I was trying to play them off against each other with my crimp-ing and my gay act. They may have begun to shrink physically in photographs but in other ways they continue to grow.

To Ingrid, my family situation is like a Special K advert – sugar-coated, somehow untruthful, a life unlived – and frankly, it irritates her. The bonhomie at Simon's wedding in Taunton irritated her. I irritate her.

She gushes tears, like a broken pipe. It's as if her whole face is leaking, pink and raw. The fight's gone out of her. Does that mean I've won this round?

Won? What am I talking about? What am I doing?

If my parents could see me now. If they could see behind the united front of smiles and cheek-kisses we present to the world. We try to keep our local difficulties behind closed doors and to an extent we do, but Ingrid's always threatening to take it outside, like a fight in a pub. That's how we got here this evening: we spun the wheel on the Twister of love and ended up frozen in this dramatic tableau with me looming over her on my bed with my fist buried in the pillow and she bawling her eyes out in frustration as much as misery. Adjust the lighting and we could be making love, not war. Is this how those with an artist's temperament live? Is that it? Or do botany students and undergraduate PE teachers also behave this way?

This particular argument, precipitated by a discussion about where we were sleeping tonight, started in my room on the ninth floor. Because we reside on separate floors of the same building – a normal relationship only in terms of the artificial ecosystem of halls – there is a lot of storming-out potential. Despite or perhaps because of the easy access, we sleep in the same room only occasionally – mine as a rule, because of the telly – but the reality of sharing a tiny single barrack bed usually cancels out the romance of the arrangement and Ingrid frequently gets up and returns to her room in the dead of night. I pretend to be asleep as she slides out from under the bedclothes and tiptoes across the lino. This is no basis for a steady domestic attachment. Too much to-ing and fro-ing. Too many turf wars. Remember when that bloke broke into the Queen's bedroom and it became public knowledge that she and Prince Philip slept in separate rooms? I couldn't understand that. My grandparents share a bed. Why would a couple sleep apart? Why do Ingrid and I sleep apart? We're in the prime of our life.

Things have been fractious ever since Brighton, if I'm honest, even though I like to think I was the model boy-friend that term, supportively driving her to and from the south coast every weekend at sometimes unearthly hours, crawling back into London on the A23 past Redhill without a word of complaint. My moving in with Rob set up a trian-gle that was never apparent before: it strengthened our friendship and imperceptibly weakened my relationship with Ingrid. Eventually taking her on as a lodger, even for a couple of weeks, created tension. Rob's relief when Jersey girl moved to Ralph West was palpable. Then inclement weather and an unscrupulous landlord forced us both to follow her here with our tails between our legs. It was a step backwards for all of us.

So Ingrid and I split up the night before the bursary and got back together again the next day. I accept that we're not the first couple to do that. Adults call it trial separation and it can be healthy. Even Sally and I did it and we were kids. But I'm 22 now. I graduate in a matter of months, finally enter the world, still a partner in what is far and away the longest relationship I've ever been in, well into its second year. A relationship with no better half. We're no better than each other.

'Sometimes I think you're only going out with me because it's convenient,' she says.

'What does *that* mean?'

'Well, when term ends I'll be going back to Jersey and you'll be leaving Chelsea.'

'So?'

'Perfect time to end it.'

'We're not ending it.'

'It's a natural cut-off point.'

I can't say the thought hasn't crossed my mind. And I mean I *can't* say it. I *can't* say what I think.

'You don't like this music, do you?'

'It's just men shouting.'

'It's supposed to be.'

'Can we put Suzanne Vega on?'

'The cassette's in the car.'

She tuts. I get up and take the Beastie Boys off. I think *Licensed To Ill* is a magnificent LP. She doesn't. Yet another wedge between us. I admire the gatefold sleeve as I slip the disc inside its paper cover, hoping at least to pique her interest in the artwork: a plane crashing into the ground, or the side of a mountain, depending on which way up you hold it. The nose of the plane is concertinaed and drawn, I presume, so that it looks like a joint if you half close your eyes. I love it, even though drugs-talk is another wedge between Ingrid and I. She tells many a tale of getting high in Jersey on pot romantically smuggled in by rowing boat from France; my experience of it is limited. I remain, through ignorance, suspicious of drugs. The fact that Ingrid has had so many good times on drugs makes me resent them. I resent her for having had those good times without me, even though she'd never met me. There's no logic in the land of retroactive jealousy.

'Kate Bush all right?'

'Suppose.'

The Hounds of Love reminds me of when we first fell in love, over a year ago, in this very building, albeit in different rooms. I was in 313, she was in 611. I think of those days I spent locked in my room making an opera with snatches of Kate Bush to dramatise our packet-fresh love.

Things were so much simpler then.

'Just think,' she says provocatively. 'At the start of July you'll be rid of me.'

'Who said I want to be rid of you? I still want to come out to Jersey.'

'What if I don't want you to come out to Jersey?'

'You can't stop me. It's a free country.'

'We don't have sex any more.'

'We never sleep in the same bed do we? Anyway, what about the other night?'

She snorts. With good reason.

'Stay here tonight.'

'Too uncomfortable next to the radiator.'

'I'll sleep on that side.'

'I always fall out of the other side.'

'All right, go back to your room.'

'I will. This is stupid. We should have had the guts to finish the first time.'

'Well, why didn't we?'

'Because you refused to go back to your room. You can't accept it.'

She's got me there. I did indeed refuse to leave her room the evening after the bursary. After an exhausting night of fags and pacing and hair-tearing – self-administered – she went to sleep and turned the light off and I curled up on the floor at the end of her bed in some form of embryonic protest. I was transported back to the second year when I slept on people's floors, except this time I had no sleeping bag and I didn't actually need to be here. We'd both been dry-crying and I found myself muttering to myself as I lay coiled there on the cold hard lino, a bit like a nutter. I wonder perhaps if I thought I could prove to her that I was just as nuts as she was. I rocked against the wardrobe door in the dark in a frankly unimpressive display of forced insanity until it was clear that she was fast asleep, at which I slunk off home.

Actually I slunk off to the lift lobby and curled up on one of the easy chairs until Lenny found me and prodded me gently awake. I lied that I wasn't feeling well and needed to be near the toilets. He left me there, probably more concerned with why I was in a pink spotted towelling dressing gown. When you're suffering as a way of life, all humiliation is welcome.

'Let's finish it when term ends then,' I suggest, in curt mockery of Ingrid's suggestion.

'Let's finish it now,' she snaps.

'Go away then. If we're not even going out with each other, I don't want you in here.'

'All right. I'm going to tear up that card you made me.'

'Do it then.'

'I will.'

'No, don't.'

'Why not? It says you love me and you don't.'

'Give it back to me then – I like that picture.'

'It's mine. You gave it to me.'

Un-fucking-believable. She storms out of the room with intent burning in her eyes. I let her go, even though I fear she really will tear up that card. It's perhaps the most self-pitying token I have ever presented anyone, a lovingly rendered caricature of Ingrid as some kind of celestial nymph in diaphanous robe. Inside the card I have drawn myself as this grubby little cartoon heading for a door marked 'EXIT'. Even this soon after the event I wonder what I thought I would achieve with this pathetic freight-train symbolism. It was a card for heaven's sake. A gift from me to her. A handmade token of – what exactly? She must not tear it up!

Recognising from the familiar diminishing slap-slap-slap of her determined footfalls the precise moment before her slippers reach the fire escape at the end of the corridor, I opt to chase after her. She must not reach those stairs. I find I am in a rage. Possessed by a Hulk-style fury that rises in my chest like mercury in a thermometer. In my mind I leap down the corridor in two giant strides.

I hear myself hissing, 'Get back in here!'

Thankfully there's no one around to see as I drag Ingrid back to my room. Using all my strength, I manhandle her all the way back down the corridor. She thrashes about like a zebra in the jaws of a crocodile. Like any couple in the white heat of battle, we cut an absurd shape. But we are beyond embarrassment.

'Get off me!'

This is intervention of the most physical kind. I am, by brute force, altering the trajectory of another body in motion. My girlfriend. This is no longer discussion, or debate, or even emotional tennis, this is basic physics, a force pushing against another force, two planets colliding. If this is feeling alive, perhaps I'd rather be dead. But there's no time for thinking.

I barge Ingrid through the door to my room and slam it

behind us with my back. She is shrieking now and trying to hit me with both fists. What will the neighbours think? Fuck the neighbours. I grab her wrists and she hammers the air. I attempt to throw her onto the bed. She bounces back and digs her fingernails into my arms, drawing blood. I gather all my might and push her onto the bed, pinning her down with my body.

Then – pull back and – *thwack*!

An innocent Ralph West pillow caught in the crossfire of a disintegrating relationship.

Needless to say, we made up afterwards and slept in my room.

A week later we had another fight and split up. For good. After an unresolved evening of backbiting and voice-raising, she woke me up in the middle of the night by steaming into my room like a pink-towelling banshee with what felt like every intention of killing me in my bed. Instead, in an echo of my own redirected punch, she diverted her bloodlust and brought her fists down so hard on my Hitachi stereo that she cracked the plastic lid. We wrestled on my bed in the dark and I intimated that this was it. The final straw. She had crossed the thin red line and she knew it. The gouges in my arm would heal, but not this crack in my stereo lid. If I hadn't pulled her off she would, I feel sure, have gone for the tone arm.

The actual denouement the next day was rather calm and reasonable. It should of course have played out like the goodbye on the tarmac at the end of *Casablanca*, but it was nothing like as dramatic. No grabbing or restraining either, just a sensible discussion in her room in the aftermath of this final bout of violence. There was sadness, but mainly of inevitability. Neither of us shed any tears. Suddenly we were free, with a couple of weeks still to run until the end of term.

That evening, feeling empty because we'd missed the evening meal, I told myself that staying in moping around my room in my dressing gown was not the answer and went instead to the pub with Rob, to fill him in and find a sympathetic ear for my tale of hi-fi abuse. A gaggle of Chelsea first-years saw us in the lift lobby and invited themselves along, Jennifer, Debbie, Suzi and Suzi's boyfriend 'from home'. Chris worked for a proper advertising agency. He regaled us with details of the latest account he was working on – something involving famous film director Michael Apted – and for a few blessed moments, I forgot about Ingrid and the last year and a half and the scabbed nail marks in my forearms and found myself laughing and joking about little things all the way down Worfield Street. I was experiencing what I didn't know was an unbearable lightness of being. Then there was a flash of remorse for having a good time on such a grave day but I was used to carrying my low-level Eighties guilt around with me and I was able to rise above it.

Unfortunately, unknown to me, the sound of our merry laughter carried up into Ingrid's open window. She recognised the voices, looked out, saw me and found my behaviour both inappropriate and insulting. Especially when she was dutifully staying in moping around her room in her dressing gown.

After the pub, aglow with Fosters, I went back to Rob's room to listen to some life-affirming indie noise. There was a knock at the door.

Rob answered it to Ingrid in her dressing gown.

'Is Andrew there?' she asked, curtly.

'Certainly is,' he replied, hiding his discomfort.

'Ask him to come out.'

Rob turned to raise his eyebrows at me. I got up off his bed and did as she had asked.

'Close the door,' she instructed, calmly. Too calmly. I did so.

She swung her arm like a spin bowler and slapped me hard around the face, clenching her teeth and screwing up her eyes with the effort: a grim parody of the face I still secretly loved. The sound echoed around the dark, deserted corridor.

'That's for going out and having a good time.'

With that, she turned and fled. My ears were ringing. The left side of my face was stinging. I was too staggered to respond either in word or gesture. I wondered if Rob had heard the mighty slap from inside. This time I wasn't going after her, and neither was I expected to. All I had to do was stand there, stunned, absorb the pain and wait for the ringing to stop.

So how and why did the divine Angharad become Linda Blair? Was it the culture clash in Jersey? The traffic on the A23? Rob? Her parents? My parents? Whitby? A thoughtless comment about a woman driver? The Beastie Boys? The puffball skirt?

It's hard to say for sure, although they all played their part in our protracted downfall. Love and hate are only ever a set of knuckles apart – that was something I learnt.

Insecurity goes hand in hand with security – that was another. Temporary domestic bliss is a dangerous game. Living on an island is for the summer season not for life. But none of these platitudes really explains why a relationship as promising and vivacious as ours turned so sour in under eighteen months.

We were no doubt at that strange and naïve age when you tend to project your desires on to those you are physically attracted to – sketching in the missing details in their profile as you'd have them, with scant regard for reality. Sustained by the glow of first contact, your dream love at first seems real, even operatic. Then the cold drip, drip, drip of reality starts to seep in and you discover neither of you has the ability to live up to the other's fantasy creation. Time does the opposite of heal, and you begin blaming each other for the failing relationship as it is steadily exposed to the truth and then the roof falls in.

My happy home life rubbed a lot of salt in the wounds of Ingrid's imploding family. The artificiality of halls, the lack of difficult questions, certainly prolonged the agony of our demise, but part of me was still desperate to cling to Ingrid. I entertained fantasies about living with her in Jersey, beating those island dilettantes by joining them. When the nuclear bombs started dropping on London, we would be kissing in a field in Breton shirts at the centre of a splash of ultramarine.

But it wasn't just fear of Armageddon that kept us together after the love had gone. Why hadn't we just called it a day when I was forced to pour water over myself to get her attention?

You have to go back to the week I spent with Rob in

Tooting, flat-hunting. Not to put too fine a point on it, I was experiencing some embarrassing itching. Having reluctantly returned from an active summer in Jersey I suspected the affliction with the garden bird's name and, without any fuss, paid a visit to St Stephen's Hospital, there to set my mind at rest and to get a prescription for some cream.

As I sat there in the waiting room, nonchalance personified, leafing through a copy of *Zigzag* I had brought with me, I noticed two things that made this visit different from the last. The waiting room was much busier and all the new patients were obviously gay men. And I suddenly knew precisely why they were here and it made my blood run cold. They were getting HIV tests. I expect in Northampton AIDS seemed like a world away in the summer of '86. Here in London I could smell its cologne.

AIDS had been in the news for a while, but this unsettling glimpse of the panic that had clearly taken hold among London's gay community gave me a real scare. Ingrid and I would never have admitted it to ourselves but one of the reasons we worked hard at staying together was AIDS. We can't have been the only couple at that time to go off sex. Sex didn't seem so sexy with a gravestone at the end of your bed. As well as the default guilt for all those flings I'd had, I was now filled with selfish regret for not wearing a condom. I'd never had sex with a condom.

I spent an awful lot of time in '86 and '87 counting backwards to my last encounter before getting together with Ingrid. It had been Jill, the old sixth-form friend at Kate's party in Bath. Frank discussions with Ingrid about whether or not we were going to die meant that I had to come clean about the Bath quickie with her. The gap between me and

Ingrid and her previous last time had been much greater, which gave her the moral advantage: if we *were* HIV positive, it would be my fault. Aged 22, I began to think a lot about my own death. I decided if I was going to end up like Daniel Massey in *Intimate Contact* or the factory worker on *Brookside*, then I wanted to face it with a girlfriend at my bedside.

But finally even this fate paled next to living with Ingrid. She stopped being my nemesis after the Hitachi-lid incident and became simply my ex-girlfriend. The price I would pay was no more sex – ever. It was a sign of how far we had descended that it was a price worth paying.

eighteen

I Warn You Not to Grow Old

A cross with a stubby pencil on a string in the box next to Labour candidate John Dickie and I'm done. I have voted for the second time in my life in the constituency of Northampton South and it feels good. Giddy on Ben Elton and the Blow Monkeys and the *NME* and Neil Kinnock's speech at Bridgend – 'I warn you not to be ordinary, I warn you not to be young, I warn you not to fall ill and I warn you not to grow old' – I am helping to change the political landscape of this country.

'I won't ask,' says Dad ruefully, as we emerge with Mum from the church hall into the sunshine of this day of great change: 11 June 1987.

I don't need to ask either; I know he's voted for Michael Morris, sitting Tory candidate in Northampton South since the town was divided in two in 1974, and a former advertising exec who wears a dicky bow. Quite. Even Rob's put that particular fashion gambit behind him. Mum declines to reveal whom she voted for, as is her unalienable right, though I suspect she has slavishly followed Dad.

We stroll back up to Kestrel Close wearing our imaginary coloured rosettes. The act is done. Change is in the air. I am single again after eighteen months, something I considered not telling Mum and Dad on this particular visit, but Mum guessed because she is a woman and a mother. A month from now I will no longer be a student and I will graduate with a second-class BA Honours in Graphic Design and Illustration.

David Williams has quit Imagination after five years to set up a new design company with his two farting rugby player friends Bob and Keith, and they're talking about me as their chief freelance illustrator, which is what I call good timing. To add to this I am in the process of applying for my first mortgage. After the disastrous spell at Drewstead Road, Dad became convinced that the most prudent thing to do vis-à-vis accommodation was to buy.

'Rather than line the pockets of some crook like Rabit, you'd be better off paying back a mortgage. At least you get something at the other end of it.'

The other end of it is, according to the building society, 25 years away. I will be 47. Is that old? It sounds old. It's older than Dad. I don't expect to be living in a flat when I'm 47. Actually, I don't know what I expect to be doing at 47. Perhaps I'll still be single and celibate, or perhaps they'll have found a cure for AIDS. Leaving college is about facing up to the passage of time and making decisions, and I don't much like it. I should have done an MA. I can feel it in my ageing bones.

Because I will be a humble self-employed graduate with

no guaranteed income my dad has magnanimously agreed to act as my guarantor, which means he is legally responsible to meet my monthly mortgage repayment if, for whatever reason, I'm unable. That's the official, on-paper agreement. The private gentlemen's agreement between us is this: he won't pay a penny. He'll guarantee me if I guarantee him. So the pressure is on me to earn enough each month, starting in July, to cover the mortgage. That sounds suspiciously like responsibility.

I signed up with a South London estate agent called Folkard & Hayward and they arranged some property viewings within what Abbey National had calculated to be my price range. I'll be honest, it was a lot more fun than queuing up to see rented hovels – just me and a gelled estate agent who looked about Simon's age and who treated me as if I was very important. Even though Drewstead Road had been the bane of my life, I'd liked Streatham itself and started looking in that area for somewhere to buy.

The very first details they came up with looked like this:

TELFORD AVENUE, SW2
FLAT E – SECOND FLOOR FLAT
ACCOMMODATION: ENTRANCE HALL
LOUNGE/ BEDROOM KITCHEN BATHROOM
Entryphone, thermostat, wall mounted Saunier Duval
boiler. Neff oven and gas hob with Franke extractor
fan, tiled splashback, ample floor and wall units,
plumbing for washing machine

It was – new terminology for me – a 'studio flat' with sloping walls at the top of a Victorian semi. I'd be very much living in one room up in the rafters, but the place was recently converted which meant newly fitted kitchen, new bathroom and fresh paintwork, and I could always think of it as an artist's garret. It was small and the hardboard floor sort of bounced underfoot but I found it romantic. Though it goes against all the rules of this new Eighties game of property-hunting, I'd fallen in love with the first place I saw and enticed Dad down to London to inspect it the next day.

Dad agreed it was a perfectly serviceable one-person flat. We co-signed the mortgage agreement and I moved one step closer to owning about 450 square feet of London. I say 'owning', I was actually leasing it from the freeholder, a concept I still haven't really got my head around. I'm buying it and yet I will still have a landlord. Hmmm. One thing I do understand is that without sufficient funds in my current account to cover the direct debit to Abbey National on the 21st of every month, I've got egg on my face and bailiffs banging on Dad's front door.

I don't feel guilty about owning property, nor about the leg-up. I know Mrs Thatch was returned to power in 1983 off the back of the Housing Act and the sale of half a million council houses, but buying mine's not going to turn me into a Tory.

'If your lot get in, they'll tax people like me out of business.'

Dad tried to convince me of my voting folly earlier today. He's the one who says never discuss politics, religion or money, but he just couldn't stop himself at the breakfast bar. Here was his eldest son, 22, a month away from getting his degree and setting up shop as a London entrepreneur, returning to his birthplace to vote for the Other Lot. Dad's argument against them seems to be: if you vote Labour in,

I'll be hit by higher taxes and you'll suffer in turn. This, if I may say so, is typical me-me-me Tory thinking. It won't wash I'm afraid. I've seen too much *Spitting Image* and listened to too much Billy Bragg. I've read this week's *NME* interview with Neil Kinnock with its elegant cover shot and he may as well have been speaking directly to me. What about the old? What about the young? What about the sick?

'If Kinnock gets his way, the bloody Russians'll be marching down Abington Street by the end of the week!' Dad exclaims.

'No, they won't, Dad.' I'm not sure whether or not he really believes the election posters featuring a surrendering soldier under the line 'Labour's policy on arms,' or whether he's just trying to scare me into crossing the floor. Again, it won't wash.

'All right, what about Dennis Healey? His wife went into a private hospital for treatment. Good Labour man he is.'

'So he's a hypocrite.'

'He stormed out on breakfast TV when Anne Diamond asked him about it.'

'It's not about breakfast TV is it? What about the old people? What about young people? What about—'

'Stop arguing, you two, and eat your grapefruit,' interjected Mum. 'Agree to disagree.'

'Fine,' I said, casually, even though I was enjoying winding him up.

'Well, he's bloody daft,' grumbled Dad, disappearing back behind his *Telegraph* before having one last pop: 'Don't come running to me when you can't pay your mortgage, because I'll be out of a job, counting my pennies.'

I'm not sure if Dad was uncharacteristically combative because election day brings out the ideological passion in him or because he actually felt threatened by me and My Lot getting in – a thrilling prospect either way and it was an enjoyably free and frank exchange of political views. Perhaps he's only helping me out with my mortgage in the first place so that he can blackmail me into voting for His Lot. It was his idea to buy after all. I would have happily lined the pockets of a crook for a while longer – I'm only 22.

Anyway, Dad's last-minute campaigning has failed. I have just voted for John Dickie (Lab). Let's hope he swings it. I have a good feeling. I'm single, I'm going to be chief free-lance illustrator and live in a garret under a new Labour government. And we're going to get together and get rid of sexism in comedy and everywhere else.

Michael Morris increased his majority in Northampton South from 53.6 per cent (26,824 votes) to 55.3 per cent (36,882 votes). John Dickie and Labour were roundly thrashed. Without my vote, Dickie would have amassed only 14,060 votes, so I made a difference in my own way. I pushed his total to 14,061. See that 1 there? That's me.

Mrs Thatcher was swept back to an historic third term of office, albeit with a reduced overall majority (144 seats down to 102). She'd famously threatened in the run-up to 'go on and on' and no one in the party was arguing. No one in the party ever did. The campaign message worked – 'Britain is great again, don't let Labour wreck it.'

I graduated from Chelsea School of Art under a Conservative government. Our degree show took place under some stairs in the Royal Festival Hall on the South Bank. Perhaps unsurprisingly, we had a boat party. I wore the

Top Man suit I had bought for Simon's wedding and I got myself a really short flat-top at an old man's barber's in Parson's Green. How different I looked from the sockless, neo-Gothic scruffbag who went in at the other end. Mum and Dad attended and met Mr and Mrs Mills for the first time.

'I never did like that gas pipe in the front room,' said Mum.

'Nor did I – it was the first thing I said, wasn't it, John?' said Mrs Mills. They bonded. Both our dads are called John.

I moved into my studio flat in July, bought a BT ansaphone called Robin ('the friendly answering and recording machine'), started a proper, green, hardbacked accounts book and met the first mortgage payment on the 21st thanks to a commission to provide David Williams with full-colour artwork of a cartoon owl in a mortar board. I thought about Ingrid a lot and began to contemplate a life without sex in the time of AIDS.

I had hoped to be doing all this under Prime Minister Neil Kinnock, secure in the knowledge that the old, the young and the sick would be looked after, but it was not to be. The greater failure though should not detract from the personal victory. Voting for That Lot on 11 June 1987 was a major turning point for me, a watershed, an exorcism. It may have been my second general election, but it was the first in which I'd actually voted Labour.

In 1983, aged eighteen, A-level student, boyfriend of Sally, borrower of Mum's Metro, drummer of Absolute Heroes, I had put my inaugural stubby-pencil cross next to the name of Mr Michael Morris (Con), slavishly following Dad.

Did I mention carrying a kind of low-level Eighties guilt around with me? Try living with that.

nineteen

Great Cash Prizes To Be Won!

I have started to hang around train stations. There are a lot of them in London: Euston, Kings Cross, Paddington, Charing Cross, Clapham Junction. I even loiter at smaller overground stops like Farringdon, Balham and Streatham Hill. Tubes too. I have developed a sixth sense for rooting out crossword and puzzle magazines, and the best place to look is often the news kiosk at a station, for self-evident reasons.

They're always low down, near the kids' comics and Marshall Cavendish partworks, but I expect the puzzle junkies know where to look, just like me. I'm at Farringdon now, mooching – not much of a kiosk here actually, but it's served by a well-stocked newsagent over the road from the station entrance. *Pippin, Postman Pat, Murder Casebook* ... there's one! Almost obscured between a *Scrabble Challenge* and a *Find It Fun Book*, a pristine copy of the new *Puzzled*. The blocky two-colour 'P' is unmistakable. It's volume 12, number 5 from the *Master Collection* range – not to be confused with your basic *Puzzled* or of course *Bumper Puzzled*, which costs 95p to the regular magazine's 80p.

The regular *Puzzled* (Family Fun For Everyone!), whose covers feature cartoon animals reading *Puzzled* in appropriate places – bears in the wood, penguins on an ice floe, koalas up a eucalyptus tree – is full of mazes and grids and word chains to complete.

Bumper follows the same format, except the cartoon animals are larger like hippos and walruses, to convey the fact that you get more puzzles for your money inside. Also, a gaudy flash on the cover promises Great Cash Prizes To Be Won!

The *Master Collection*, easily identified by the cartoon wizard who appears on the cover in various poses and situations (A Wizard Brew Of Puzzling Fun!), aims to be a little harder inside. Accordingly, with this imprint you can win a Volkswagen Polo, a Haven holiday or a Dreamland Electric Superduvet!

Then there's the related series *Brain Teasers*, trademarked by a cartoon owl in a mortar board, perched on a spray-painted delta symbol to get across the fact that these are even harder logic problems. You'd have to be quite a wise owl to master these! Big Cash Prizes though!

I draw the cartoons on the front of *Puzzled* books.

I pick up the new copy of *Master Collection*, rifling behind it in case there are others not in view. I'm quite pleased with this one, it's Christmas themed. The wizard is stirring a large cauldron, except it's decked with tinsel and closer examination reveals the potion within to be a kind of festive stew, with a turkey leg and some holly poking out. The wizard's cat is playing with a bauble and the rat who always turns up in the craziest places is actually working the bellows that fan the flame. I take my prize to the counter, along with the latest *Murder Casebook* (The Acid Bath Killer) and pick up a Boost while I'm there for the journey home. Part of me wants to tell the old man behind the counter that I drew the picture on the front of the magazine but he might not believe me and, if he did, *so what?* Why should he, or anyone else, care?

I do the cartoons on the front of *Puzzled* books. T.S. Eliot's J. Alfred Prufrock, from which I can still quote four years on, measured out his life in coffee spoons. I measure mine out in cartoon animals.

Puzzled books, published by Mirror Publications, pay my mortgage. Or at least, Mirror Publications pay David Williams, who art-directs the drawings, and his company pay me £50 per full-colour artwork, which goes towards my mortgage. That's not bad money, especially when they order up a couple at a time and with the four titles running parallel, that's common. I am now truly a sausage machine. My signature does not appear on the artwork, nor am I credited anywhere on the inside of the magazine: I am the Unknown Cartoonist. Nor do the names of the valiant men and women who compile the puzzles appear: they are the Unknown Compilers. The credits, in tiny type, recognise only Mirror Publications Ltd, Puzzle Promotions (who design and typeset the inside pages), Creative Print & Design Ltd (who print the cover) and Benham & Co Ltd (who bind and print the magazine itself).

I have illustrated the covers of so many *Puzzled* books,

Mum and Dad have stopped ooh-ing and ah-ing at them when I take home the latest batch. *So what?* I can sympathise. Once the brief thrill of spying a new one on a low shelf of a news kiosk has dissipated, I too am blasé about them. Not the money though – I'm never blasé about that.

Like Prufrock, I know the evenings, mornings and afternoons. I am a professional freelance illustrator. That's what it says on the business cards I had printed at Kall-Kwik on Streatham High Road. This means I wake up in the morning, get dressed (optional), eat a bowl of Start, watch a bit of *Good Morning Britain*, then haul myself to work at my draughtsman's table, there to colour in my latest wizard with the help of Mr Winsor and Mr Newton. It is, in many ways, a sad and lonely existence, paradoxically colourless after the merry larks of halls and the community spirit of college.

It's not as if we didn't know the end was coming and, unlike sixth form, we had a boat party and a glamorous private view to marks its passing, but nothing prepares you for the jolt of leaving higher education. There is no counselling. There is no training. There is no factsheet. Just a blur. And of course it hits harder than simply leaving school because you've had four more years to get used to it, to atrophy into a grant-maintained, deadline-surfing, Boost-eating bus-stop jockey with a can in one hand and 10p for the phone box in the other. Unlike school, on reflection, you pretty much had a good time all the time at college. Even the bad times were all right: the frozen pipes, the veggie laz, the fights. On reflection, it was one long holiday, with holidays. Why didn't I make more of it? Go out to more galleries? Watch less telly? Have more profound conversations? Demonstrate more often? Drink in a different pub?

More to the point, why didn't I apply for an MA?

Rob's at the Royal College, Jane's at the Royal College, even one of my old Nene buddies Keech from Kettering is at the Royal College, having completed his three years at North Staffs Poly and moved down to London. The Royal College, apart from being royal, is a student utopia. It is the world's only wholly postgraduate art school – like four years of sitting on your arse and doing some drawing isn't enough! These students, and there are about 800 of them doing MAs and PhDs, have managed to postpone entering the real world for another *two years.* At the end of it they'll have been in higher education longer than doctors. The sculptor Barbara Hepworth went here, Ridley Scott, David Hockney, Ossie Clarke – not one of them could face getting a job when it was so obviously time. They were all too scared to leave college. I wish I'd had the guts to admit that.

I can't complain. My flat is habitable. I have work. I am warm. I have Robin. But I wish I was still at college. Telford Avenue, where I now live *and* work, is a mere three streets away from Drewstead Road, but it may as well be in another country. It's a year since Rob and I lived in Flat 2, and I occasionally take the long route and walk past it when I'm off to Safeway's for mince, bin bags and Budweiser. It looks the same from the outside – no gate – but I wonder if Rabit still owns it, and if he's had the loft lagged in time for the coming winter. I feel infinitely more secure now than I did then, but at the same time the element of danger is missing. And Ingrid.

Ingrid and I are no longer boyfriend and girlfriend. When I graduated from Chelsea, I set myself free. Just as Valeria had unknowingly eased me into college life, Ingrid more consciously helped me out of it. When the end came, it came on two counts, one of them a blessed relief. She went back to Jersey for the summer holiday, while I got my head around the fact that I didn't actually *have* a summer holiday. (I've had the same two-month summer holiday every year since I was five – you grow kind of accustomed to these things.) The Chelsea degree show under the stairs closed on 12 July. A week later, BT connected my phone line at Telford Avenue. I was in business and my cards came back from Kall-Kwik. No time to cry.

I can't help but regard my current day-to-day existence as cold turkey. In newly decorated isolation, I'm coming down from college. This process, tricky enough, is exacerbated by trying to kick Ingrid. (Oh, how I have wanted to kick Ingrid.) I was hooked on her for five terms and one summer. Towards the end, I gave up pretending that I could handle it. If I had ever controlled her – and that's debatable – she now controlled me. Even from afar. Especially from afar: when my parents reported seeing her socially while on holiday in Jersey I didn't know where to put my emotions.

I've started an intensive daily regimen of sit-ups and dumb-bell exercises. There's not a lot of room in here, but I've found that if I clear the coffee table it doubles as a bench and that I can hook my ankles under the legs of my draughtsman's table. I refrain from actually holding my hand above the flame of the gas hob to build up my pain threshold, but apart from that and shooting pimps, I *am* Travis Bickle. If things had worked out between him and Betsey, maybe he wouldn't have gone on that killing spree.

Things didn't work out between me and Ingrid, but I'll

get over it. I have my hippos and my wizard and his crazy rat always popping up somewhere and there are great cash prizes to be won.

Now I'm off to the Royal College bar to hang out with some students.

twenty

This Is This

'Does it always feel like this the morning after?'

It's a fair question. I feel distinctly delicate; it's a low-level foreboding liquidity that seems to be sloshing round in my socks and threatening to rise up at any moment. It's as if what I ate last night has left gates open throughout my alimentary canal. I am, or soon will be, undone.

Last night was my first ever visit to an Indian restaurant, an experience I never actually managed to tick off when I was a student, although I understand it's a very studenty thing to do. In mitigation, I spent most of my four years at college being cooked for, and the rest of it too mean to eat out. I am no longer a student, but I feel like one; eating dangerously, drinking too much, staying out too late, surrounding myself with other students, experiencing student firsts.

It was Matthew's birthday and he and his more cultured medical student friends walked me patiently through the bamboozling menu and, to their credit, didn't con me into ordering the super-hottest curry – which, being students, they probably should have done. I had a korma and bits of other people's, and the waiter gave us all a free liqueur to finish. I chose Cointreau because I'd heard of it. It was a good night, and the food, all hot and yellow and varied, made a mockery of the pale, raisin-based Birds Eye boil-in-the-bag curries I've been buying from Safeway's of late.

The curry and the lager has also made a mockery of my naïve guts. I don't really want to be here on a wheezy fold-out bed in somebody else's rented house. I want to be at home. A few strides from my bathroom. You're never more than a few strides from anywhere in my flat.

Though I graduated the best part of a year ago, blowouts like last night's extend the happy illusion of still being under the wing of higher education. I still *feel* like a student. I still *dress* like a student. I still *make tapes of John Peel* like a student. I spend my weekday evenings doing student things like drinking in an old man's pub and talking student bollocks loudly with other students, then staying up till the early hours with cans and coffee in a rented student hovel.

It's close to noon, half the day gone. I opened my eyes about 20 minutes ago in Nigel's room, with no change of clothes and no toothbrush, distinctly delicate and flushed with guilt for an imaginary essay I should be finishing, or an imaginary lecture I should be attending. In truth, I should be at my draughtsman's table drawing a cartoon sheepdog for ICI, but the remorse is the same even though I am my own boss. I'm bunking off. I'm sleeping in. I'm a student in all but name and, of course, an actual seat of learning.

Instead I find myself a willing surrogate of St George's Medical School in Tooting. An undercover undergraduate. Since September I have become so used to drinking there and striding confidently down its antiseptic-smelling corridors doing my best not to look like a lost hospital visitor, I have actually broken my lifelong fear of hospitals. If I ever need Accident & Emergency, I'll know precisely where to park and will as likely as not recognise one or two of the staff working there.

'I expect Indians are used to it,' says Nigel, throwing on an unironed shirt and tie while he slurps coffee from a cracked mug. He really does have a lecture to go to. A dissection actually. Of a human cadaver. And he has to wear a shirt and tie under his white coat. It's another world.

'Let yourself out,' he adds, picking up an armful of notes and textbooks with gory pictures in. 'See you at rehearsals tomorrow?'

Tomorrow? I'm gathering up every fibre of my body in order to concentrate on getting through today.

I didn't expect it to be like this. The big lie that I'm living. But leaving college is harder than you think. All my immediate friends are students. And who else am I going to hang out with? David Williams? He's effectively my boss and virtually *thirty*. The couple who live in the flat below me? They're yuppies *and* a couple. If they're not still at Chelsea, like Suzi and Debbie and Jennifer, or at the Royal College, like Rob and Jane and Keech, my friends are training to be doctors – and nurses – at George's. I don't know anybody with a job.

In an average week I spend about two nights up at the Royal College bar in the shadow of the Royal Albert Hall, and the rest at either a designated medical student pub in Tooting or else at the St George's union bar, signed in as a guest. You'll recall that Chelsea never had a union bar, so

I'm actually spending more time at one now than I ever did when I was a student. So my beer and discos are still subsidised, even though I am registered self-employed, keep a green accounts book and have a 25-year leasehold mortgage. I wonder if anyone but me can tell?

I met the trainee doctors – and nurses – through Matthew, Rob's old friend and now his partner in struggling cabaret double act the Hall Brothers. Matt and Rob could easily be brothers, so identical is their sense of humour and delivery, but Matt is not like other medical students. As with Rob he was creamed off by Cranbrook School and comes from neither money nor privilege. Nor are his parents in medicine, which seems to be just about compulsory at medical school. There are enough pint-swilling, fart-lighting twits here to form an entire rugby league, boorish and loud and drunk and probably performing a practice operation on a human eye the following morning. Most of them are called Giles or Jeremy and have debts that would make even a cadaver's eyes water because the course is five years long and involves buying a lot of really expensive textbooks full of gory pictures.

So how did I manage to infiltrate their ranks and find acceptance?

It all started when the Hall Brothers were booked to provide some live musical entertainment at a St George's bash – Beatles standards in a music hall style with banter in between. The Brothers invited me to accompany them on some borrowed drums. I was chuffed, and began to spend more and more time at the hospital, practising 'Lady Madonna' and 'Can't Buy Me Love' in the hospital music room. It wasn't long before I'd joined the school's amateur dramatics group. Again, no one seemed to bat an eyelid that I didn't actually attend the school, and I ingratiated myself by offering to design posters, programmes and tickets for our sporadic shows. I even wrote a couple of sketches for the medical school revue, which were accepted and performed, and ended up co-writing the next production with Matt. It's like having a milk round in Cambridge and being allowed to join Footlights. I'm enjoying all the trappings of proper university life that weren't available to me at my little art school. Perhaps I'll run for Ents Sec? Come Rag Week you may yet see me bandaged up and wheeled down Tooting High Street on a gurney, rattling a bed pan for money. Or perhaps I'll go all the way and after five years start posing as a locum at a busy hospital near you.

I clicked immediately with Nigel, who, like me, fancies himself a bit of a movie buff. A comp-educated kid from Bournemouth whose dad works at the post office, he immediately stood out from the rugby-shirted herd. Nigel invited me to assist in the running of the St George's Film Society, for which I now design posters and help choose the Mickey Rourke films.

I am a fraud, an interloper, a foreign body and do you know what? It's a good feeling. What's more, Matthew, Nigel and the collected Jeremys have another year of study left after this one, so there's no need for me to leave college just yet. I'm not at college, but you know what I mean.

I'm not at college because I'm not a student.

Did I mention nurses? I'm in a nurse's bed, in the nurses' home, next to a nurse. The sun's peering through the curtains but she's still fast asleep, facing the wall which at least gives me the option to slide out and get dressed before she notices my absence. I slept only fitfully, balanced on the edge of the bed watching the fluorescent hands on the clock, wondering what exactly I was doing. There was no sex last night, despite the Red Stripe and vodka and the fact that I think I was invited round for sex.

Ruth and I, that's the nurse's name, didn't have sex because I don't have sex any more, not since Ingrid, not since AIDS.

Every time I think I've worked out that I'm safe, they seem to extend the incubation period, meaning I could have caught it before I'd heard of it, which is massively unfair. And still no news of a cure. Perhaps that's why I choose to hang around with doctors and nurses – very reassuring. Matthew seems certain that the figures quoted on the news are inflated and that there's nothing to worry about. 'We're not going to catch it,' he says. You can imagine the enthusiasm with which I have been clinging to that controversial piece of medical opinion. Despite this, my once insatiable carnal appetite remains permanently on hold. My ardour dampened. My desire taken away. The only person I've had sex with since Ingrid is Ingrid. Once. For old times' sake.

Perhaps you won't be surprised to learn that after our messy, protracted split-up, Ingrid and I have been enjoying a messy, protracted post-split. It's a year since we broke it off and still she haunts me – because I let her. She lives now in a rented hovel in Brixton, just up the road from Streatham, and she still has a spare set of keys to my flat from when she was homeless at the start of term and threw herself on my mercy. Because I have come to terms with the idea that I won't be sleeping with or going out with anyone for the foreseeable future, I don't mind her dropping by unannounced, which she usually does at a late hour, to unload her latest woes on me 'as a friend' and make me fancy her, then leave.

SCENES FROM A PRETEND DIVORCE (1)

The flat, Telford Avenue. Dead of night. I am on the precipice of sleep after a long night's driving around from Nigel's to the King's Head to Matthew's to the Ning Fung to Rob's to Chris and Suzi's for a late-night game of Triv. I'm knackered. Part of me – the weak part – was disappointed to arrive back at the flat and not find the light on, as it occasionally is. The other part of me was relieved. I crashed out at 12.30.

I am awoken by the sound of the spare key rattling in the front door of the flat. I switch the light on before Ingrid actually enters.

'You up?' comes the voice.

'Yeah,' I say, lying.

She enters, looking ravishing and flushed, which is unfair, made-up and bright-eyed as if she's just home from a party. Except she's not home.

'I didn't phone in case you were asleep,' she says.

So she just turned up instead. I refrain from questioning the logic of this. The weak part of me, the part that's undressed under my quilt, thinks I've hit the jackpot. Perhaps tonight's the night she'll stay, the only girl in the world I can safely have sex with – or at least, if it's not safe and we are both carrying the virus, it won't make any difference, if that makes any logical sense

'Been out?'

'With my friend Antoine,' she nods.

I bristle at the mention of his name: 'my friend Antoine', a moneyed ponce from Kensington whose dad owns a private club and who holidays in Monte Carlo. It's one of those on-off, is-it-or-isn't-it relationships, about which I've heard more than my fair share during the 'off' times when Ingrid's called upon my late-night counselling services. Looking ravishing.

I lean casually out of the bed to hook my dressing gown off the floor for the sake of modesty, asking, 'Is it on or off?'

'Oh God, off,' she says. 'We're still friends though.'

'What brings you round here?' I ask, circumspect, climbing out of bed now.

'Just came to catch up. What have you been doing? Who have you seen?'

She's as anxious that I stay single as I am of her. This pleases me. Perhaps there's a chance she hasn't shagged Antoine.

'The usual,' I shrug. 'Nige, Rob, Matt ...'

'Not *Anna*?' she says, with sadistic relish. She's never met Anna. Anna is Chris and Suzi's flatmate. My friend Anna.

'How do you know about Anna?'

'I read your diary.'

'When?' I'm suddenly offended by her intrusion.

'The other night,' she says, as if it's obvious. 'When you weren't here. Sorry, I couldn't stop myself. You left it open. It was just lying there on the table.'

'That's because I live here!' I didn't mean to raise my voice. It is late. 'I can leave things lying around.'

Now it's her turn to be offended. 'All right. You can have the keys back if you like.'

'I only lent them to you when you had nowhere to live. You've got somewhere to live.'

She purses her lips. 'I'll go shall I?'

'Have a cup of tea first.'

I'm already filling the jug kettle. I spent one night with Anna but nothing happened beyond snogging, a monument to my new celibate lifestyle. I wrote in my diary about how I wished I could relax with other girls but that the spectre of Ingrid haunted me. These words were not for Ingrid to read. I didn't leave the diary out for her.

Did I?

There is definitely something liberating about being in another woman's bed, even on the edge of it. Something prescriptive about being with a nurse too. Perhaps Ingrid will have dropped in at the flat and discovered me absent. That's a stimulating thought. A year without a girlfriend and a year without sex. I'm Morrissey at last. I've slept in two other beds with two other women since leaving Chelsea – Anna and a jolly-hockey-sticks med student called Carol – but nothing took place, underwear remained on, and the ghost of Ingrid slept alongside us. I never knew adult relationships could stain your life like this. Anna grew tired of hearing about Ingrid, even though she started it by offering a sympathetic ear. Carol never stopped talking about her wacky tennis-club friends long enough to find anything out about me.

Before you ask, yes, I am more than aware of the cliché value in fancying and getting off with a nurse – but in my own defence I've hardly ever seen Ruth in her starchy blue uniform. The white tights and sensible shoes aren't even an issue. We met through the drama group, where she is usually in her non-starchy civvies. Though younger than me by a year or so, she is rather matronly in shape, quite a change from my usual crispbread-eating arty type, and I think the novelty appeals. She's a strong character, as I now realise nurses have to be, and Welsh, which they don't. She's no *Carry On Doctor* bit of stuff.

A planned inevitability about this evening has sapped it of any romance. She invited me round. Her flatmate's away. The only place to actually sit in her tiny halls-like room is the bed. Our consumption of alcohol was deliberate and numbing and the moment I threw caution to the wind and had the decisive can that took me over the driving limit we sealed our own fate. I was flattered by her attention, she was flattered by my presence. No harm has been done, but I already regret being here as I sneak out of the nurses' home expecting at any moment to have my collar felt by some imagined actual matron.

Arriving home, dying for a cup of tea, an aspirin and a supplementary nap, I put the door key in the Yale lock. Lovely heavy front doors, these Victorian houses. There is no give. It's unlocked. Strange. The other people who live in the building are usually very security-conscious and one of them even went to the trouble of putting a finger-wagging reminder up on the inside of the door to double lock it when going in or out. I put my other key in the Chubb and let myself in.

Not that I really care but I wonder what the professional couples who live in the other flats think I do? My name tag next to the multiple doorbells is the only one that's actually Letraset rather than scrawled in pen – that must tell them something – but none of us has ever socialised beyond a cursory hello on the stairs. That's London. The couple in Flat B, who I think are responsible for the double-lock reminder, were quick to knock on my door when the water from my overflow pipe was splashing on their side window. They were very nice about it, but no drinks invitations were exchanged. I fixed the washer on my toilet cistern and never heard from them again.

I fight my way past the bicycles in the front hall to the old dresser where the mail goes, sifting through it and extracting just the one letter. I don't recognise the handwriting which means it might be from someone enclosing a postal order for a copy of my fanzine. It's called *This Is This.*

I actually had a couple of indie types ring the bell one afternoon and buy one on the doorstep. They'd seen the plug in *Underground* magazine. My only plug. But I've already sold three copies to strangers by mail order.

I open the envelope with my thumb as I go up the stairs. Being a studio flat, it's right at the top, past the missing chunk of plaster where the couple in Flat F attempted to have a huge Heal's sofa delivered. In the end the delivery men gave up and took it back to the shop. Yuppie nightmare. Oh, the letter's not from an indie kid, it's a demand for ground rent from my landlord, who may well be unscrupulous, I've never met him. He is based in the Isle of Wight and has never, to my knowledge, visited the property. He bought the freehold in an auction and now collects ground rent from all six tenants. If the roof falls in, it's our problem.

Once through the front door of my flat, I launch myself gratefully on to the sofa. It was once Nan's sofa, and plenty small enough to get up three flights of stairs. No flashing light on Robin the ansaphone, but there's a sheet of paper left on the coffee table, a note. I don't need to read it to know who it's from or what it says. It's held down by Ingrid's spare set of door keys.

That's the end of that then. That was that.

I am undone. I should have shagged Ruth while I had the chance. I'm going to bed. The ICI sheepdog can fuck off.

twenty-one

Down in London

Since moving into the flat and entering the world of work I have relaxed a little about returning to Northampton and now pop back every few weeks without feeling as if I am in some way surrendering my independence. No more bags of dirty pants though. I do those.

I'm here this weekend for a reason – Nan and Pap's joint birthday lunch. She turns 70 on Tuesday, a landmark age, and he's 72 today, Sunday, 29 May 1988. I arrived home last night and sat with Mum and Dad and watched the last of Alan Bennett's *Talking Heads*, *A Cream Cracker Under the Settee*, in which Thora Hird – who's always reminded me of Nan – fell and couldn't get up. It made me thankful that my own grandparents are mobile and none of them live alone.

'Are you getting enough work down in London?' This is Nan's new catchphrase.

'Is he getting enough work down in London, our Christine?' she'll constantly ask my mum.

'Yes, our Mum,' she'll say.

'Yes, Nan,' I'll say. She worries. She's always been a worrier and if she had her way, I'd move back to Northampton forthwith and get a job up here. She could never see why I had to go all the way to London to 'learn art'. What was wrong with Nene College? she'd ask. They don't do degree courses, I'd explain. What do you want a degree for? she'd ask.

What did I want a degree for?

At the time, swept along by the runaway momentum of destiny and the overconfidence of youth, I found her constant questions silly and unworldly. I was going to London because, well, Chelsea seemed like the place. All right, because I'd seen Alexei Sayle on telly talking about his time there. But more than anything – like in those nature programmes about migrating birds or buffalo – I was going because it was time to go. Buffalo don't get asked why they're going, do they?

Nan and Pap have lived in Northampton all their lives; in the same bungalow since 1939. All of their three children have married into families who have also always lived in Northampton. They now all live in Northampton with *their* children. Three generations, all represented at the Saxon Inn in town, except one, Simon, who is in Germany with his wife, Lesley, and his mistress, the army. And Melissa's boyfriend Graham, who's playing football.

I've never seen inside the Saxon before. To my knowledge it's one of only two hotels in Northampton – the town doesn't attract many visitors – and I'd seen inside the other one, the Westone, one New Year's Eve with my old school friend Craig. The Saxon is very nice. Everything's a very subtle pink and grey – the upholstery, the carpet, the print curtains, and the low coffee tables are in a modern pale wood and glass-topped. They must have recently done it up because the Saxon, like this family, has been here for years.

Nan and Pap look very smart too. We all do; the men are in jacket and tie, the ladies an assortment of Sunday best blouses. Melissa's perm has calmed down and she looks every inch the NatWest cashier, her chosen career since leaving school at sixteen. This means she can live at home for a good while longer. In Northampton.

I am lurking to one side of the main group as we sit in the lounge and wait to be seated, not because I am somehow infected with a Metropolitan otherness and feel detached from the tight-knit nucleus of the family, but because I am hiding an unwieldy gift for Nan and Pap.

'Ah, here they are!' declares Mum as the stragglers arrive, Uncle Brian and Auntie Janis.

'We had a job parking,' says Brian, by way of explanation.

'Hallo, Andrew!' says Janis, warmly, as if perhaps she hadn't expected me to turn up. Why wouldn't I? It's Nan and Pap's birthday do. I only live fifteen junctions away. Still, it is nice to be received as some kind of homecoming hero: when you live apart, you don't have to do much to earn that status except come home.

In fact, they all make a bit of a fuss of me, which I don't really deserve.

'How's London?' asks Brian.

'Brilliant!' I say. You'd have a job parking.

'Your mum tells us your flat's very nice.'

'Well it's not very big, but—'

Dad interrupts. 'Why don't you—'

He nods at the huge and conspicuous Sketchley's bag at my feet. I put my glass of Britvic down on the glass table-top and remove the large, framed picture from the bag, moving through to where Nan and Pap are seated in the soft-furnishing equivalent of thrones.

'I've got you a present,' I say, handing over the picture.

'Ooh,' says Nan, sitting up.

When I say 'got', I 'got' the frame from the Reject Shop on the King's Road, where I still occasionally shop for old times' sake but that's not important. The picture I did myself – it's an affectionate caricatured portrait of Nan and Pap in pen and ink. Good likeness, I think, but then I have lived with their faces all my life. In the top corner I have carefully reproduced two old photographs that Mum lent me, of Nan and Pap on their wedding day and in the first years of married life. Next to these I have written, 'That was then … ' and at the bottom it says, 'This is now.' The fact that it's the title of an ABC song is just something to amuse me – the thrust is that, yes, things used to be different, we all used to be younger, but the present is just as worthy of celebration. It's something I believe, and something I think Nan, especially, needs reminding of.

'I shall have to put my reading glasses on,' she says, getting them out of her handbag.

The last time I was in Northampton, another Sunday, Nan and Pap were round at Mum and Dad's. For no special reason other than easy, inclusive entertainment – Nan doesn't like playing Triv – Dad got the slides out.

The slides go back to 1965, the year I was born, and run

to 1977, the year we graduated from slides to prints. But nothing beats the lowered lights, bared wall and shared spectacle of a slideshow to induce familial nostalgia. So many of those plastic Kodak boxes, each one carefully labelled by Dad: 'Xmas 1970', 'Holiday Wales 1973', 'Silver Jubilee 1977' ... so many haircuts and fashion crimes and was *all* our furniture at Winsford Way either brown or orange?

Ooh, look, there's Simon, aged about ten, in Wales, investing a family walk up a gentle hill with all the jeopardy of an orienteering course, rope slung around his shoulder, trousers tucked into thick socks and a map sealed inside a plastic bag to keep it dry. I never see Simon any more. There's Pap dressed in shirt and tie even though we're at the seaside – is that Torquay, or Brixham? And there's Dad looking like Leslie Phillips in a cravat! Hell-oo-oooo!

By the end of the slides, we had all laughed so much it hurt – laughing at ourselves, but ourselves in another time. Nan had tears rolling down her cheeks, and threatened do herself 'a mischief'. When the houselights went back up, she came out with another of her catchphrases, 'I shan't sleep tonight.' What she meant was her mind was buzzing, turning over, alive with memories. There was a sense of melancholy, as there always is with the old, that the best days are behind us, that things ain't what they used to be.

Back at the Saxon, Nan's now inspecting the portrait through her reading glasses, noddingly appreciative but not bowled over. I don't know what sort of reaction I expected, but one less subdued than this one, perhaps.

'It's very nice,' says Pap.

'I don't know where we shall put it.'

'What about in Brian's room?' suggests Mum.

'Party of eleven?' interrupts a waitress.

We are led through to the dining room: Nan, Pap, Mum, Dad, Brian, Janis, Allen, the other Janice, myself, Melissa and cousin Dean, now a 21-year-old windsurfer who I'm sure has a job too but I don't know what it is. If Simon and Lesley were here that would make a more representative quorum of thirteen – in fact, we should now add the absent Graham to our extended family, as he and Melissa have been going steady for some months – to the point where his parents, Dave and Jackie, met ours for the first time on the occasion of her seventeenth birthday meal at the Cromwell in Kislingbury. It must be serious; Mum and Dad have a framed photograph of Graham and Melissa up on the right speaker cabinet in the front room. There's one of Simon and Lesley on the left speaker cabinet, and – oh, irony or ironies – one of me and Ingrid taken two summers ago on the windowsill in between. I've asked Mum to take it down, but she says, 'It's a nice photograph,' and I suppose it is. Anyway, when the curtains are drawn, Ingrid and I disappear.

It's raining outside in honour of the bank holiday weekend but it cannot dampen our familial spirits in this subtle pink and grey paradise with napkins folded into little fans and a bread roll each already on the side plate. It's a happy occasion, the conversation is light-hearted and the food is excellent: melon starter, followed by turkey and all the trimmings, then Black Forest gateau for afters. I think Nan and Pap liked their portrait, they were perhaps just a little overwhelmed by it. I produced a similar one for Mum and Dad's silver wedding and that's up on the wall in 'my room'. They call it my room, though technically it isn't any more, but then we all call it 'Brian's room' at Nan and Pap's and he hasn't lived there for over 20 years.

Quite why this afternoon is making me feel so sensitive about the past I don't know, but there is something sentimentally splendid about three generations around a table in their home town. Fancy two people having amounted to that many bread rolls! How proud Nan and Pap must be of their clan, happy, healthy, together. It would no doubt make Ingrid sick, if she were still here.

Am I getting enough work down in London? Yes. Did I have to go to London to learn art? Yes. What did I want a degree for?

Good question, Nan. To draw cartoon animals on puzzle books? To draw cartoon reindeers for corporate Christmas cards? To be the chief illustrator for David Williams? No. He's never asked to see my certificate. Nobody has. This is just as well, as it's up in a frame in 'my room', but it's only a piece of paper anyway. I didn't even meet David in London – I met him in Northampton. Perhaps this is where I'm meant to be. Am I hiding out in London with my brave face and meals-for-one because I think that's what the next inexorable step in adulthood is? Perhaps I should end the pretence, stop living apart and come home. The room's still waiting for me after all.

I can't blame the drink that's being knocked back for making me maudlin. Straight after the cheese and biscuits I'm driving back to London, so I'm on orange juice.

'Do you have to go back?' asks Nan, in the immediate rather than the bigger sense.

'I've got work to do.'

'Are you getting enough—'

'Yes, Nan.'

I give her a kiss and touch Pap's sleeve and he pats my arm. I kiss Mum, and Dad grabs my arm and they all thank me for coming and it's as if I'm leaving early purely to guarantee a big send-off and I'm not. I've got a job on and the rain will slow me down on the M1. I have to get back. It's time to go.

Happy birthday for Tuesday, Nan. Happy birthday, Pap. Down in London, I shan't sleep tonight either.

twenty-two

No Sleep
Till Leicester

Back from the shops. One message flashing on Robin. Click.
Beeeeep.

'This is a message for Andrew Collins … '

Don't recognise the voice. Northern. Slight speech impediment. Music playing in the background, unidentifiable.

'My name's James Brown. I work for the *New Musical
Express* … '

I am frozen to the spot.

'Why don't you give me a call back tomorrow morning
after ten o'clock and we can talk about your magazine. My
number's 01 404 0700. OK, cheers, bye.'

Click. Beeeeep.

Now I'm leaping unself-consciously around the flat,
bouncing off Nan's old sofa, grinning at myself in the
mirror, doing a little dance. James Brown from the *NME* has
just left a message on my ansaphone. For me. About my
'magazine'. I sent him a copy of *This Is This* when I mailed

out all the others to would-be sympathetic people in the music press, and to be honest, after that lone plug in *Underground*, I was beyond hope of hearing anything. I replay the message, this time with my head right next to the tiny speaker, to make sure I've caught everything and to identify the music playing in the *NME* office. I can't but it doesn't matter. Tomorrow morning after ten o'clock I shall call him on that number.

For a Wednesday, this is really shaping up. James Brown, who edits the 'Thrills' section at the front of the paper, is going to write something about my fanzine. Sales will rocket! I might have to produce a second issue!

I think I'll replay the message one more time.

James Brown was full of compliments for *This Is This* when, not wishing to appear too eager, I called him at precisely 10.30 this morning. He said I had good 'magazine sense' and asked if I was 'formally trained'. I said I sort of was, although nobody at Chelsea ever actually taught me how to make a magazine. Rob, Run and I had just worked it out for ourselves in classic DIY style.

As a faithful reader I've had a couple of letters printed in the *NME* over the last couple of years. I even sent them a couple of film reviews, but they never responded – not even with a rejection slip. I suppose their snub was, in truth, one of the main motivating factors for producing my own fanzine. Yet until James Brown's message yesterday I had imagined a huge, yawning, impassable gulf between me and my beloved music paper.

Then James Brown said these words:

'I might be able to use you.'

He wasn't interested in the fanzine, he was interested in its editor-in-chief. He invited me to go up to the office for a chat next Tuesday and he said he'd find me an assignment to try me out. I was too dumbfounded to sound sufficiently grateful.

'Thanks.'

I phone Nigel and Rob and Mum and Dad and Suzi's advertising boyfriend Chris and even Ingrid to tell them my news: I've had a call from the *NME*! Whether it's *the* call yet, it's too early to say, but it feels like something significant has occurred. The offer of an escape.

Well, that's typical. I'm drunk, I'm at college, I'm wrapped around a toilet bowl and I'm having trouble piecing together the last couple of hours.

Having met James Brown at the *NME* office in June I managed to land a part-time job in the paper's layout room, designing pages, three days a week. Not only was it a lightning apprenticeship in how a newspaper worked, it gave me the financial stability to start turning down puzzle-book jobs. Though still effectively freelance, being at the *NME* gave me a weekly payslip (the first since my shelf-stacking, trolley-pushing Sainsbury's job in 1981). It also gave me a platform from which to start bothering the paper's section editors for some bits of writing work. I started to write the odd review and eventually, they gave me my first feature-writing job. This is it, Leicester Poly, 25 October 1988, a Balaam & the Angel gig, my graduation from groupie to the inner sanctum.

The last thing I remember was the band taking to the stage and launching into a furious, headbanging set to a hall-ful of pissed students. And a pissed cub reporter from the *NME*. I had already conducted the interview and placed the cassette safely in my bag. Flushed with the sense that I had successfully completed my mission, I decided to celebrate by drinking all the vodka in the band's fridge. Then I allowed their PR to ply me with lager and Pernod chasers at the dirt-cheap bar. The spirit of rock'n'roll, the spirit from the back-stage fridge and the excitement of just being here on behalf of the *NME* all conspired to make my head spin. There was a glorious moment of composite ecstasy in there, possibly during the song 'Live Free Or Die', then it all goes a bit hazy.

I am awoken by banging and shouts of my name. I vaguely remember having staggered backstage with my access-all-areas sticker to violently throw up in the toilet that I am now hugging for dear life. I had subsequently decided that the toilet floor was the safest and most comfortable place in the world to be. I curled up and surrendered to the dead sleep of the spent.

Thump thump thump. I can hear the voice of the band's PR, Roland.

'Andy – are you in there?'

Thump thump.

I am unable to answer, my faculties still in a holding pattern, circling way, way above Leicester. It sounds as if Balaam & the Angel are with him. They were one of Kevin's bands, all those years ago. If he could see me now. Perhaps not.

'You'll have to go over,' Roland says and I can make out the sound of one of them getting a leg-up over the high cu-bicle wall. And then she appears. My girlfriend. Tereza.

'Yeah, he's there,' she tells them and drops down on my side. She makes sure I'm all right, unlocks the door and between them she and Roland get me to my feet. I am led out of what is by now a semi-deserted polytechnic into the reviving shock of cold night air. The band are no doubt delighted that the boy from the *NME* passed out in the bogs.

It was supposed to be a big night for Tereza and me. Delectable, infectious, curly-bobbed, slightly boyish Tereza. We've only been going out for about a month but already it feels different. She's the best friend of Ruth the nurse, from the same small town in South Wales and she captivated me from the moment I first saw her. She's quite the comedian and works at Sainsbury's. At last, someone who isn't a student. I knew our relationship was special when we didn't get off with each other the first night we met, and we didn't sleep with each other the first night we got off with each other and we didn't even sleep with each other the first night we slept with each other.

Which is why the trip was quite a big night for us, staying overnight in a double bed in a hotel, even if it is more of a B&B, and even if it is in Leicester. But any notions of romance are dashed by the fact that I am now throwing up again on the landing carpet while Tereza unlocks the room door. Worse still, I have no idea where my bag is. The bag with the interview tape in it. All I'll have when I get back to the *NME* is a headline, No Sleep Till Leicester, and a headache.

Despite Leicester, I have definitely entered a new phase in my life. I have a new girlfriend who I'm mad about but who doesn't at this stage appear mad. Like Ingrid, she's a vegetarian, but that's where the similarities end. The ghost of Ingrid is laid to rest. I have burned my diaries for 1986 and 1987 out of respect for Tereza, who was frankly getting sick of Ingrid's ghostly lingering presence. Tereza lives in a rented hovel in Tooting that makes Drewstead Road seem desirable – it actually has no bathroom – and as a result I have asked her to move in with me. I surprised myself when I asked her, even though her situation is desperate, but realised I do want to share my life with her. That's got to be a good thing. We have made a pact: she'll give up smoking if I give up meat.

I plan to buy my first double bed.

And yes, Nan, I'm getting enough work down in London. Though I doubt you'd call the *NME* work and sometimes neither would I.

epilogue

Another Polytechnic

It's almost exactly three years later: 29 October 1991. Now an *NME* journalist to the core of my being, I'm covering another band at another gig at another polytechnic.

The band are called Catherine Wheel, emerging proponents of what's known in the music press as shoegazing – fuzzy, effects-heavy, overwrought guitar music usually made by ex-students from the Thames Valley, although this lot are from Great Yarmouth. The polytechnic is Middlesex – its well-appointed Trent Park campus, which is almost off the top of the tube map in Enfield. I've spend a lot of time in their union bar recently, taking advantage of the cheap lager, but not in my capacity as an *NME* wild child. And anyway I'm not drinking tonight as I'm in the car.

I'm still going out with Tereza, which is a record for me, although we are no longer living together. My studio flat in Streatham was never big enough for two people anyway. I still live there, constantly dismayed by how little my mortgage seems to be going down at the end of each year, but otherwise content. Tereza now lives in a shared hovel in Wood Green in North London. We're together but we live apart.

Catherine Wheel are belting out their most famous song, 'Black Metallic'.

So why do we no longer live together, Tereza and I? Because she is now a student at Middlesex Poly. Fed up with shitty shop-floor life, and perhaps buoyed with confidence in our blooming domestic and romantic stability, she applied for a Media Studies course and got in. Because of the slump in the Eighties property dream it simply wasn't practical to sell, so I'm stuck there while she lives the student lifestyle up here. I can hardly deny her that – I believe everybody should be given the chance to go through those three years of self-discovery.

So Tereza and I have the weekends, when she usually insists we go back to Wales to visit her parents. We make like nothing's changed, and I sometimes spend the night at hers during the week and hang out with her student mates, all four or five years younger than me of course. It's a workable compromise but there's still something wrong with this picture.

I have become the boyfriend 'from home'.

And we all know what happens to them.

So our days are numbered and it was higher education that did it. I can hardly complain, can I? At least I have the wisdom of age to understand it, even if I can't do anything about it. I suppose that's what it was all about in the end, 'my student struggle': pulling away to find out who I was, where I was going and how the world worked. Not really finding answers, but making headway and getting there slowly nevertheless – knowing a bit more, but never enough to do anything about it. Life would be intolerable if we knew everything.

At least Catherine Wheel perfectly match my mood of doomed melancholy with their chiming guitars and their self-pitying lyrics.

There is one consolation – although I won't know it for at least another two years – my future wife is in the room. She's the band's PR, and she can't stand students.

Before *Heaven Knows I'm Miserable Now*, there was *Where Did It All Go Right?*

Andrew Collins

Where Did It All Go Right?

Growing up normal in the 70s

'Every word is nostalgic, warm and funny'
DAILY MIRROR

They tucked him up, his mum and dad

Where Did It All Go Right? is Andrew Collins' memoir about his happy, everyday childhood years – being normal, coming from nowhere and not doing much – where the worst thing that happened was Anita Barker mocking the stabilisers on his bike.

With the help of his diaries (kept from the age of six) Andrew delves back into his first 19 years. With tales of playing out, bikes, telly, sweets, good health, domestic harmony, happy holidays and 'going down the field', he aims to bring a little hope to all those out there living with the emotional after-effects of a really nice childhood.

'An unashamed nostalgia fest… comic gold'

Time Out

'Anyone who grew up in the 70s will love this funny and sharply observed memoir'

Hello!

You can order this book now by post:

Where Did It All Go Right? by Andrew Collins
ISBN 0-09189-436-0 £6.99

FREE POST AND PACKING
Overseas customers allow £2.00 per paperback

BY PHONE: 01624 677237

BY POST: Random House Books
C/o Bookpost, PO Box 29, Douglas
Isle of Man, IM99 1BQ

BY FAX: 01624 670923

BY EMAIL: bookshop@enterprise.net

Cheques (payable to Bookpost)
And credit cards accepted

Prices and availability subject to change without notice.

Allow 28 days for delivery.

When placing your order, please mention if you

do not wish to receive any additional information.

www.randomhouse.co.uk